EYES
WIDE
OPEN

EYES
WIDE
OPEN

LOOKING FOR GOD IN POPULAR CULTURE

Revised and Expanded Edition

William D. Romanowski

BrazosPress
Grand Rapids, Michigan

Published by Brazos Press
a division of Baker Publishing Group
P.O. Box 6287, Grand Rapids, MI 49516-6287
www.brazospress.com

Second printing, August 2007

Printed in the United States of America

Library of Congress Cataloging-in-Publication Data
Romanowski, William D.
    Eyes wide open / William D. Romanowski.—Rev. and expanded ed.
        p.   cm.
    Includes bibliographical references and index.
    ISBN 10: 1-58743-201-3 (pbk.)
    ISBN 978-1-58743-201-9 (pbk.)
    1. Popular culture—Religious aspects—Christianity. 2. Popular culture—United States. I. Title
    BR526.R646 2007
    261.0973—dc22   2006021101

Photos on pages 97, 142, 151, 168, 173, 189, and 192 were supplied by Photofest, New York, New York.

To my sister and brother
—Kim and Michael—
and for the next generation

Michael, Lucy, Nellie, Tara,
Nora, Sam, Claire, Max, Spencer,
Abraham, and Molly

CONTENTS

PREFACE TO THE REVISED AND EXPANDED EDITION

One of the challenges in writing about popular art and culture is its constant movement: films are out of theaters and on DVD in a matter of months, television shows cancelled, and a CD can move up (and down) the *Billboard* charts with a bullet. For this second edition, I've updated a number of the illustrations but retained many others that have proven to have "legs." My own personal tastes and preferences will become obvious. I like Bruce Springsteen's music, for example, and use it to model the kind of analysis that a reader can do likewise with a favorite artist. Since my teaching and research interests are in film studies, I rely on movies for many illustrations. But it is also the case that popular films like *Pretty Woman* or *Titanic* (though not personal favorites) have an advantage as illustrations because so many people have seen them, unlike television programs and music that reach more specialized audiences based on age or genre. Also, examining the same artwork in different contexts can show that there are multiple ways of thinking about a film, television program, or music video.

Language is another issue. For convenience, I sometimes use "Hollywood" as a generic term to refer to the entertainment media, and not just the film industry. Since my original writing, the term "Christian" has acquired a measure of ambiguity. It has been used in reference to the music of Amy Grant, Jars of Clay, and U2; Christian romance, Anne Lamott books, and the Tim LaHaye/Jerry B. Jenkins Left Behind series; films like *The Omega Code* and those of Paul Schrader and Martin Scorsese. As an adjective, "Christian" has taken on multiple meanings—both positive and pejorative—depending on the source and audience. In thinking about this I found talking about faith perspectives and a cultural orientation more useful and descriptive in most contexts. Even so, I still use the adjective Christian to refer to popular art and cultural orientations that resonate with basic beliefs and assumptions that people claiming the Christian faith adhere to.

Categories that mark social, religious, and cultural distinctions have also been politicized to a great extent. Analyses of a society marked by diversity and the existence of subcultures need to be able to distinguish dominant and subordinate cultures, for example. I read recently that some evangelical Christians with a "for us or against us" mentality have added "mainstream media" to a list of terms like "liberal" and "secular humanist" that they use to divide groups of people into hard and fast categories of good and evil. It is only realistic to draw observable distinctions where they exist between ideals, beliefs, and assumptions valued by members of a particular Christian subculture, for example, and those of the broader (mainstream) culture. And so I still make use of "mainstream" to refer to the entertainment industry or the dominant American culture. Marking these differences does not mean that I share the hostile attitudes of any particular group or even their polarized mind-set. I have also tried as much as possible to be specific in naming particular Christian groups like evangelicals, mainline Protestants, and Catholics.

For this second edition I recast the original material to situate it amidst contemporary events and trends and also for a more specific audience. I have added new chapters, reworked, expanded, and updated others keeping in mind those people who are using this study in educational settings, especially liberal arts courses in film, media, and popular culture. Supportive material and documentation has been included so that readers so inclined can follow up these sources as part of their own research and investigation. I refer to critics regularly not just to glean insights into particular artworks but also to show how we can benefit from critical reviews and to demonstrate different kinds of criticism.

Finally, I took this revision as an opportunity to advance an approach to popular art as art. This edition, like the first, is meant to be exploratory and suggestive. I write in that spirit. A reader does not necessarily have to accept my particular faith-informed cultural orientation in order to find something of value in the prospective model presented here. You will have to judge for yourself the viability of my critique of the popular artworks treated in these pages and the cultural perspective they represent. Our society benefits from having people of various faith persuasions participating honestly and intelligently in the cultural conversation.

I owe a debt of gratitude to a number of people. Rodney Clapp, for his editorial support and friendship, and Rebecca Cooper, Bobbi Jo

Heyboer, and the Brazos team for their good and diligent work on this project. My thanks to Robert Woods for his helpful suggestions toward this second edition, my neighbors (and co-workers) Rick and Michelle Zomer, and my colleagues at Calvin College and especially in the Communication Arts & Sciences department. The Calvin Media Foundation supported production of a three-part video/DVD series based on *Eyes Wide Open* for classroom use. Reworking the material for a different medium enhanced my own understanding of popular art. The Calvin College McGregor program provides opportunities for a faculty member and student to work together on a research project during the months of summer. Jennifer VanderHeide worked tirelessly with me on this revised edition. She did outstanding work, dazzling me with her reading, research, and editing skills. Jen, I can't say thanks enough. Donna, Michael, and Tara—I love you.

INTRODUCTION

Individuals differ in their capacity to handle challenges to their faith, but each of us in our own way should endeavour to be both distinctive and culturally engaged.

John Coffey, *Cambridge Papers*

One of the favorites at the Museum of Modern Art's 2003 film series, "The Hidden God: Film and Faith," was *Groundhog Day* (1993). It tells the story of Phil Connors (Bill Murray), an obnoxious Pittsburgh weatherman who is trapped by a Pennsylvania blizzard while covering the annual appearance of Punxsutawney Phil, a groundhog whose sight of his shadow predicts more winter to come. The next morning Connors wakes to the clock radio and Sonny and Cher singing "I Got You Babe." He discovers that it's February 2nd again. This happens again the next day, and the next, until he learns his lesson, wins the heart of his producer, Rita (Andie MacDowell), and is "released from the eternal cycle of repetition," as one reporter put it, adding, "Of course, this being an American film, he not only attains spiritual release but also gets the producer into bed."[1]

People from different faith groups all laid claim to *Groundhog Day* as representing their teachings. One scholar said the film "perfectly illustrates the Buddhist notion of samsara, the continuing cycle of rebirth that Buddhists regard as suffering that humans must try to escape." A rabbi saw the film as an allegory, finding "Jewish resonance in the fact that Mr. Murray's character is rewarded by being returned to earth to perform more mitzvahs—good deeds—rather than gaining a place in heaven, which is the Christian reward, or achieving nirvana, the Buddhist reward." A film critic for a Jewish publication read it differently. He said, "The groundhog is clearly the resurrected Christ, the ever hopeful renewal of life at springtime, at a time of pagan-Christian holidays. And when I say that the groundhog is Jesus, I say that with great respect." A Catholic scholar argued it was "a stunning allegory of moral, intellectual, and even religious excellence in the face of postmodern decay, a sort of Christian-Aristotelian *Pilgrim's Progress* for those lost in the contemporary cosmos." On the other hand, an evangelical in Punxsutawney (the film's setting and shooting location) said her organization did not use the film as an educational tool: "We stick pretty much to Scripture."[2]

This is a book about popular art and culture. As the *Groundhog Day* illustration suggests, it is more specifically a book about the interaction of faith, perspective, popular art, and culture. *Time* film critic Lance Morrow once likened the "philosophical emanations" of a movie to gases that "may enter undetected and start to affect the brain." He recommended that "we should each carry a canary into darkened movie theaters. If the canary starts to gasp and keel over, we should run for our lives."[3] Morrow's assertion of the importance of critical engagement contrasts with those who maintain, "It's only a movie. You can't take it so seriously."

Before a church service one Sunday morning, I was having a conversation with two friends. Jonathan said he "loved" a movie he'd seen the night before. "That script could only be written by someone coming out of a Calvinist background," he said. This surprised Nancy because she had also seen it with some of her friends, and they "hated it." Jonathan responded quickly: "Well, it's not a happy movie." The conversation continued as they debated the merits of the film.

People participate in popular art and culture for many reasons. We all need different kinds of recreation. People like to be entertained and enjoy creativity and storytelling, a catchy chorus in a song, the humor in a TV sitcom, and so forth. Going to a movie with friends is a fun social activity. Curling up in a chair to watch a favorite television program or listening to music can be relaxing, a diversion from the cares and concerns of life. At the same time, these experiences can also serve as a celebration of common values and even life itself. They can enlarge our sense of the world and our place in it and increase our sympathies and understanding of other people and cultures.

While much popular art can be enjoyed with little intellectual effort, this does not mean that it must or should be enjoyed in this way or that the arts cannot be provocative and make people think. Moreover, developing good critical skills and practices need not diminish our enjoyment of popular art. Instead it promises to enhance the experience and make it more rewarding, especially as we become better at it.

Developing a critical approach helps us reach conclusions about the meaning and value of particular artworks. It can sharpen our judgments and increase our awareness and understanding of both art and life. The critic's quest is to arrive at a "place of wakefulness and clarity," as one scholar put it.[4] The best criticism sends the reader back to the artwork with a new understanding or with fresh ways of looking at it. I suggest that much aesthetic delight can come from intentional involvement that is informed by one's faith perspective.

However, rather than make faith the *issue*—turning popular art and criticism into religious propaganda—I propose instead to think of faith as providing the *context* for artistic engagement. This counters the widely held belief that subject matter is what makes a popular artwork "Christian" by putting the emphasis instead on artistic qualities and the perspective brought to bear on that subject. This approach affirms the essentially artistic character of popular art while recognizing the many roles and purposes it fulfills in serving our neighbor.

Movies, television, music, and videos provide a common experience for many people by addressing widespread concerns, fears, and prejudices and nurturing aspirations. They can give us a sense of belonging to a larger community and affirm important myths and heroic adventures. These forms of entertainment media can provide general knowledge, stimulate our thinking, and get us to look at things in new and different ways. They might explore challenging political, moral, economic, or religious issues by questioning gender relations or pointing a finger at sexism, racism, elitism, homophobia, and social or economic injustices. In short, the popular arts can comfort and affirm, challenge and provoke.

The realm of popular culture can be seen as an arena for argument or debate in which different ideas and perspectives find voice in stories, videos, songs, and pictures. Artists often mine tensions and conflicts for dramatic or comedic purposes and explore contradictions in what people believe and how they live. When Col. Nathan R. Jessep (Jack Nicholson) thunders, "You can't handle the truth!" in *A Few Good Men* (1992), he points to the ambiguous reality that the need for a military contradicts the values of the civilization it must protect. And the general would rather not be questioned about the methods he uses to train soldiers to be able to kill.

Artists live in and find inspiration from the real world. They give us *maps of reality*—symbolic representations (i.e., *re-presentions*) of life in sounds, stories, and images—that suggest the meaning of things. Determining meaning is a matter of perspective and interpretation. There is a close relationship, then, between the arts and life perspectives: the latter shape the former as much as if not more than the other way around.

It is only to be expected that artists, scholars, and critics have employed various approaches centered on the contribution of faith to the popular

Introduction

art enterprise. This concern with a faith distinction, or a specifically Christian distinction, is worthwhile and valuable if only because perspectives can and do make a vital contribution to the artistic experience.

Faith-Informed Perspectives

The authors of *The Transforming Vision* wrote, "Faith is an essential part of human life. Humans are confessing, believing and trusting creatures."[5] That's also how I see it. The relationship between faith and culture is creational, part of our humanness. To be God's image bearer is to be human, and to be human is to be a cultural agent carrying on God's creative work by fashioning ways of life that promote love, creativity, kindness, mercy, justice, truth, and stewardship.

Cultural activity is a creational given, but after the human fall in sin, culture is oriented away from God's intentions for it. Some Christians take this to mean that God requires minimal cultural engagement. I disagree. I believe Christians should be studying, discerning positive and negative aspects, and working to redeem culture.

I approach the popular arts, then, as part of the historical cultivation of God's creation carried on from generation to generation. The popular arts are not outside God's judgment—or beyond God's redemption. The challenge is to discover what it means for us to be faithful to God and responsible to our neighbor through these media.

The Christian tradition is diverse, and there is no single Christian view on any subject. Actually, there are probably as many different "Christian" perspectives on the media as there are critics who label their work as such. They might not all agree on what "Christian" means for media criticism, but they nevertheless conduct their work based on pre-existing beliefs drawn from a certain understanding of scripture. By my way of seeing it—to speak only of the Christian tradition—whether a critic writes for *The Christian Century* (mainline Protestant), *Christianity Today* (mainline evangelical), *Commonweal* (Catholic), or Focus on the Family's *PluggedIn* (conservative evangelical), their work qualifies as *faith-informed*, a phrase historian George Marsden suggested to refer to "belief systems built around organized religious faith."[6]

My own faith-informed perspective affirms commitments to a certain Christian set of beliefs and also represents particular assumptions about the relationship between faith and culture. I make no apology for working out of a particular tradition. It is not as though in our postmodern culture an individual or community cannot stand on some perspectival ground for thought and action. From these beliefs and assumptions comes a certain attitude, one that recognizes and values diverse perspectives while also maintaining the importance of one's own in thinking critically about popular art and culture.

The relationship between religious groups and the entertainment media has over time been characterized by a variety of attitudes coalescing around concerns with the communicative power of these popular art forms and their ability to influence. A range of approaches exist; the one presented here finds its way among extremes. On one side are those reactionary Christians who might regard popular art as hostile to people of faith or even an apostate cultural form; on the other are those who simply shrug it off as mere amusement. Somewhere in between are those who judge an artwork solely on its accord with their own moral or ideological position and others who think it necessary to resist making any judgment at all in order to respect an artist's vision and take an artwork on its own terms. While TV programs might represent beliefs and values that are not consistent with my own, I do not see that as reason for complete dismissal of them, just a fair and thoughtful critical appraisal. And movies can be fun, delightful, and entertaining, but they can also communicate perspectives that I think deserve our careful consideration. Admittedly, it can be a difficult course to navigate at times, trying to avoid the imposition of a particular perspective while also thinking of the popular arts as exploratory. That can be a challenge, but it can also make watching movies and TV and listening to music more enjoyable and enriching. Ultimately, I hope my own analysis plays itself out along the borders between conviction and humility.

Popular artworks look at life in a fallen world that is at once hostile to and also in search of God. People of whatever faith persuasion have the capacity for truthfulness and sinful conduct and can offer artistic insight into life in God's good but fallen world. We can appreciate and evaluate these efforts by asking what kind of perspective this artwork offers on the matters of life it addresses. Viewers can try to come to terms with an artist's position by weighing the viability of her "message," trying her perspective on for size, so to speak, even as they might render judgments about whether they find it true or false. This attitude not only respects the artist's right to express ideas but also calls for people to take those ideas as seriously as they would like others to consider theirs. Christians who would dismiss a film or television program because it does not affirm their viewpoint on a given issue still want those with opposing viewpoints to take seriously Christian perspectives in the media. Why do they expect others to be fair and open, but think they do not have to tolerate what they perceive as non-Christian beliefs in popular art?

It is often in the sphere of "entertainment," as Margaret Miles observed, that "values are formulated, circulated, resisted, and negotiated."[7] We live in a media-saturated society where popular artworks enter into our cultural discourse regularly. I argue that we need to act *as people of faith* discerning perspectives in these representations of life in God's world.

Popular Art Is Art

The critical approach presented here is concerned with faithful cultural engagement. What distinguishes this approach is its locus, animated as it is by a certain understanding of how the popular arts serve as art.

"Art needs no justification," the late art historian Hans Rookmaaker once wrote. "Its justification is its being a God-given possibility."[8] In other words, creating positive works of culture is a legitimate and worthy endeavor in and of itself. While the arts serve many purposes and are understood in terms of those purposes, they should not be identified simply by their usefulness. "Art is not a means to an end, it is not a function of something else," philosopher Calvin Seerveld maintained. "Art stands or falls on its own *artistic* contribution in God's world."[9] A critical approach to popular art has to focus on popular artworks *as popular art*. Otherwise, it is not popular art criticism.

Recognizing its communicative power, I think of popular art as art that embodies meaning for people and contributes to one's cultural orientation. We can understand television, movies, music, and videos as popular art forms that function in society, communicating and criticizing cultural values, providing social unity, and contributing to our collective memory. But we cannot forget that popular artworks are the products of a profit-driven commercial enterprise, made in a crucible of entangled concerns. Since popular art is multidimensional, it is profitable for us to think about it not exclusively in terms of inherent aesthetic properties, but as a complex phenomenon including aesthetic, moral, social, political, industrial, technological, and other dimensions. Young people especially can benefit from learning to think critically as well about the cult of hyperbole, sensation, consumption, and mass identification that the media propagates.

I have met many people who have told me that they don't really know how to discuss a movie or television show very deeply or talk about the latest CD. They think their faith should matter when it comes to popular art, but in the absence of a workable critical approach, they simply defer to vague personal tastes and preferences. People like or dislike particular movies, concerts, or TV shows, but are not always sure why. As we would expect, there are people who are uncertain about what they are experiencing and what effect it might be having.

There is no doubt the popular arts have some kind of effect. But what is the nature of that effect? The persuasive power of the popular arts comes from their roles and capacities as art. As representations of life, popular art can influence behavior, shape attitudes and opinions, and inform perspectives.

One of the most frequently debated questions is whether the entertainment media reflects or shapes society. To argue that it reflects society is to oversimplify what is really a complex process. Popular artworks are a reflection of society insofar as they address contemporary issues and treat them in ways consistent with current perspectives. But the popular arts are never merely a reflection. By portraying our lives and culture, the popular arts popularize and glamorize ideals, values, attitudes, and beliefs that exist. In this way, the popular arts contribute to the power of culture to shape lives. The popular arts reflect a culture they help to create.

In that regard, and to some extent as a requirement for popularity, the entertainment media is more likely to affirm people's beliefs than to introduce new ones. People want to be entertained while also being affirmed in what they already believe—witness the different audiences in 2004 for *The Passion of the Christ* and *Fahrenheit 9/11*, for example.

Studies also show that whatever impact the popular media has is not universal but particular to individuals and, in some sense, communities, and is mediated by a host of variables. We might have very different reactions to popular artworks based on age, personal temperament, viewing skills, gender, sexual orientation, race and ethnicity, family and neighborhood, education, community standards, political perspective, or social and economic status. And it is the cumulative effect of viewing the world portrayed in these media that has the power to persuade—over time and with the influence of many films, TV shows, and CDs.[10] And so all people of goodwill ought to be concerned with the cumulative impact of a steady diet of American movies that often exalt self-interest as the supreme human value, glorify violent resolutions to problems, make finding the perfect mate one's primary vocation and highest destiny, and offer material prosperity as the most reliable source of meaning and satisfaction in this life. Such a value system arguably runs against the grain of most religious traditions.

It is important, then, to be able to understand and think critically about the dominant themes in popular art. More often than not, Christian appraisals are variously entangled in the dominant American mythology. We need instead an engaged, critical, and productive involvement with the popular arts grounded in a faith vision that encompasses all of life and culture.

People understandably like those artworks that affirm their view of life. But a good faith-informed criticism should not simply be a matter of applauding artworks that advocate a certain moral or ideological position (on abortion or capital punishment, for example) or contain recognizable theological themes (tales of redemption). Would it not be of greater value to direct our energies toward developing an approach that considers the significance and quality of artistic endeavors, and the extent to which various artworks deepen our understanding of God's world? Such an approach will not simply forewarn people of potentially offensive material or ideas they may not agree with. Instead it will help us distinguish redemptive aspects, determine appropriate participation, and develop tools for constructive criticism. This in turn will illuminate art, ideas, and visions of life in ways that can be a significant blessing to us all.

Considering a Cultural Landscape

The focus in this study is on the intersection of popular art and faith perspective. As Andrew Greeley observed, the correlation of religion with creativity is largely "because both are metaphor-making, meaning-bestowing processes."[11] In other words, imagining is part of the way we construct meaning; we imagine the way the world is and ought to be. One theologian talked about imagination as "the general sense of the way people give shape to their world, in particular through the images and practices that express this shape."[12]

Scholars have been preoccupied with the relationship between faith and imagination for a long time. "Such is our nature, that we cannot think of things invisible, without a degree of imagination," Puritan theologian Jonathan Edwards wrote. "I dare appeal to any man, of the greatest powers of mind, whether he is able to fix his thoughts on God, or Christ, or the things of another world, without imaginary ideas attending his meditations?"[13] Imagination is necessary to faith and cultural activity. The capacity of popular art to create imaginative worlds has been a source of controversy in the church for generations that reveals something of the similarity between the institutions of art and religion; both are concerned with values, meaning, and visions of life.

It is at this juncture that what I call a cultural landscape messes with artistic features in popular artworks. *Cultural landscape* refers to the collection of ideals, beliefs, attitudes, values, and assumptions that are represented by theme, character traits and actions, storylines, symbols, images, and so forth. Looking at the artwork itself, then, is key to understanding communication of a perspective on the human condition and the world.

Engaging popular artworks is an imaginative activity; that it is one of the ways we envision the way the world is and ought to be relates it to faith. As Miles wrote, "We cannot begin to live a life we cannot first imagine, and images stock the imagination's repertoire."[14] During the creative process, artists imagine the world according to a system of beliefs. The worlds they invent exist materially on paper, CD, film, or videotape, but also in our minds by drawing on our cognitive abilities—emotion, reason, imagination, desire, and so forth. While any number of factors might inform artistic creation or critical appraisal, these activities are certainly animated by what people believe. Such perspectives make an important and even necessary contribution to the popular art experience, and it is at this level that we can talk about "Christian" distinctiveness in popular art and criticism.

For example, a common American belief about the human condition represented in countless Hollywood films is that "God helps those who help themselves." People are basically good, temporarily wayward, but capable of redeeming themselves. I hold a more ambiguous view of humans as both sinful and yet having inherent dignity as God's image bearers. Based on these assumptions, then, I am often critical of the kind of stock melodramatic depictions we regularly see on TV and in Hollywood films that divide the world up all too easily into good and bad people.

Emphasizing the matter of perspective ought not to lead to some kind of simplistic equation of "Christian" with good art, and "non-Christian" with art that is bad or evil. Writing about film, theologian John Lyden observed "if one only looks for how a film differs from the Christian view, or how it is like it, one may overemphasize either similarities or differences and fail to hear what the film itself has to say."[15] This is an ever-present complication if only because perspectives play such an important role in the aesthetic experience. For that reason, however, being aware of a cultural landscape should help make us better at understanding and interpreting movies, television shows, popular songs, and videos.

The criticism surrounding *The Incredibles* (2004) makes this point. There were critics who raved about the Pixar Studios hit as a celebration of family values. Others, however, found political undertones in the movie's radical individualism and drew comparisons with Ayn Rand's novel *The Fountainhead*, in which the hero uses his individual talents and initiative to break free of society's mediocrity. Perceiving it this way, a *New York Times* critic thought the world of the film represented a "kind of misguided egalitarianism" that was "not just stultifying but actively, murderously evil."[16] For precisely the same promotion of libertarian ideals, another reviewer applauded the film because it "explicitly defends the value of talent and achievement against the leveling values of egalitarianism."[17] As you can see, perspective matters in popular-art criticism.

Engagement with a popular artwork centers in part on its treatment of the issues of life. It is only natural to ask what this artwork suggests about the matters of life it addresses and what we think about this treatment. Whatever we think is going to be based to some extent on the ideals, beliefs, and assumptions that we bring to the artwork, among them an attitude about the value of others' viewpoints. Even so, understanding the dynamics of faith, culture, and popular art should help us to look at and listen to popular artworks from the inside out, that is, in terms of their own cultural perspectives. In that regard, popular artworks can increase our awareness and deepen our understanding of people and the world we live in.

But gaining insight into contemporary culture is only part of the reason Christians should analyze popular art, for as I already noted, the popular arts not only represent people's values and beliefs but also inform our understanding of life and the world. As examples, a viewer can appreciate the depth of love and devotion exhibited by the main characters in *The Notebook* (2004) while also criticizing the myth of romance the film draws on for its emotional energy. *Titanic* (1997) depicts God as impotent and uncaring, but that does not make the film worthless for people who believe God is intimately involved in human affairs. Indeed, considering *Titanic*'s record-shattering box-office performance in the United States and around the world, there must be an incredible number of people (including professing Christians) who were not disturbed enough to stay away.

Conclusion

In an interview in the Los Angeles magazine *BUZZ*, actress Rene Russo talked candidly about being a Christian. In a letter to the editor, one reader thanked the writer for giving a "positive portrait of Rene Russo and her Christian faith." She wrote: "There are thousands of us 'believing Christians' in and around the film industry. As with Miss Russo, our faith is more than form, it's the substance of our life. . . . I hope (and pray) that there will be further exploration of this stream of living waters running through the film industry."[18] This "stream of living water" is one group of people that I hope will find this book of interest.

It is not enough for artists alone to contemplate faithfulness in the arts; they have to be supported by investors, production companies, critics, and audiences. And so this book was written with a wide audience in mind—producers, artists, executives, and critics, but most of all for those of us who like to attend concerts and movies, watch television, and listen to music. Those searching for a faith-informed criticism are a key component of the audience that I am addressing with this book. I hope that people of faith and also those who hardly, if ever, darken the door of a place of worship will also find something of value here.

The ultimate goal is to have a positive influence in our media-saturated society. To that end, I would like this book to contribute to the larger task of developing and sustaining a fair and rigorous faith-informed criticism, one that investigates weaknesses, takes pleasure in achievements, celebrates virtues, and laments failed opportunities. Our aim should be to preserve the best features, improve the weakest parts, and eliminate the worst traits of popular art.

I suggest no more than that readers consider taking the approach presented here as a kind of case study or model for a faith-informed engagement with popular art and culture. As with all critical approaches, certain artworks afford the possibility of deeper analysis than others; the one presented here is no exception. One advantage of this approach, however, is that it allows us to consider a wide range of artworks, not just award winners, since even the most mundane and uninteresting narratives exhibit something of a cultural orientation. This accords with the world of popular culture where we cannot always equate artistic excellence with popularity or commercial success. You will have to decide for yourself how valuable this approach is by asking questions: How useful is it? What kinds of insights does it yield? Does it open up possibilities for the creation and criticism of popular art?

Summary

- This book is about the interaction of faith, perspective, popular art, and culture.
- Faith, which is an essential part of human life, gives people a context for artistic engagement, and employing a faith-informed critical approach is not only necessary but also enriches encounters with popular artworks.
- A critical approach to popular art has to focus on popular artworks as art that embodies meaning for people and contributes to one's cultural orientation.
- Being aware of a cultural landscape in popular artworks should help make us better at understanding and interpreting movies, television shows, popular songs, and videos.

Discussion Questions

1. How does your own faith affect the way you experience popular artworks?
2. Given that we live in a media-saturated society, why is it important for people of faith to be discerning about perspectives represented in the entertainment media?
3. The author suggests that "the popular arts reflect a society that they help to create." What do you think? Does the entertainment media reflect and/or shape society?
4. Think of a movie, television program, or song/music video that you really enjoyed. What made it enjoyable? To what extent did your appreciation have to do with whether or not it represented ideals, beliefs, or values that you support? Are there popular artworks you enjoy even if they don't seem to affirm your beliefs and values?

PART
ONE

I

STATE OF THE ART

WORLDLY AMUSEMENTS NO MORE

For decades, America has embraced a baffling contradiction. The majority of its people are churchgoing Christians, many of them evangelical. Yet its mainstream pop culture, especially film, is secular at best, often raw and irreligious.

Richard Corliss, *Time* Film Critic

I wish there were the kind of programs that could get huge ratings, like wrestling, and yet bring people into the Kingdom.

Lowell "Bud" Paxson, Founder of PAX TV

Summer is the season of movie blockbusters: *Mission Impossible, Spider-Man, Shrek, Pirates of the Caribbean*. But even with *Revenge of the Sith*, the eagerly awaited final installment in the celebrated *Star Wars* series, the summer of 2005 turned out to be a rough one for Hollywood. Ticket sales were down 9 percent from the previous season. Fourth-quarter releases *Harry Potter and the Goblet of Fire, King Kong*, and *The Chronicles of Narnia: The Lion, the Witch and the Wardrobe* closed the deficit gap, but the year ended with movie attendance down for the third straight year.[1]

While industry experts contemplated the dismal summer box office, another trend was garnering increasing attention. "The Narnia film arrives as the entertainment industry is taking notice of—and trying to profit from—what it views as the increasing influence of religiosity on American culture," a *New York Times* reporter observed.[2] What was considered a fringe group of born-again Christians protesting Martin Scorsese's *The Last Temptation of Christ* to no avail in 1988 had become a potent box-office force behind the stunning success of Mel Gibson's *The Passion of the Christ* (2004).

The numbers were an eye-opener for Hollywood. These same religious consumers were already spending hundreds of millions of dollars on religious books and Christian-themed music. The film industry wanted a piece of the action. Movies in 2005 with clear religious themes like *Constantine* and *The Exorcism of Emily Rose*, and even those without any sort of explicit Christian connection, like *Cinderella Man* or *The Greatest Game Ever Played*, were being pitched by studios to reach the "Christian" market, and more specifically, those fundamentalists and evangelicals who embraced *The Passion* with such enthusiasm.

Film distributors had balked at Gibson's project, convinced it would be a flop. It was, after all, an extremely violent depiction of the torture and crucifixion of Jesus of Nazareth in Aramaic and Latin with English subtitles. Not exactly a Friday-night date film. Moreover, even in production *The Passion* was steeped in religious controversy with charges the film was anti-Semitic. Studio executives no doubt recalled conservative Christian protests of *The Last Temptation*. But a TV writer and producer said in retrospect, "Ask them today if they would have financed *Passion* knowing then what they know now, and you'll see enough green lights to make Hollywood look like a Christmas tree."[3]

Producers and others identifying themselves as Christians even speculated that the film's success might "fundamentally reshape the nature of the movie business when the final numbers come in."[4] *The Passion* earned $370 million in the United States and over $600 million worldwide, finishing third on the money-making list for 2004 behind *Shrek 2* and *Spider-Man 2*. Film producers were looking for ways to exploit what a *Premiere* writer called "an incredibly loyal, hungry, and potentially vast audience of religious consumers."[5] The dual aim, a writer in *USA Today* observed, was "to use faith-based hits to help staunch a three-year box-office slide and to convert those with little faith in Hollywood fare into permanent moviegoers."[6]

Where Satan Has His Throne

This interest in churchgoers on the part of Hollywood was not entirely new. Film studios courted Protestant and Catholic audiences regularly at least until the mid-1960s, when the disastrous box-office performance of *The Greatest Story Ever Told* (1965) signaled an end to the biblical spectacles. Since then, studios targeted the church crowd occasionally for pictures like *Jesus Christ Superstar* (1973), *Chariots of Fire* (1981), and *The Prince of Egypt* (1998).

Nevertheless, *The Passion* put churchgoers on the entertainment industry's radar in a big way. This was all the more remarkable given the long history of unease, and sometimes outright antagonism, that has existed between the church and entertainment media. Allegations that popular musical styles were demon-inspired have been commonplace. Blues and jazz artists, crooners like Frank Sinatra, and rock 'n' roll greats Elvis Presley and the Beatles were all fiercely condemned as barbaric and uncivilized.

At one time ministers even preached against novel reading. "I cannot believe that a person who has ever known the love of God can relish a secular novel," nineteenth-century revivalist Charles Grandison Finney declared. "Let me visit your chamber, your parlor, or wherever you keep your books. What is here? Byron, Scott, Shakespeare and a host of triflers and blasphemers of God."[7]

Finney's diatribe against the popular art issue of his day found new form in the campaign against "the menace of the movies" in the twentieth century. The movies were a critical issue in many denominations where discourse revealed underlying concerns about the function of entertainment and the possession of cultural power. For that reason the history of church and Hollywood relations can give us insight into the whole discourse about faith and popular culture.

Protestants, who were the dominant religious group, perceived themselves as bearers of a God-given responsibility for the moral and religious character of American life. They spearheaded the movie reform movement during the first quarter of the twentieth century. However, as the increasingly pluralistic and secular character of American culture eroded the Protestant hegemony, non-Protestant and non-Christian players gained a new voice in the public arena. In part to combat this loss of influence, mainstream denominations emphasized church unity and advanced ecumenical forms of action on a national scale. The "movie problem" was thought to be too large for individual churches and even denominations.

Protestant leaders, however, were unable to galvanize their constituents around a consensus on goals and strategies. Some cooperated with Will Hays, a Presbyterian who became president of the film industry's trade association in 1922. While some Protestants advocated federal regulation of the film industry, still others adhered to a strict policy of abstinence; descriptions of Hollywood as the "place where Satan has his throne" were common among conservative church writers.[8] In contrast, Catholics formed the Legion of Decency and threatened a massive boycott of movies in the early 1930s. Hays put a Catholic in charge of the Production Code Administration (PCA), an industry agency that monitored film content according to the tenets of the 1930 Production Code. That Jewish studio heads employed a prominent Protestant to head their trade organization and Catholics to write a code of ethics and administer it shows the importance of religion for understanding the cinema.

The discourse about film changed dramatically after World War II. In 1948, the Supreme Court dismantled the film studio monopoly over production, distribution, and exhibition of movies. This weakened the apparatus of the Production Code Administration. Beginning in 1952 the Supreme Court rendered a series of decisions that extended First Amendment protection to film. The courts gradually undermined the practice of prior censorship, and by direct implication, church control over movie content. Censorship and boycotts were now seen by many as violations of constitutional rights.

Protestant and Catholic organizations advanced a two-pronged strategy in the decades after World War II. First, they pursued film education for church members and tried to encourage filmmakers by presenting awards to films that offered honest portrayals of the human situation. James Wall, a key Protestant player at the time, argued that movies were "a vehicle through which the artist presents his vision. The task of the churchman is then to evaluate that vision in the light of his own understanding, informed by the Christian faith."[9] They also lobbied for a film industry rating system to protect young moviegoers as well as the freedom of the filmmaker.

In the wake of Supreme Court decisions that differentiated obscenity standards for adults and minors, the Motion Picture Association of America (MPAA), in cooperation with Protestant and Catholic agencies, abandoned its Production Code and in 1968 adopted the movie rating system we still use today (with some modifications). With the advent of a movie classification system, however, these Protestant and Catholic organizations saw their role greatly diminished; in the 1980s, they either closed their doors or dramatically shifted goals and priorities.

Parallel Universe

In the meantime, evangelical Christians were changing "from embattled minority to the most visible and vital sector of American Protestantism," as a *Christianity Today* writer put it.[10] This coincided with the rise of the evangelical consumer culture in the 1970s and '80s centered on publishing, Christian-themed merchandise, and the emerging contemporary Christian music (CCM) industry. As late as 1970, however, a writer claimed that "evangelicals do not patronize the movies."[11]

But that was changing. The source of much Hollywood criticism since the 1980s has come from fundamentalist and evangelical Christians who still harbored early twentieth-century assumptions about the cinema. They conceived of movies as entertainment, not art, and believed that film producers should be responsive to church officials as society's moral guardians. Given these assumptions, it followed that they adopted many of the tactics employed by earlier generations of reformers. Some evangelicals protested films they disapproved of and tried to pressure the industry for biblical stories and stories that favorably depicted religious groups, not unlike other consumer advocacy groups. In the spirit of the "culture wars," many divided movies, music, and television programming into either "Christian" or "secular" categories with an artwork's merit riding on simplistic moral, theological, or ideological evaluations. Others just ignored popular art and culture based on elitist attitudes about the superiority of the traditional high arts.[12]

Christians exhibit a variety of approaches to popular art and culture, but the evangelical framework wielded considerable influence on the public discourse, not only among evangelicals, but also in the larger church community and the entertainment industry. Even mainstream trade and news reports assumed that explicitly religious content separated "Christian" artworks from nonreligious or "secular" ones. When members of a British rock band announced that they were Christians, a London critic admitted he was "expecting Dodgy-style guitar pop and happy-clappy lyrics about Jesus." Fortunately, this group was an exception to the norm and the reviewer was surprised when there was no "overt evangelism or self-righteous babble."[13] Because of its significant weight on the whole matter of faith and popular culture, I want to examine the evangelical perspective more closely.

Two central tensions existed in the evangelical model. First, the popular arts had to be used to evangelize if they were to be considered "Christian." The hallmark of evangelical media became an explicit statement of religious belief, what I call *confessional* artworks. While the sound of CCM, for example, varied wildly—from Adult Contemporary (AC) to hard rock to rap—a clear declaration of faith, usually expressed with evangelical catchphrases, distinguished easily enough this "Christian" fare from its mainstream counterpart.

The result, however, was a lot of embarrassingly poor-quality productions marketed in the name of evangelism. A review of the movie *Left Behind* (2000) began with: "Immediate disclaimer: This is not to denigrate the religious beliefs that inform *Left Behind*, an adaptation of the best-selling Christian thriller of the same name. This is simply to address the hilariously bad manner in which those beliefs are expressed." This critic concluded, "Whatever the central message, the movie's still a blundering cringefest, thanks to unintentionally laughable dialogue, hackneyed writing and uninspired direction."[14] A desire to communicate the gospel could not make up for a lack of artistry; evangelical popular art had a difficult time finding an interested and appreciative audience outside the evangelical market.

But if popular artworks could be used to evangelize, it was reasonable to think they could also be used for spiritual corruption. Media was also feared, then, as a potential threat to the faith. For that reason, some evangelicals condemned mainstream popular art as apostate and advocated abstinence, while others issued moral or spiritual warnings.

Wanting to convert the unsaved while remaining spiritually pure justified their appropriation of trends and practices in the broader culture. The evangelical consumer culture provided a religiously safe harbor they hoped would attract others to the faith. As Gospel Music Association (GMA) president John Styll put it, "Essentially a parallel universe has emerged: below the radar of pop culture, but emulating it directly."[15] Entrepreneurs exploited the evangelical market with CDs, videos, and merchandise all explicitly labeled "Christian" (including for women—or perhaps really for men—a thong with WWJD on the front). The Christian retail industry grew from an estimated $1 billion in 1980 to over $4 billion by 2003.[16]

The second tension in the evangelical model resulted from the tendency to privatize faith, confining religious belief to personal morality, family, and local congregation, while conducting their affairs in business, politics, education, social life, and the arts much like everyone else. They gave "*full* reign to the blood of Christ within a *limited* area," as Fuller Seminary President Richard Mouw put it.[17]

Drawing boundaries between "religious" and "secular" is certainly nothing new in American life. But this dualistic conception was central to the way evangelicals thought about, produced, and consumed popular art. An emphasis on *confessional* appearance and a concern with *personal* morality distinguished their approach. As an adjective to describe popular art then, "Christian" came to mean two things: overt religious themes and appropriateness for the "family" audience.

"I don't think we're here to replace the church," Lowell "Bud" Paxson said, but his family-friendly PAX TV network counted on the large population of people who claimed to be Christians to tune in for its slate of syndicated shows like *Touched by an Angel*, *Diagnosis Murder*, and *Highway to Heaven*.[18] And the Dove Foundation, an evangelical nonprofit, pro-family group, petitioned Hollywood for more "wholesome family entertainment" based on the existence of "the huge untapped market of consumers who want exciting movies, but without explicit portrayals of sex, violence and profanity." Even if Hollywood was making more family-oriented films, "it will take years to get the supply anywhere near the demand," President Dick Rolfe contended.[19] For these and other entrepreneurs, that "untapped market" of churchgoers was the winning ticket—a huge audience not only for family-friendly popular art and criticism but also for advertisers and merchandisers.

Along with a dogged belief that the entertainment media must somehow be used for evangelism, a penchant for sentimentality and the demographics of the "family" market greatly influenced the character of evangelical entertainment. And for better or worse, these ideas, attitudes, and practices largely shaped popular perceptions about the relation of Christianity and popular culture.

But while this evangelical model generated industry growth, it began drawing criticism for both frustrating the original evangelistic ideals and limiting artistic and commercial potential. The CCM industry was caught in a paradox of its own making: the music had little appeal outside the evangelical subculture, where critics easily dismissed most of it as clichéd and redundant. One evangelical songwriter even acknowledged that CCM "for the most part is a homogenized knock-off of pop music."[20] Perhaps that's why artists like Jars of Clay, Switchfoot, Mercy Me, and Stacie Orrico tried hard to avoid being labeled "Christian." Wanting their music to have appeal outside the evangelical market, they either signed with mainstream record companies (like Sixpence None the Richer) or shied away from publicly discussing their Christian convictions (like Creed). In the meantime, a significant trend was underway that would eventually create a crisis and lead to a dramatic change in evangelical attitudes.

A Paradigm Shift

By the mid-1980s, Amy Grant had reached unprecedented stardom in the contemporary Christian music field. Featuring songs like "El Shaddai" and "Sing Your Praise to the Lord," her *Age to Age* album (1982) became a milestone in gospel music; it sold over one million copies and topped the Christian sales charts for almost two years.

Grant's phenomenal success in the gospel music business paved the way for her music to cross over into mainstream radio and record stores. This was a dream come true for many evangelicals who hoped that Christian music "would be so compelling, so cool, that waves of radio fans would convert on the spot."[21] To flourish outside the evangelical

Amy Grant's music exposed tensions in the dominant model for "Christian" popular art.

market, however, Grant had to abandon overtly Christian lyrics; most of her songs now focused on wholesome romantic love. After several projects, *Heart in Motion* (1991) sold over 5 million copies. One song, "Baby Baby," reached the top of the *Billboard* charts, an achievement that *CCM Magazine* called "the most significant event in the history of contemporary Christian music."[22]

The brouhaha over Grant's crossover success garnered considerable press coverage. A writer in the *Los Angeles Times* asked, "Has Amy Grant traded in hallelujah for hubba hubba?"[23] But Grant met fierce criticism in the evangelical community. Religious radio stations refused to play "Baby Baby," and many removed the singer's records from their libraries in protest of her new musical direction. Fans were both perplexed and angered that Grant was not singing about God and even felt betrayed by CCM's brightest star. The absence of any explicit Christian content in *Behind the Eyes* (1997) seemed like a breach of contract, a violation of the rules; there was nothing now to separate her music from secular AC songs. Fans likewise accused Sixpence None the Richer, a self-described "pop band with a Christian underside," of selling out when the band scored a *Billboard* hit in 1998 with "Kiss Me."[24]

Was an evangelical artist like Grant still "Christian" if she sang innocent, if also jejune, love songs that reviewers described as "shallow wholesomeness" and "one step out of the elevator"?[25] Even Grant was unsure. "Am I a Christian? Yes, yes, yes!" she said, adding, "I don't know if *Behind the Eyes* is a Christian record."[26]

Grant's nonconfessional music exposed tensions in the evangelical model and also demanded a new—or at least a revised—justification if it was still going to be considered "Christian." "Some feel that if music doesn't have some kind of evangelical content, it doesn't have any value," Grant said in response to her critics. "I feel differently. I want to be able to turn on the radio and hear fun songs where I'm not being pressured materially, sexually or violence-wise."[27] And other evangelicals eventually began singing a different tune. "People always try to put gospel music in a box, but God is bigger than that," gospel and R&B singer CeCe Winans said. "Gospel music is not always going to be a song that says 'Jesus, Jesus, Jesus.'" In contrast to the traditional CCM rationale, Winans argued, "A lot of time, we feel like if it's not 'Amazing Grace' then it's not gospel music or (it's) something that's watered down—and that's not true."[28]

Comments like these from Grant and Winans represented a dramatic shift in evangelical thinking about popular art. They were a sign that a paradigm shift was taking place. A *paradigm* is an accepted model that has explanatory power for a community; it provides answers to questions about the nature of problems and acceptable solutions. When a paradigm becomes so fraught with problems it is unable to resolve, tensions result and eventually a new model replaces the original—a paradigm shift occurs. The change is signified by a remaking of cultural perceptions and the introduction of new questions and standards for acceptable solutions.

Regarding popular art: Is confessional appearance (which can often be very superficial) the *only* way to characterize "Christian" popular art? And if not confessional appearance, how might we judge these productions as being faithful? Likewise, how can Christians remain faithful in their engagement with the films, television, and music produced in the broader culture?

No Longer Worldly Amusements

Of course there are still some Christians who think that avoiding "secular" popular art altogether is the mark of a true believer. Matthew Crouch, producer of the evangelical sci-fi film *The Omega Code* (1999), said, "My dad was sincerely told by his mother, 'If you go into the theater and see Roy Rogers and Dale Evans ride their horses, you're gonna go right into hell.' We're just waking up to the fact there can be entertainment."[29] Today, however, even the most conservative Christians participate more freely than ever in a world of popular art and culture dominated by huge media conglomerates.

In 2005, the Southern Baptist Convention and American Family Association called off their boycotts of the Walt Disney Company after having no effect. This was just one event revealing changes already underway in the evangelical world.

The *Dallas Morning News* ran a story in 1998 about the growing number of Christians who advocated going to movies, even R-rated ones. Dan Allender, a senior editor of *Mars Hill Review*, said, "We want people to be involved in culture because Christ has revealed himself in culture."[30] Evangelical filmmaker Dallas Jenkins asked, "For those of us GenXers who aren't really into family films, where are the thought-provoking, morally important rated-R films? Every year there are dozens of big, successful family films, but only two or three landmark, important films for adults. Can't at least one be made by a Christian?" He went so far as to say, "Non-Christians are just as capable of producing God-honoring and spiritually uplifting products as Christians are, and I've been as equally offended by a Christian's product as I've been moved by something from a non-Christian."[31]

Changes at the evangelical magazine *Christianity Today*, which began publication in 1956, also revealed this shift in attitude and practice. In contrast to the mainline Protestant publication *The Christian Century*, *Christianity Today* initially reviewed only "Christian" films or mainstream ones that were explicitly religious and would have been acceptable to their readers. When in the mid-1970s the magazine began sporadically treating films that were not directly religious, the reviews were "characterized by negative overall attitudes," according to one scholarly report.[32] That started to change during the 1980s; there was an increase in the number of Hollywood films treated and more mixed critical reviews revealing a penchant for moral and theological themes.

In February 2004, the magazine launched a movie website featuring reviews, interviews, commentaries, and a discussion forum. The stated purpose was "to inform and equip Christian moviegoers to make discerning choices about films through timely coverage, insightful reviews and interviews, educated opinion, and relevant news—all from a biblical worldview."[33] Clearly a paradigm shift had occurred in the evangelical world, a remaking of cultural perceptions that worked to overcome not just spiritual denigration but also elitist assumptions about popular art.

Christianity Today's highbrow publication, *Books & Culture*, published a review that was critical of the popular animated film *Shrek* (2001).

Without much attention to the extent that Disney versions sentimentalized their originals, the reviewer dubbed *Shrek* "a twisted fairy tale" that subverted "the glorious and mysterious and ennobling idea of fairy tales themselves."[34] The flood of passionate reader response (most of it tearing the review to pieces) was unprecedented. "Leaving aside the specifics of agreement or disagreement, what's striking is not only the sheer volume of response—evidently an astonishing number of our readers saw *Shrek* almost as soon as it was released—but also the degree of engagement," the *Books & Culture* editor observed. "Movies, for better or worse, are the lingua franca of our culture, or as close to a common language as we come."[35] And in contrast to earlier generations that banned the "worldly amusements," evangelicals were clearly participating in that cultural conversation.

This transformation drew increasing attention as evangelicalism assumed greater significance in the national interaction between religion, politics, the media, and popular art. In a feature story in the *New York Times Magazine* a writer observed, "Over the last 50 years evangelical Christianity in the United States has moved away from fundamentalism, which is still dedicated to the idea of separation from an ungodly world." And based on the results of a national survey, a writer for *U.S. News & World Report* concluded that "evangelicals—their distinctive faith aside—are acting more and more like the rest of us." But not entirely; these journalists also noted that evangelicals participated "albeit with caution" as they sought "to walk the walk in a pluralistic culture."[36] The posture of aversion to mainstream popular culture that once distinguished evangelicalism has shifted to a model of engagement. But what kind of engagement?

Walk the Walk in a Pluralistic Culture

In the fall of 2003, I participated in a seminar in Los Angeles designed for church leaders, academics, and laypeople to interact with filmmakers. One panel session resounded with the themes of the earlier CCM crossover. These evangelical filmmakers were also pressed by commercial imperatives while still harboring a sense that their work should somehow have evangelistic value. As they saw it, the choice was either make movies with "universal themes" for appeal in the broader culture, or create "a parallel universe of Christian movies."

Panelists also talked about artistic integrity, moral message, and market viability. One producer almost apologetically asked if we could talk about "film as a product that needs to be marketed and sold." It was not an easy course to chart, and given the commercial pressures it was not hard to imagine evangelical filmmakers simply making "homogenized knock-offs" of Hollywood productions that, while wholesome perhaps and friendly to sentimental touches of the divine, could hardly be characterized as representing an integral Christian perspective.

Amy Grant's career shift—from "El Shaddai" to "Baby Baby"—aptly illustrated the effects of commercialization on popular art. In one sense, by overcoming some of the limitations of the evangelical industry's ideas about music making and cultural separation, her music reached a much larger audience. But the process of popularization had its effect as Grant's music, lyrics, and thematic content conformed to the general tastes of the AC market.

As gospel record labels improved production quality, marketing, and distribution, executives remained puzzled by the fact that the market they served was so small in proportion to the size of the churchgoing population. One record executive admitted, "Even if the music product measures up on so many levels—creatively, artistically, commercially— there's still the spiritual dimension, and sometimes at least, our Christian agenda continues to be an obstacle."[37] It was no surprise, then, that evangelical bands were told by mainstream executives that their explicit Christian content limited their crossover success.[38] This should make producers ambivalent at least about presenting the gospel message in a consumer culture.

As evangelical demands for an explicit "Christian" message gave way to producers shooting for mainstream success with a "softer sell," the threat of losing any Christian distinctive became increasingly real. A *Christianity Today* writer wondered, "If Christian culture becomes less of an alternative to the culture, if it *does* bow to mainstream pressures to win more listeners, why bother with exclusively Christian festivals at all?"[39]

Writing about the changes taking place in the CCM industry, Mark Joseph asked, "In a post-CCM world, what kinds of songs should be written by musician Christians who seek to impact the wider culture without alienating listeners who share their faith?"[40] At the center of this whole affair was a central question: What, if anything, constituted a distinctive faith-informed engagement with the popular arts, whether music, movies, or television?

Comfort with Popular Culture

If previous generations were too willing to throw the proverbial baby out with the bathwater in their condemnation of popular culture, were some evangelicals and others going to the opposite extreme now? This is a fairly naïve position that leaves them vulnerable to cultural accommodation—the very thing many of them wanted to resist. Nevertheless, values and practices shunned by previous generations had become commonplace among evangelical Christians, who were "becoming more like their fellow Americans in their comfort with popular culture," as one scholar observed.[41]

Barna Research Group studies showed that "born again Christians" have bought into media technology as much as anyone. In recent years the marketing research firm reported that almost three quarters of Americans subscribe to cable TV; just over one quarter have a satellite dish. Ninety-three percent of Americans own a VCR and 59 percent have Internet access. And there was no significant statistical difference between Christians and the general population. Evangelicals were also numbered among the most frequent moviegoers.[42] Moreover, researchers at MarketCast, a leading Hollywood marketing firm, found religious and nonreligious people indistinguishable when it came to watching movies and television shows.[43] And so while it was true that evangelicals flocked to *The Passion* and shunned Michael Moore's *Fahrenheit 9/11* in 2004, everything in between seemed to be fair game.

In one sense we can understand this as an affirmation of culture. But these studies also suggested that many people who identified themselves as religious did not think much about popular art and culture in terms of their faith, even though for various reasons they might have deemed "Hollywood" antagonistic to God and faithful living. Indeed, a 2004 survey showed that 70 percent of Americans thought movies, music, and television were having a negative effect on the country's moral standards.[44]

There are probably a number of issues at work here. Apparently people are often willing to pay for what they disapprove of. For example, in one survey, three-fourths of single Christian adults thought "movies containing vulgarities, explicit sex, nudity, and antibiblical messages had an adverse effect on their moral and spiritual condition," but at least half of these same people approved of films that included these very ingredients.[45] Despite a reputation for denouncing Hollywood for undermining "traditional values" with R-rated products, a survey showed that Christians were only slightly less likely to see an R-rated movie than non-Christians. And even though Christian leaders have condemned the series because it features witchcraft and wizardry, four out of five teenagers have still read a Harry Potter book or seen a movie with the majority having no discussion with church leaders or parents about the supernatural elements.[46]

People might share attitudes about the popular arts—that television is having a negative effect on individuals and society, that most movies aren't worth the price of the popcorn, that pop singers and Hollywood celebrities have too much influence with young people—but these attitudes do not necessarily reflect their behavior. These same people still go to the movies, have more than one television set in their homes, and purchase videos and CDs.

Despite fears and warnings about the potential dangers of the entertainment media, most people believe that they are personally immune. Scholars call this "the third-person effect"; other people might be negatively affected, but they are not.[47] Also, like most people, churchgoers generally think of popular art as entertainment, downtime after a long day, or a social activity to be enjoyed with friends. They don't think too much about the films and videos they watch or the music they listen to.

But as I will show in the following chapters, critics were right to worry about the potential influence "the market-driven, therapeutic, narcissistic and entertainment-oriented culture" can have on church and society.[48] We should not fall prey to a naïve consumption of popular culture without a faith-informed appraisal.

Conclusion

Popular art can be used for confessional purposes—to enhance worship, make statements of belief, exhort believers to faithful living, or attempt to evangelize. Problems arise when these are perceived to be the *only* legitimate reasons for Christian involvement. As the controversy over Amy Grant's music showed, many Christians believed it was evidence of secularization if a Christian artist treated other topics or served other purposes. I think a more persuasive counterclaim can be made.

Believing that the only reason to create popular art is for evangelism, these Christians portrayed religion as a narrow aspect of life instead of as a life orientation. But if Christ is Lord over all things, then the popular art that Christians produce should not only affirm but also demonstrate this profound belief in God's sovereign rule. Insofar as Christians do not create popular art and music, giving artistic insight into every aspect of life from a faith perspective, *that* is evidence of secularization.

When confessional intent overrides artistic concerns, it constrains the imagination by prohibiting artists from treating a broad range of topics. And restricting the concerns of a faith-informed approach left whole aspects of the entertainment media without critical appraisal. The evangelical music industry, for example, uncritically adopted the secular goals and strategies of the commercial market—the cult of celebrity and hyperbole, sensation, consumption, mass identification—and ultimately equated these with doing ministry.[49] Impersonal forces, like marketing and demographics, can have a great impact on media production and content, and the values of consumerism, like self-indulgence and immediate gratification, can harm individuals, families, and communities.

Especially during times of conflict, groups will attempt to persuade others to their vision of the world using "all the possible instruments of persuasion the culture provides," as cultural historian Warren Susman put it,[50] including the popular arts. For that reason, culture itself can be contested terrain with people trying to convince others of the rightness of their way of life. We all need to be able to identify and think critically about perspectives that show up in the media marketplace, offering us an endless array of choices but limited perspectives on matters that concern us most.

To lay a foundation for the popular art approach presented here, we need to explore the relation of faith and culture to some degree. For as we have already seen, ideas about culture not only set parameters but also shape the character of people's involvement by marking out specific roles for popular art to serve. Culture, then, is the concern of the next chapter.

Summary

- The long history of antagonism between the church and the entertainment industry revealed underlying concerns about the function of entertainment and the possession of cultural power.
- The evangelical paradigm for popular art was distinguished by its emphasis on *confessional* appearance and a concern with *personal* morality. "Christian" popular art came to mean two things: overt religious themes and appropriateness for the "family" audience.
- Popular art can be used for *confessional* purposes, but problems arise when these are perceived to be the *only* legitimate reasons for Christian involvement.
- While earlier generations might have rejected many of the values and practices of the dominant culture, there exists today a sizeable group of Christians who more or less affirm contemporary culture.
- A paradigm shift has taken place regarding evangelical views of popular art.
- According to national surveys, the viewing and listening habits of Christians are hardly different from other groups in terms of both what and how much they watch and listen.

State of the Art

- Most people feel immune to the messages of the popular arts because they view them as mere "entertainment." This is known as the "third-person effect."

Discussion Questions

1. Discuss Amy Grant's "crossover" into the mainstream music market and the ensuing controversy among Christians.
2. Are all "family" films worth watching? If not, what separates worthwhile family films from those that are not?
3. Do you think Christians can or should make or watch R-rated films? Defend your answer.
4. Does removing objectionable content make a film better? Conversely, does including objectionable content make a film better?
5. What, in your opinion, makes a popular artwork "Christian"?
6. How does your Christian faith influence the way you watch movies, listen to music, and read books?
7. Why do you think Christians are generally more attracted to mainstream films, music, radio, and TV than they are to "Christian" alternatives?
8. An observer of British culture contended that many Christians "look at culture more positively and testify to feeling more stimulation—even spiritual stimulation—from 'secular' sources than they do from sources within the evangelical sub-culture." Is this consistent with your own experience? Explain.

2

THE SMOKE GOES UPWARDS

FAITH AND CULTURE

Showbiz is shamanism, music is worship. Whether it's worship of women or their designer, the world or its destroyer, whether it comes from that ancient place we call soul or simply the spinal cortex, whether the prayers are on fire with a dumb rage or dove-like desire, the smoke goes upwards, to God or something you replace God with—usually yourself.

Bono of U2

So at the crux of a Christian conception of culture is that it belongs inescapably to the office or task of being human, is cosmic in scope, and is actually performed as a service of reconciliation and praise or as a wasteful, fruitless attempt to regain paradise for ourselves.

Calvin Seerveld, *Rainbows for the Fallen World*

The day before *The Last Temptation of Christ* opened in select theaters in 1988 an estimated twenty-five thousand people staged a demonstration at Universal Studios in Los Angeles. Most of them were fundamentalist and evangelical Christians carrying Bibles and wooden crucifixes in protest of Martin Scorsese's "blasphemous" film. They chanted "J-E-S-U-S" and waved placards with slogans like "Universal is Anti-Christian," "Stop This Attack on Christianity," "Read the Bible; Know the True Story," and "Scripture Not Scripts." That they also shouted "Jewish money, Jewish money" stained this campaign with racism; mailings and public pronouncements from religious leaders included threats that the film would "create a wave of anti-Semitism."[1]

Coleman Luck was working on the Universal lot then as a television producer and writer. Luck is also a Christian, but he found it "frightening" driving with a colleague through the crowd of people picketing. People "were shoving placards with 'John 3:16' written on them in front of our car," he said. "These were Christians, but believe me, they didn't look very loving. My friend, who was not a Christian and was a producer for [the television program] *Equalizer*, turned to me and said, 'I would hate these people if I didn't know you.'"[2]

The dramatic contest over *The Last Temptation of Christ* garnered media attention as one of the most visible confrontations between the religious community and Hollywood in recent times. The event also showed how different and even conflicted Christians can be in their engagement with popular art. Some Christian critics condemned Scorsese's film as "the most blasphemous evil attack on the Church and the cause of Christ in the history of entertainment," but there were others who concluded that the film's treatment of Christ as both fully human and fully divine was "consistent with all important streams of Christian theology."[3]

Cultural engagement is as varied and conflicted as are attitudes toward popular art. Within the same faith community one group of Christians may give strong support for one political party or another, while others may shun politics altogether. There are some Christians who argue for prayer in public schools; others establish alternative faith-based schools. Some Christians do not have a television in their homes; others have several. There are Christians who believe that a woman's place is in the home; others say a woman's place is outside the home and even in the pulpit.

So what is culture, and why should Christians be concerned with it? Culture is not simply about reading the right books, knowing the right wine to order with dinner, and being familiar with Beethoven or Monet. Culture, I will argue, has much to do with faith; it is part of being "fearfully and wonderfully made" in the image of God (Ps. 139:14). Culture represents human responses to God's first and foundational command: "Be fruitful and increase in number; fill the earth and subdue it" (Gen. 1:28). God entrusts ordinary human beings with the continuing process of creation. That we are God's co-creators is a fundamental assumption and overarching theme in scripture.

This chapter explores the concept of culture as the way humans define and live in God's world. Understanding the dynamics of culture is important for this study. Ideas and attitudes about popular art center on a fundamental question: how are people of faith to be *in* the world but not *of* it? Some Christians take this to mean that God requires minimal cultural engagement, but that view does not resonate with Jesus's petition for the disciples: "My prayer is not that you take them out of the world but that you protect them from the evil one" (John 17:15). Instead, I believe Christians should be actively engaged with culture: studying it, discerning positive and negative aspects, and working to redeem it.

Created with Purpose

We learn from scripture that God brought the created order into being and claims ownership of the entire creation. The Psalmist declared, "The earth is the LORD's, and everything in it, the world, and all who live in it" (Ps. 24:1). The whole creation is the realm of the kingdom of God—the place where God rules. And all "things," all creatures, are God's servants (Ps. 119:91).

The opening chapters of Genesis affirm that everything was made with a purpose, that is, a role for service in God's kingdom. That purpose is its *meaning*, the reason for its existence. The vegetation is to bear fruit with seed in it according to its kind. The sun, moon, and stars are there to light the earth, to separate the day from the night, and to serve as signs to mark seasons and years. The fish in the sea, the birds in the air, and the living creatures on the land are to be fruitful and increase in number according to their kinds. The human creatures were created in God's image with a unique and special purpose—to be the caretakers of the creation.

God called the creation "good"—meaning perfect—even as it was unfinished. The creation stood poised on the threshold of its historical development, with all its vast potentials awaiting their realization. The magnitude of that potential staggers the imagination. Think about the vast applications—from technologies to transportation—that followed the discovery of the wheel, or how ideas like democracy, capitalism, and socialism have shaped human social relations. Consider the effects that theories like psychoanalysis or behaviorism have had on our understanding of human behavior. We've made discoveries about the natural environment, such as photosynthesis, and others related to human biology, such as penicillin and DNA. God's co-creators have used the stuff of creation to develop imaginative art forms—literature, poetry, painting, sculpture, theater, music, and film—and incredible means for human communication, including languages, printing, photography, sound recordings, radio and television broadcasts, satellite transmissions, and the Internet.

God delegated the ongoing work of creation to men and women. This is known in theological circles as the *cultural mandate*, God's command at creation that humans *do* culture. Our calling as God's co-creators does not make us into gods, but it does highlight our humanness. We alone among earth's creatures are accountable to God for the *care* and *cultivation* of human life and the potential of creation.

See the connection? The Latin root of the word "culture" is *colere*, which, as one scholar explained, "can mean anything from cultivating and inhabiting to worshipping and protecting."[4] The term culture, then, is nuanced and complex, embracing multiple meanings that collectively imply a sacred purpose to all human activities in God's world.

All Things Are Servants

Personal identity, communal concerns, the meaning of life and work, culture and history are all inextricably bound up in this call to stewardship. In Hebrew, a steward is literally a person who is "over a house," a guardian or ruler who has been given authority and power to accomplish a task. A steward, or manager, has been delegated responsibility and put in charge of something and is accountable to someone for getting the job done. Joseph was made chief steward in charge of Pharaoh's land, resources, and possessions (Gen. 41:39–41). In the parable of the shrewd manager, the servant must give an account of his stewardship of the master's possessions (Luke 16:2). In a more profound sense, stewardship refers to our calling to administer over God's entire creation: "The highest heavens belong to the LORD, but the earth he has given to man" (Ps. 115:16). This is a tremendous responsibility, for we are accountable to God for the welfare and potential of all earthly creatures.

We read in Colossians that Christ is Lord of "all things": "things in heaven and on earth, visible and invisible, whether thrones or powers or rulers or authorities; all things were created by him and for him." And further that "God was pleased to have all his fullness dwell in him, and through him to reconcile to himself all things" (Col. 1:16, 19). Jesus is the Lord of all created reality—visible and invisible—the lilies and trees in the fields, powers and authorities, the whole realm of ideas, emotions, and imagination. I want to emphasize that the meaning of "all things" has to do with service in God's created order (Ps. 119:91).

How do we work toward realizing the rich potentials of God's creation? In this important endeavor, Christians can rely on the Word of God to prepare, inform, and correct us as we learn through observation, study, and experience (2 Tim. 3:16). The Bible is the historical narrative of God's work for the redemption of his people and the whole creation. It is a guide, not just for personal salvation but also for right and faithful living. The Bible is a light for our paths, informing our journey through a history that is not static but filled with changes of all sorts—technological, social, aesthetic, economic, and so forth. Thankfully, God's plan for restoration is a dynamic, ongoing process involving generation after generation.

So our experience in God's world cannot be discounted in efforts to bring all things under the Lordship of Christ. We know that the Spirit's ongoing illumination of scripture is progressive in the sense that it moves steadily forward, increasing our understanding while building on the knowledge that came before. As our findings advance, we make new discoveries that show the glory and honor of God, and we can rely on the Bible to give us insights into how new developments and different situations can be put into service.

God established principles for all of life and creation. We inhabit a created order, not a world in chaos, and God's principles for that order are knowable. These principles apply across the spectrum of life, and the realization of them enriches our lives and affirms God's handiwork. We know, for example, that trust is important for deep and meaningful relationships, that justice is critical to good government and jurisprudence, that ecological stewardship is necessary for the health of our natural environment, that truth is essential in providing news and information, that discipline and diligence contribute to solid scholarship, and that creativity enlivens drama and storytelling.

Naming Things for Service

In the Genesis account, Adam first cultivates creation by naming the other creatures (Gen. 2:19–20). Adam imaginatively invents words that represent things in God's creation. A word is a symbol—a representation of an idea or thing. The word *symbol* is derived from the Greek term *symballein*, to "throw together." We symbolize by throwing together a word and the reality it represents. There is such closeness between a symbol and what it represents that they are like two halves of the same thing; a symbol shares in the reality of what it symbolizes. Symbolizing is a key to living because it helps us to establish meanings for the things in God's world, including love, sex, romance, work, play, success, masculine and feminine ideals, and so forth.

At first, symbolizing might seem rather simple. If you want to get out of a building in the United States, look for signs marking the EXIT. But in France look for SORTIE, and in England the WAY OUT. In the United States, you get in a "line"; in Britain you get in a "queue." Same thing, but a different name. As this suggests, there is an arbitrary quality to a symbol in that people assign meaning and share interpretations of it. The door leading outside doesn't have to be—and isn't—called the EXIT all around the world.

The process of creating and interpreting symbols can very quickly become rather complex and even contentious. When we name or identify something with a symbol, we assign meaning to it with a certain attitude that reveals what we believe. Think about terms in the popular vernacular that describe a sexually promiscuous woman: "whore," "slut," "tramp," "bimbo," "sleaze." Compare these to the more flattering words like "stallion," "stud," "playboy," "macdaddy" that describe sexually promiscuous men. These terms or symbols represent different meanings—attitudes, values, and beliefs—regarding sexually promiscuous people based on their gender. In this culture a promiscuous sexual encounter devalues the woman but heightens the status of the man. Men and women can come to understand these symbols as guides for conduct and behavior. As this suggests, once we create a culture, we are largely bound by it. We have to live up to the ideals, share the same attitudes, and hold the same beliefs, or take a stand against them and try to fashion alternatives. Either way, we have to work within the existing cultural system.

These same meanings about sexuality can also be communicated in fashion, advertising, television programs, music videos, movies, songs, and so forth. These media images draw their power as affirmations of the larger cultural system—in my example, the culture's story of masculinity and femininity, what it means to be a man or woman. It is in this sense, as I noted earlier, that the popular arts reflect a society they help to create.

Knowing how language works can help us understand culture, for culture also has to do with establishing meanings that people share. So much so, in fact, that anthropologist Clifford Geertz described cultures as systems of shared meanings.[5] But language is only one sort of symbol we use to create shared meanings. Paintings and instrumental music are also symbolic. If we think of the creation—all that is, visible and invisible—as a primary environment, culture refers to the secondary, symbolic world that humans construct as we continually cultivate the creation. Cultural formation has to do with interpreting and defining reality.

The ideals, beliefs and values, attitudes and assumptions that make up a cultural system are invisible in the sense that they have no material existence. You can't hang an ideal or a value on the living-room wall, although you might find a painting that represents them. A culture is communicated through what anthropologists call *texts*. Cultural texts are human actions, events, and material works that embody meanings that are widely shared. As the term suggests, a text can be "read," or interpreted, to understand its meaning; cultural values find social and material existence in our actions and products.

As Geertz put it, a culture is "an ensemble of texts."[6] These texts include conversations, rituals, ceremonies, news reports, songs, poems, theatrical plays, dances, theories, political rhetoric, myths, legends, stories, icons, advertising, films, television programs, popular songs, literature, speeches, architecture, works of visual art, and so forth. We use the term *culture*, then, to refer to the realm of human activity and its results, both material and nonmaterial products.

Scholars often talk about cultures as "dramatic conversations about things that matter to their participants."[7] Since meaning is negotiated through means of communication, popular art is an important area for study. The popular arts can show us the meaning of things, and in that regard they are one way that we communicate our culture. Determining meaning, however, is a matter of perspective and interpretation. We have to ask, *What* are the stories about life the popular arts tell? *Who* tells the stories? *What* is their inspiration? *From what perspective* do *these artists* approach the issues of life and *what meaning* do *they* give to them?

Culture and Religion

"All the world's a stage, and all the men and women merely players."[8] This well-known line from Shakespeare suggests a relation between life and drama that gets at the idea of culture. Some theorists even argue that life *is* drama and that people live and act in ways that can be analyzed in terms of roles they play in the acts and scenes of everyday life—at home, school, church, work, or weekend parties. In this sense, we can compare a people's culture to the script for a film. Like a screenplay, a culture determines viewpoint and priorities while also representing a particular way of looking at life and events. So culture can be likened to a script that guides and explains people's actions, giving us a sense of identity and purpose.

A culture, then, is a collection of ideals and beliefs, values and assumptions, that makes up a kind of master plan for living and interpreting life. Of course, these are only analogies to help us understand a very abstract concept, but it is important to realize that when people belong to a culture, they share common ways of understanding and interpreting their experience and guiding their behavior. Culture involves both creating meaning for things and living according to those meanings. It shapes experience and expectations, and gives us a means of coping with the new and unexpected. A cultural system gives people assurance about themselves and certainty about existence. It brings order, clarity, and direction out of the complexities and contradictions in life. A culture can shape what we come to know and value—how we understand God's world.

The Bible gives us a complex understanding of culture. Culture is a gift from God, as well as a religious duty and obligation. All human beings are made in the image of God and share in God's original commission to cultivate the creation. The cultural mandate, then, unites us in our communal responsibility to manage God's world. In this regard, culture is universal, a common endeavor and historical process carried on from generation to generation that binds us together in the community of humankind. Cultural diversity is also an assumption in scripture. The Christian faith is not restricted to any one culture, but is "for every nation, tribe, people and language" (Rev. 7:9).

To be "religious," then, means much more than going to church, praying, and evangelizing—what I am calling *confessional* life. In scripture, the word "heart" is used to represent the religious core of human existence. "Religion, centered in the heart, is the response side of our covenantal relationship with God," one theologian explained. "The heart is the key to who a person really is before the face of God."[9] Human beings, created to love and worship God and serve their neighbors, are religiously centered, whether one believes in God or not. For example, "Who are humans?" is a deeply religious question with profound implications for how we live and treat others. Do all humans bear God's image regardless of their avowed religious beliefs, race, sex, gender, or class? Are humans the supreme beings in the universe, or are we accountable to God in all that we do? Do we tend a creation in obedience to the Creator, or is this a natural world over which humans rule supreme?

I understand *religion* to describe an innate condition of human existence that is both fundamental and universal. Religion, as Calvin Seerveld put it, refers to "that inescapable, structural God-relatedness of humans, that deep-down unconscious bent of being dependent upon some Absolute that every person has, that *sensus deitatis* (sense of deity), the directedness of one's self toward the true God or toward whatever one takes to be divine, final."[10] By this account, worship of money is idolatrous, but still religious. The hope that progress through technological development and economic growth will bring *shalom*—peace, prosperity, security—is religious. The belief that human beings have limitless possibilities and power is religious.

We can distinguish between religion, in this sense, and organized or formal religion. Religion—a life directed in service of God or something less than God—is not restricted to confessional life. Instead, we are religious in every dimension: the social, political, economic, and aesthetic, to mention some. Theologian Paul Tillich, for example, talked about religion as "the meaning-giving substance of culture, and culture is the totality of forms in which the basic concern of religion expresses itself." In short, he wrote, "religion is the substance of culture, culture is the form of religion."[11] In other words, faith is articulated in culture. This understanding of religion lets us see all human thought and activity as grounded in basic religious convictions; Christian freedom and service then is meant for every area of life.

In these terms, the issue is not *where* we serve God, that is, in which aspects of life. The Christian life should represent the fullness of our humanity as image bearers. The issue is *how* we serve. It has to do with the way we conduct business and family life, the way we worship, and how we spend our leisure time. Whether shopping at the mall, writing stories or composing songs, watching television or movies, our dealings in all of these activities should be offered to God. The translation of Romans 12:1 in *The Message* puts it nicely: "Take your everyday, ordinary life—your sleeping, eating, going-to-work, and walking-around life—and place it before God as an offering." It is in this sense that life is worship—a living sacrifice to God. While sacrifice contains an allusion to death, this verse strikes a contrast since we are called to be "living" sacrifices—heart, soul, body, and mind. This principle holds regardless of one's faith convictions, for all humans are created as believing, worshiping, and cultural beings.

The writer of Ecclesiastes tells us that there is a time for everything under the sun. There is a time to eat, drink, and find satisfaction in our work (Eccles. 3:13). God also expects us to feed the hungry (Matt. 25:35–36), to pass just laws (Prov. 8:15), and to be fair in business (Prov. 11:1; 16:11). Those skilled in the arts are to perform with excellence while cultivating the potentials of their medium (Exod. 31:1–6; Prov. 22:29). There is also time for cultural discernment: "Do not conform any longer to the pattern of this world, but be transformed by the renewing of your mind. Then you will be able to test and approve what God's will is—his good, pleasing and perfect will" (Rom. 12:2). These are all worthy endeavors that, when carried out with integrity and character, can give praise and honor to God by affirming a Christian presence in cultural affairs—including the realm of popular culture.

Sacred and Secular

Christians who fragment God's creation into sacred and secular realms or distinctions between "the holy and the common," as one writer put it, often conclude that culture cannot be redeemed, "since it is 'common,' shared by believer and unbeliever."[12] This view is based on a belief that since the Fall, culture is a necessary evil, its only worth being to serve "lesser" human needs. But how could culture be of "lesser" importance? It is our central task as image bearers.

That Christians draw lines making distinctions between religious and nonreligious aspects of life is an effect of secularization. The term *secular* should not be used to refer to specific activities in God's world—politics, business, education, or popular art—but to the orientation, the spiritual direction that is represented by the way people carry out these practices. Secular refers to the absence of faith conviction and perspective in performing these activities. As secularization occurs, a Christian faith orientation loses significance for our thinking, practices, and institutions. The effect is to weaken the influence of faith in public affairs, making it primarily a private matter having to do with personal devotional life and morality, family, and local congregation. It is as though God has no jurisdiction in public life. This is a complete fallacy. As the Dutch theologian and statesman Abraham Kuyper said: "There is not a square inch in the whole domain of human existence over which Christ, who is sovereign over *all*, does not cry: 'Mine!'"[13]

In other words, Christians cannot be selective in their responsibility to the God who lays claim to all of life and creation. We cannot try to be faithful when it comes to personal morality and church life but then employ "secular" tactics, values, goals, and ethical standards for business, politics, education, art, and so forth. Our entire life is meant for service in God's kingdom.

It follows from this understanding that a Christian approach to popular art is not relegated to a delineated "religious" sphere (made up of practices like evangelism, worship, and prayer), theology, or even issues of personal morality. Instead, this understanding of religion and culture draws our attention to how beliefs are represented in the world of a popular artwork.

Redemption Means Restoration

God's first command to us as image bearers is easily overshadowed by the fall of humans and the creation into sin and the focus of the Bible on the history of redemption that culminates in Christ. The Fall, however, does not negate or abolish the original cultural mandate, even though this central human task to administer the potentials of the creation is now corrupted by sin, which has become part of the human condition in a fallen world. We all bear the image of God, but now everything—our reason, imagination, emotions, cultural patterns, and achievements—is entangled in our rebellion against God.

It is not hard to see that cultivating the creation is a complex affair. While different and even conflicting perspectives exist, people of whatever faith conviction have the capacity to develop and enjoy humanizing aspects of culture and also promote and suffer under sinful developments. Together we have to support cultural advances that are life affirming—promoting growth, justice, freedom, and human dignity for all—and work to reform those that are dehumanizing or oppressive.

The effects of sin are not limited to the human heart but involve culture, society, and creation. The Old Testament prophet Isaiah described a Messiah that transforms the entire creation (Isa. 11, 65, 66). What effect does this have? There is no more weeping and death is ended. Harmony comes to the creation—the wolf and lamb feed together—and to our cultural endeavors. Swords will be turned into plowshares and spears into pruning hooks (Isa. 2:4). People will inhabit the houses they build and eat the fruit from vineyards they plant. They will not toil in vain, but "will long enjoy the works of their hands" (Isa. 65:22). In other words, there is continuity between this life and the new life to come. Human labor and culture are redeemed, restored in meaning and purpose in the New Jerusalem, the peaceful City of God.

As many writers have noted, humankind began in a garden—a creation filled with potentials yet to be realized—but the Christian life is directed toward a city, the New Jerusalem. The ultimate result of Christ's return will be the consummation of God's creation or kingdom into the new heavens and new earth (Rev. 21–22). The Hebrew word for "new" means renewed or restored to its original purpose. This implies that the creation we now inhabit will *not* be destroyed (meaning wiped out of existence) and replaced by an ethereal place where the redeemed wear white robes and float around playing golden harps. When God finished his creative work—on earth as well as in heaven—it was perfect. The atoning work of Jesus Christ restores *this* creation—redemption means restoration. At Christ's return, the creation will be purified from the presence of sin and restored to its original purpose as a dwelling place for humankind to rule for God. What kind of world do we want to present to the Lord upon his return?

So we see that, from Genesis to Revelation, humans are called upon to rule in many different ways in God's world. It is vanity to think that we could usher in the new heaven and the new earth ourselves, for humans cannot finally remove sin from the creation. Nevertheless, God has entrusted us with the created order, and like the servants in the parable of the talents, we will have to settle our accounts when the rightful owner returns.

The Eyes of Your Heart

Cultural activity itself is a creational given, but Christian participation is marked by an overarching purpose. We are called to be salt in the world, working to enrich culture and preserve life-affirming aspects. We are also called to be a light to show the way for cultural development, uncovering and disentangling forces for good and evil, working to restrain evil and advance redemptive potentials by redirecting unhealthy or destructive patterns toward principles in line with loving God and serving our neighbor.

When Jerusalem was seized by the Babylonians, Daniel and his friends did not separate themselves from, nor were they assimilated into, the now dominant culture of their foreign conquerors. They showed wisdom and discernment in trying to be *in* the Babylonian culture but not *of* it. Although they served in Nebuchadnezzar's court, they refused to bow and worship the king's gold idol. Rather than be defiled by the royal food and wine used in heathen idol worship, they requested an exemption and found nourishment in vegetables and water. They used the talents God gave them to learn the language, literature, and diplomacy of the Babylonians. As a result, the king entrusted them with positions as stewards that allowed them to have influence for God's sake.

Likewise, when in Athens, Paul demonstrated an understanding of Greek culture—including its art and literature—and was able to communicate with a wide range of people. "So he reasoned in the synagogue with the Jews and the God-fearing Greeks, as well as in the marketplace day by day with those who happened to be there" (Acts 17:17).

Scripture encourages people of faith to engage their culture in positive ways, while also providing a framework for critique of that culture. As I noted earlier, people are bound by their culture to a large extent. They identify themselves, think, feel, and act according to established ideals, beliefs, attitudes, and values. Christians should understand that popular art engages what is common among people in the arena of human affairs. While we ought to be able to enjoy much of what other people enjoy, we should also be mindful of the biblical imperative to be distinct and live in the light of our convictions.

The Bible is filled with images and metaphors about seeing. To open one's eyes, to see, is to comprehend the truth, to understand the meaning of things. Seeing with the "eyes of your heart" (Eph. 1:18) is a way to think about culture. Culture is anchored in faith. To carry out our cultural duties, we have to be looking at things from the perspective of faith, for as much as we need to be able to see, "we live by faith, not by sight" (2 Cor. 5:7). In their own unique way, the popular arts help us to "see." As British film and TV producer Norman Stone pointed out, movies "can move people into thought, into facing things, into challenging themselves in a different way from a textbook or novel or sermon."[14] Whether as producers or patrons, people have a responsibility to understand this vital means of cultural communication.

The late George Gerbner, a media analyst, observed, "For the first time in human history, the stories are told not by parents, not by the school, not by the church, not by the community or tribe and in some cases not even by the native country but by a relatively small and shrinking group of global conglomerates with something to sell."[15] This is especially true in our postmodern world, where global media companies pay little attention to national borders, and new forms of communication—cable, satellites, DVDs, the Internet—can override any nation's attempts to protect its cultural heritage and boundaries. As Gerbner indicated, is it not clear that in contemporary society the producers of popular art inform our understanding of culture as much as any other single factor?

The popular arts can make our cultural values known to others and invite consideration of them. In other words, they show both how humans live and how (some think) they ought to live. As such, they can be "read," interpreted, and evaluated as maps of reality, humanly constructed representations of the world. By considering the popular arts in this way, we approach them as a dramatic conversation that we can take part in as producers, critics, and audience members.

So it is that the creation and evaluation of popular art is one way we turn faith into a vision both of and for life. How does this occur? In the next chapter we will consider some of the concepts used to explain the process by which people make sense of the world and engage popular art.

Summary

- God made *everything*—visible and invisible—and claims ownership of *everything*. Further, all things were made with a purpose—to serve in God's creation—and so all things are God's servants.
- To be God's image bearer is to be human, and to be human is to be a cultural agent, carrying on God's creative work by *doing* culture. This is known as the *cultural mandate*.
- *Culture* is our common, historical endeavor to define and live in God's world, but after the human fall in sin, culture is a complex affair because the effects of sin are not limited to the human heart, but involve culture, society, and creation.

The Smoke Goes Upwards

- Symbolizing is a key to living because it is the means by which we establish meanings for all things in God's world.
- That a culture reveals what humans believe about "things" shows the close relation between faith and culture.
- Culture is communicated through *texts,* which are human actions, events, and material works that embody meanings that are widely shared.
- The term *religion* refers to an innate condition of human existence that is both fundamental and universal. Being religious is not restricted to confessional life, but we are religious in every dimension of life.
- The popular arts are cultural representations or texts that give substance to cultural values and perspectives. Creating and evaluating popular art is one way we turn faith into a vision both of and for life.

Discussion Questions

1. What is culture, and why is it important for Christians to think of themselves as cultural agents or stewards in God's creation?
2. How should this biblical understanding of culture and stewardship affect the way we think about the popular arts and culture?
3. That all *things* are intended for service in God's world is a central motif in scripture. How might this idea affect the way we think about symbolizing and engaging culture?
4. Name some ways you can actively and intentionally fulfill the cultural mandate as an individual and as a community.

3

TERMS OF THE TRADE

STUDYING POPULAR ART AND CULTURE

The thing about writing and directing a film is that you are presenting a view of the universe. Each time, every scene, every line. Every time you put the camera down you are saying here's a version of the universe as I perceive it. And that is being tested by everyone who sees that movie.

Lawrence Kasdan, Filmmaker

Why do people go to movies, watch sporting events, read novels, or turn to "extra-ecclesiastical (or, loosely, 'popular') religion"? They participate in such activities because these and other forms of popular culture function in the same way traditional religion has always functioned: to provide ways for one to make sense of one's world and life.

Editors, *Screening the Sacred: Religion, Myth, and Ideology in Popular American Film*

When the shootings at Columbine High School in Littleton, Colorado, occurred in 1999, I was living in London, England. This shocking tragedy captured the attention of the British press, and one journalist summarized American responses.

The religious right blamed what happened on the federal ban on prayer in the schools. The internet, where one of the suspects had a web site, was severely criticised, as were violent movies, television shows and video games. Child psychologists were happy to talk about how we don't encourage boys to share their feelings. . . . The anti-gun lobby used the shootings to rail against the easy access to guns. But the pro-gun lobby, incredibly, blamed the shooting deaths of the 15 people on the fact that we don't have enough guns. . . . The perennial white racist politician David Duke could not resist labeling the massacre a product of "diversity."[1]

The people who held each of these positions claimed to know the nature of the problem and also the logical and acceptable solution. This may have seemed so obvious to each of them that they could not understand why everyone didn't see it the same way.

But such disagreement should not surprise us at all, considering the myriad factors that shape people's perceptions, attitudes, and beliefs. We know from experience, for example, that not everyone finds certainty in God and, moreover, that a common faith does not automatically or even consistently result in a certain way of life. People who sit beside each other in church every Sunday might recite the same creed but still think and live in very different ways. As I noted earlier, they may or may not share the same views on fashion, education, social life, home decor, church involvement, political issues, the economy, or the value of art. The same Christians who all confess they should love their neighbor might support or oppose public policies having to do with affirmative action, welfare, tax reform, or health care. Believing that we are all created in God's image might not prevent them from harboring racist, sexist, or homophobic stereotypes.

Actually, Christians may have a stronger sense of union with others who are of like mind on these issues than with people in general who share their common faith in Jesus Christ. This may seem strange at first. After all, aren't we all supposed to be "one in the spirit"? How can we explain the widely divergent views of Christians who all profess "one Lord, one faith, one baptism" (Eph. 4:5)? Such diversity of perspective, even among people of common faith, should make us recognize the complexity of culture and how hard it is to understand living in God's good but fallen creation.

In *Clueless* (1995), a movie about high-school life, Cher (Alicia Silverstone) is asked, "What's a Monet?" She responds: "It's like a painting, see? From far away, it's OK, but up close, it's a big old mess." Trying to understand culture as a meaning-making process can be a lot like that. From a distance perhaps, it may appear straightforward: people come to accept certain beliefs and act accordingly. But as we have seen, the closer you get, instead of a clear and consistent pattern of meaning, we discover that a *perspective*, that vision of life an individual or community holds, is fashioned through complex negotiations with faith convictions and cultural beliefs and assumptions.

Scholars employ various terms in their investigation of the human search for meaning; religion, culture, worldview, myth, and ideology are keywords in the vocabulary of culture studies. A range of definitions exist and there is often much overlap among them. One film scholar, for example, equated "ideological meaning" with "a person's view or group's worldview." Another scholar referred to worldview as a "strange collection of assumptions, attitudes, and ideas." This makes worldview seem a lot like culture. Likewise, some scholars sound like they are talking about culture when they define ideologies as "the systems of meaning within which people live in reality."[2] That writers will often use the same descriptive imagery (like lens or picture) also suggests a close relation between these concepts.

I think of these different terms as co-extensive in the sense that with some variations they all have to do with describing the cultural process by which people make sense of life and live meaningfully in the world. In the previous chapter we considered culture and religion. In this chapter we'll look at other concepts used regularly in the study of popular art and culture.

Worldview and Cultural Orientation

A *worldview* is variously described as a lens, a model, a picture, or a framework consisting of "fundamental beliefs through which we view the world and our calling and future in it."[3] The term worldview has been used to describe the way the world *is*, while also providing a model for the way the world *ought* to be. A worldview is rooted in faith insofar as it deals with the ultimate questions about the human condition—identity and meaning, sin and suffering, hope and despair, life and death—that can only be known through faith.

Worldviews are made up of "basic beliefs" that "form a framework or pattern; they hang together in a certain way," one scholar explained. And while they may lack internal consistency, "it remains true that the more significant feature of worldviews is their tendency toward pattern and coherence."[4] This is a key characteristic of worldview.

In one sense a worldview can shape itself to faith while also fashioning the world of human experience to itself. If someone believes in supernatural intervention, for example, she might believe a cancer patient's recovery is an act of God. An atheist, however, might interpret the same event as evidence of the progress and power of human knowledge and technology.

Terms of the Trade

In another sense, however, events can also shape a worldview and even affect faith commitment. A person who experiences a horrible tragedy—the death of a loved one or the ravages of war—may doubt the existence of God or question divine love and power. A young man's identity and self-esteem can be influenced more by the ideals portrayed in advertising than by a belief that he has dignity because he bears the image of God. A society's view of gender can have a great impact on how a woman might think about the ways she can serve God.

People are not born with a culture, a way of life, but are nurtured into one. Under normal circumstances all of us grow up in a cultural environment. Beginning in early childhood we learn the ideals, language, norms, values, traditions, habits, customs, beliefs, and the acceptable behavior of a particular way of life. Perhaps we can talk theoretically about worldview formation to the extent that a person or community becomes conscious of and articulates that way of life in some systematic way. But these dynamics of the meaning-making process would seem to militate against the simple idea that a worldview proceeds out of faith. A worldview, if we think of it as "a unifying perspective" or "coherent vision of life," is also shaped by personal dynamics, social and cultural environment, and other conditions that may exist in a certain place and time.[5] Philosophers aside, perhaps, most people do not think in such a methodical way or live such an orderly existence.

Let me explain. Christians may accept the Bible as God's Word, believe in the triune God as the Creator of all things, recognize sin as the cause of the human predicament, and profess that Jesus Christ is both divine and human, and that he redeemed humankind by atoning for sin. We do not get much beyond these basic beliefs, however, before things get rather complicated and even conflicted. On just about any issue—family and child rearing, military expenditures and justification for war, abortion, gay marriage, health care, capital punishment, the environment, distribution of wealth, the role of government and of church, educational curriculum, technological development, to name many—there are myriad "Christian" perspectives. It is not hard to see that these perspectives have nevertheless taken shape in ways that resulted in significant differences and even conflicts despite their common "worldview" assumptions.

Even though these Christian worldviews may all be rooted in a faith in Jesus Christ, the fact that there are a variety of Christian perspectives that don't just differ but even conflict indicates that worldview is not necessarily the paramount factor in accounting for the pattern of human action. This observable phenomenon draws attention to the limits of the explanatory power of the concept of a worldview.

"The time is long past when widely shared 'worldviews' or dominant political or religious institutions, such as the nation-state or the church, mosque, or synagogue, provided comprehensive road maps that most people follow," philosopher Lambert Zuidervaart observed. He preferred the term *cultural orientation*. Cultural orientation refers to "how individuals, communities, and organizations find their direction both within and by way of culture." Zuidervaart explained that "such cultural pathfinding is never pure or neutral. It is always already underway, drawing upon cultural resources that are historically effective to a greater or lesser extent."[6]

Cultural orientation has to do with the formation of personal identity and social solidarities and is characterized by both individual and communal matters. Rather than having it all together, it suggests still figuring it out, asking questions, finding one's way amidst life's ambiguities and the realities of suffering and injustice, however confident of one's faith. In other words, we all have much to learn; developing a cultural orientation is a lifelong task.

However we talk about the meaning-making process, it is informed by faith and culture. A cultural orientation functions as a kind of perspective; it can mold the world into a particular kind of place that may or may not reflect the truth about God's created order. Seerveld described *perspective* as "the simply lived-out, expressed, or carefully articulated hanging-togetherness of a sane person's thought, word, and deed."[7] To a certain extent, all life perspectives are grounded in some kind of faith, because we cannot know with complete certainty the answers to life's deepest quandaries. We see "but a poor reflection as in a mirror" (1 Cor. 13:12), and we all have faith, a hope that what we believe is true and trustworthy. Christian perspectives have to be shaped and tested by scripture in order to resist the temptation to wrongly appropriate secular beliefs.

"Christians' trust in God may be mingled or confused with some culturally formed assumptions, ideals, and values. Inevitably it will," George Marsden observed. "The danger is that our culturally defined loves, allegiances, and understandings will overwhelm and take precedence over our faithfulness to God."[8] Simply being a believer does not necessarily mean that someone will automatically think and act in ways that are characteristically "Christian." Such an attitude diminishes the effects of sin and the complex entanglement of cultural beliefs and values. People of whatever faith perspective can easily accept ideals and attitudes about life (and popular art) that are more representative of secular values than Christian ones. And as I will show later, cultural accommodation ought to be a real concern for people of faith.

However complex the phenomenon of popular art might be, a faith perspective is an identifiable part of the aesthetic experience that plays a role in both the creation of and experience with a popular artwork.

My own analysis tries to account for this. Concepts like cultural orientation and perspective suggest an approach to popular art that is at once grounded in a perspective and is still exploratory—one that lends itself to an understanding of artworks as representations of life based on cultural perspectives or orientations.

Myth and Ideology

The term *myth* refers to a people's collective way of thinking about something, whether life and death, good and evil, family, freedom, race, or justice. Myths help build social consensus by providing a common vision; they provide a measure of unity in a society by reinforcing its basic values, justifying its existence, and sanctifying its goals. Myths help a community understand the past and present and anticipate and plan for the future. In short, as one writer put it, "Myth reveals a culture's bedrock assumptions and aspirations."[9]

The universal nature of myth, which can be seen in cross-cultural forms, points to the inherent religiosity of human beings. From primitive gods and creation myths to contemporary beliefs in the salvific power of science, progress, or prosperity, common myths invest ordinary life with meaning. Even so, myths are social constructions, stories that arise out of the course of historical experience and collective memory offering explanations and interpretations of the world. Myths and their narrative representations help people make sense of their lives regardless of the veracity of the myth. They provide a way for people to examine their place in the world by comparing it to a shared idea.

A common mythic culture operates at the level of assumption for most people; myths exist apart from discourse and argumentation as concepts that people already accept as true and upon which they conduct their lives. Most people probably cannot articulate in any systematic fashion their society's mythic system, but they do know stories that represent those myths. The children's book *The Little Engine That Could*, for example, is a representation of the American myth of success—the belief that through determination and hard work you can achieve anything.

Believing a myth to be a true account of the nature of reality, people are driven "to make the myth something historically real; that is, to turn the utopian promise into a specific kind of ideology," Warren Susman wrote. He also noted that it is the "special meeting ground between history and myth that frequently provides a key to the central tensions within a culture."[10] In this sense, *ideology* can be understood as a specific social platform—propositions, policies, proposals, and practices—designed to put myths to work in everyday life.

For example, parents who accept as "natural" the patriarchal proposition that men (and the masculine) are superior to women (and the feminine) will often treat boys differently from girls. The proposition that the poor are all shiftless and corrupt is based on the mythic belief that anyone who works hard can increase his wealth, possessions, and social status; those who fail have nothing to blame but themselves. It might be easy then to overlook certain realities: social barriers do exist, people might live with physical or mental differences that hinder their ability to climb the social or economic ladder. If, on the other hand, someone accepts that social, political, and economic structural inequalities can negatively impact the condition of people's lives, he might be inclined to seek solutions to poverty in different public policies and not just blame individuals. It is not hard to see how beliefs and assumptions can crystallize into attitudes about the real world.

Ideological propositions can make their way into popular artworks. For example, the characterization and storyline in D. W. Griffith's classic 1915 silent film *The Birth of a Nation* are directed by the racist assumption that white people are superior to black people. White characters are shown as loving and caring, while black characters are portrayed as sinister, corrupt, and evil. As another example, in *Trading Places* (1983), the rich and pompous Louis Winthorpe III (Dan Aykroyd) manages a commodity brokerage firm owned by two conniving old rich men, the Duke brothers (Ralph Bellamy and Don Ameche). When an African-American street hustler, Billy Ray Valentine (Eddie Murphy), is falsely arrested for stealing Winthorpe's briefcase, the Dukes orchestrate a change in places, stripping Winthorpe of his job, home, and wealth and giving it all to Valentine. They make a gentlemen's wager to test their different theories of human nature. Does social environment or heredity count more in life? Given their new circumstances, will the two men take on each other's behavior? The comedic reversal played off ideological assumptions about class, race, and human nature.

Some accounts of ideology are very broad and all-encompassing, others more specific, but most accounts include to some extent relations of power in a society. In that sense ideology has to do with a group's control over the governing ideas or "official" version of reality in terms of national identity and the meaning of events, for example, or regarding issues of class, race, gender, sexual orientation, and so forth.

These things considered, my use of the term *ideology* here is oriented toward social, political, and economic relations as cultural manifestations, or one front of a cultural system. I use ideology to refer to the system of representations by which people think about, organize, and govern themselves in these spheres. These representations that take form in propositions, policies, and practices may be true or false. They may be rigid and oversimplified versions of reality (as ideologies tend to be). They may or may not be consistent with the cultural system of a person or group of people. What ideology does, however, is help people make sense of life by bringing some kind of order in the social, political, and economic realms.

Ritualistic Power

Understanding myth and ideology helps us see more clearly the role the popular arts play in communicating culture. Storytelling is obviously an important part of the cultural orientation process. We also tend to participate in the popular arts in habitual ways, like talking with friends after seeing a movie or tuning in weekly to a favorite TV program. Practices like these intersect with media content in providing emotional pleasure and satisfaction.

Susman observed something of the relation between myth and ritual that gives us insight into the way popular artworks communicate (and criticize) myths, ideologies, cultural ideals, beliefs, and values. "The function of myth is largely utopian: it provides a vision of the future without providing in and of itself any essential dynamic element that might produce the means for bringing about any changes in the present order of things," he explained. "Ritual is generally enough to assure the fulfillment of the promise of the myth."[11] An American holiday (*holyday*) like Martin Luther King Jr. Day, for example, is an annual ritual that points to the future hope that one day racism will be eliminated. The Fourth of July ritual—fireworks and barbecue—finds its meaning in celebrating the founding of the country and also the belief in the promise of the American Dream. The liturgical seasons of the church assure believers that Christ lived and died and will one day return and establish the kingdom of God for eternity.

We can see how popular art functions as mythic ritual by looking at the movie *Titanic* (1997). *Titanic* represents class distinction not only as un-American but also as a relic of the past. In that sense, viewing the film serves as a ritual with a mythical dimension. In American mythology, the pursuit of wealth and upward mobility is expected and valued; character is based on individual ability, determination, and entrepreneurial spirit. The promise of the American Dream—that by working hard enough anyone of however humble origins can advance socially—works as a mythic construct that covers class distinctions and barriers. While a representation of the past, *Titanic* provides a vision of the future, assuring the audience of the fulfillment of the promise of this myth.

Insofar as myths are enacted in rituals, writers have discussed rock concerts, television watching, and film going as communal rituals comparable to attending a church service. "*Simpsons* fans treat Sunday as a day of worship," one writer proposed. "Not early mornings at church; 8 pm in front of the holiest of holies, the TV tuned into the FOX network."[12] Another writer observed, "Many fans . . . think of U2 live as a religious experience or even 'like church' only so much better."[13] Participation in popular culture, beyond its entertainment value, reaffirms a culture's dominant values "in the same way that the rituals of worship services undergird and reaffirm religious beliefs," one theologian observed. "Popular culture is to what most Americans believe as worship services are to what the members of institutional religions believe."[14]

Television and film genres, for example, can be understood as embodying a set of cultural conventions and expectations shared by the producer and audience. They work to provide audiences with satisfaction and basic emotional security by affirming existing beliefs and attitudes and resolving tensions and ambiguities. That families and friends resolve their problems on weekly sitcoms affirms the viability of the social fabric. The detectives and medical specialists on the *CSI* television series, with their matchless investigative skills and scientific knowledge, make it seem possible to solve every crime. Likewise, the members of the medical team on *House* ruminate about symptoms, run tests, argue results, and speculate about treatments, but usually find a way to diagnosis the illness, however rare, and find a way to treat it. On the *Law & Order* series, even though detectives and lawyers sometimes make mistakes, prosecuting the wrong people and letting the guilty get off, their high motivation and determination to put criminals behind bars assures viewers that justice ultimately will prevail. Watching a romantic comedy, we know with certainty that when boy meets girl, but then loses girl, they are destined to be together and live happily ever after because their match was made in heaven. Earthlings always find a way to defeat the aliens and walk away with an even more enlightened understanding of human nature and the universe. And a plethora of songs and music videos inspire young hope that a newfound love will bring personal happiness and satisfaction.

Specific genre films can also be thought of as artistic solutions to social and cultural problems. To offer one illustration, movie westerns have been called "America's foundational ritual," a generic formula rooted in history repeating endlessly the story of the American pioneering experience as critical in the formation of the American character and institutions.[15] The western myth represents a classic form of national self-understanding, and continues to provide a framework for cultural discourse over the meaning of America as the continued reworkings of the movie western in different historical and cultural contexts have shown.

For a long time the genre thrived on its identification of persistent problems and ability to recast the nature of those problems in terms of the pressing concerns of an era. Even though movie westerns are few and far between these days (which itself indicates changes in American culture), the basic generic elements of the western myth—its formula, reluctant hero, ritualized violence, and reconciliation of ideological tensions—have influenced every genre of adventure story. And the western structure has been appropriated by the detective, science fiction, "urban vigilante," and Vietnam war film.[16] The action film *Die Hard* (1988), for example, adhered to the western formula and was filled with intertextual references to old western movies like Gary Cooper and Grace Kelly in *High Noon* (1952) and the singing cowboy, Roy Rogers.

Going the Distance

The myth we call the American Dream is a staple in popular artworks. Countless movies feature a rugged individual hero who on his own merit overcomes obstacles and trials in a climb "from rags to riches." According to scholars, the American myth "exhorts us to shake free of the limiting past in a struggling ascent toward the realization of promise in a gracious future."[17] In Hollywood renditions characters transcend their humble beginnings by working hard and exercising some exceptional gift; their accomplishments affirm the belief in America as the land of opportunity.

The Academy-Award winner *Rocky* (1976) is a celebration of the American Dream, a Cinderella story, a rags-to-riches tale. The story itself is structured in terms of the American myth. In huge white letters ROCKY scrolls across the screen with a trumpet accompaniment on the soundtrack that sounds like it's announcing the arrival of a king. The opening image is a mosaic of a Byzantine Christ on the ceiling in what appears to be a church that has been converted into a boxing arena. The camera then tilts down to Rocky (the "Italian Stallion") Balboa (Sylvester Stallone), suggesting he is a messianic figure. As the camera tracks back, it looks as if Jesus is watching over Rocky during the fight. In both senses, the shot works as a religious signifier. Later, Rocky's trainer/manager tells him, "You're gonna eat lightning, and you're gonna crap thunder!" as if Rocky were a some kind of god.

Rocky lives alone in a single-room apartment on the south side of Philadelphia. He makes a living collecting for a loan shark, and though a pretty lousy boxer, he's a "bum" who has the heart to overcome the limitations of his working-class existence and a life of loneliness. In the meantime, Apollo Creed (Carl Weathers), an African American and reigning heavyweight boxing champion, has a problem. Without a ranked contender available, Creed needs a gimmick for his next scheduled fight. He decides to give a local unranked Philadelphia fighter a shot at the title. America is "the land of opportunity," the champ explains to the promoter. "I'm sentimental. And a lot of Americans are just as sentimental." The promoter likes the idea and says, "It's very American." Creed responds, "It's very smart." Both know that "the media will eat it up," and they will profit handsomely. Rocky is selected, not because he is a competitive fighter (by all appearances he is not), but because of his name, the "Italian Stallion," that symbolically represents the ethnic American Dream.

Rocky's training represents his personal transformation and "struggling ascent," aptly symbolized by the steps of the Philadelphia Art Museum. Rocky begins his training with an early morning run; he holds his side as he struggles to make it up the museum's steps. Weeks of training culminates in a montage sequence showing Rocky going through a variety of workouts in preparation for the fight. The "Rocky" theme song blares on the soundtrack as the fighter now bounds up the large stone steps of the Philadelphia Art Museum. A shot of him with arms raised triumphantly with a panorama of the city of Philadelphia in the background signals the arrival of a champion.[18]

Intertextual references to America as the "land of opportunity" and Rocky's bout with Creed as a "Cinderella story" pepper the dialogue. But Rocky never says, "Yo, Adrian. The meaning of my life and actions is to shake free of a limiting past in a struggling ascent to an open and gracious future." Instead, the story shows us how certain character traits, hard work, and circumstances work together to allow Rocky to take full advantage of his "shot" at the heavyweight boxing title. Rocky only had to believe in himself in order to pull himself up by his proverbial bootstraps and ascend from rags to riches.

Against tremendous odds, he attains a personal victory by "going the distance" against Creed in a fight that was described as "a mythic spectacle."[19] He also wins the love of his shy girlfriend Adrian (Talia Shire). Through faith in himself and hard work, Rocky has legitimated himself, demonstrating his potential as a boxer. He can now get married, start a family, and acquire material wealth—the traditional American Dream (and the stuff of sequels). Can you see how this cultural myth *is* the story of Rocky, woven right into characterizations and the narrative itself?

Rocky is also situated on that "special meeting ground between history and myth." Many writers observed that the film implicitly captured the ambivalent mood of Bicentennial America. Released in the aftermath of the defeat in Vietnam, Watergate, and the civil rights movement, amidst the decade's second recession, *Rocky* tapped into white working-class

Rocky (1976) is a celebration of the American Dream that also represented white working-class prejudices and fears, especially resentment of African Americans.

prejudices and fears, especially resentment of African Americans. Lower-middle- and working-class whites believed America had been pushed around for over a decade, and they had personally been left out for the sake of progressive change. As Stallone said of audience response, "When they're cheering for Rocky, they're cheering for themselves."[20]

Rocky asserted an ideological explanation: political liberals and African Americans had stolen the American Dream from its rightful heirs; the world had been turned upside down. One writer proposed that the film used a "scapegoating ritual" to symbolically resolve the crisis by directing ethnic anger toward African Americans.[21] Disregarding socioeconomic realities, the film showed working-class whites languishing while African Americans thrived and Apollo Creed (patterned after Muhammad Ali) reigned as the world's boxing champion. During the fight, the American flag looms large in the background, especially when Rocky stuns Creed by knocking him down in the first round. The shot of a white man beating up on an African American symbolized racial attitudes at the time. *Rocky*, then, is a good illustration of myth and ideology at work in the popular cinema.

A Culture's Liturgy

Julia Roberts won an Oscar for her portrayal of real-life heroine Erin Brockovich, an individual who climbs from rags to riches by helping to uncover one of the biggest environmental crimes in history. Again, the three stages of the American myth correspond to the three acts in the narrative of *Erin Brockovich* (2000), a film title that exalts the individual heroine—not the victims or the social cause.

Erin is an unemployed single mother of three living in the world of lower-middle-class suburbia. A transformation takes place when, on her own initiative, she begins an investigation of a suspicious real estate case involving the Pacific Gas & Electric Company. What she discovers is that the company is quietly buying land that was contaminated by a deadly toxic waste that the company was dumping illegally. Area residents were being poisoned, their lives plagued by strange and debilitating illnesses and the death of loved ones. Her investigation leads the law firm into one of the largest class action lawsuits in history against a multi-billion-dollar corporation involving a $333 million settlement.

In this story a heroic individual exposes corporate corruption. Change is brought about initially and primarily as a result of individual ambitions, goals, and actions.

The British film *Billy Elliot* (2000) makes for an interesting comparison. The story employs the same narrative structure showing an individual overcoming obstacles to achieve something unprecedented. And like *Erin Brockovich*, *Billy Elliot* is grounded in real events—the labor strikes in Britain in the 1980s. But this social backdrop suggests that the story is not simply about an individual struggle against the odds, but about communal defiance against an uncaring society.

Billy Elliot lives in a British coal-mining town. His home is filled with tension because his father and brother are struggling to survive a crippling and heated miners' strike. Billy discovers and pursues his love for the ballet and eventually leaves his friends and family for the London stage. Billy has to break through class barriers in order to realize his potential as a dancer—an occupation that also runs against the grain of working-class notions of masculinity. Unlike Erin Brockovich, Billy's success is measured not by material gain, but the extent to which he develops his talent. The theme of liberation—the freedom to be who you want to be—is embedded in the narrative and affirmed by the circumstances of several characters.

But this theme is tempered in a way that affirms British attitudes about change, upward mobility, and accepting the inevitable. Throughout this film there are constant reminders that Billy's accomplishment is not as much an ideal as an exception. When Billy is accepted into the Royal Ballet School in London, his father hurries to the local union club to tell his friends. But his enthusiasm is dampened by news that the strike is over and they are returning to work with no gains. The scene immediately following Billy's departure for London shows his father and older brother, grim-faced, descending into the mine. *Billy*

Elliot restrains the basic optimism of a film like *Erin Brockovich*, while also suggesting a different measure for personal success and the quality of life.

There are countless movies that employ the same narrative structure as *Rocky* and these other films, testifying to power and popularity of the rags-to-riches myth: *Rudy, All the Right Moves, Waterboy, Cool Runnings, Flashdance, Saturday Night Fever, Working Girl, Cocktail, Patch Adams, October Sky, Coyote Ugly, Save the Last Dance, The Rookie*, ad infinitum. We can understand these films as part of our culture's liturgy—ritualistic stories that assure us of the promise of the myth repeated over and over again.

Conclusion

Myriad cultural orientations can exist within a society, and differing cultural values can be controversial, contentious, and even threatening, insofar as they challenge the validity of a particular way of life. The study of culture, then, involves not only charting cultural patterns and changes but also the possibility of transformation. How do people imagine different ways of living, contribute alternatives to the cultural discourse, and change their way of life?

U2's lead singer, Bono, talked about the need to develop an "empathic imagination" in order for people to understand each other. "To tell our stories, to play them out, to paint pictures, moving and still, but above all to glimpse another way of being," he said, "Because as much as we need to describe the world we do live in, we need to *dream up the kind of world we want to live in*. In the case of a rock & roll band that is to dream out loud, at high volume, to turn it up to eleven. Because we have fallen asleep in the comfort of our freedom."[22]

Now that we have refreshed ourselves on the idea of culture and key concepts in studying popular art, we are ready to return directly to the central question of this book. What is the place of the popular arts, and how might people of faith participate responsibly in them?

Summary

- A worldview consists of "fundamental beliefs through which we view the world and our calling and future in it."
- Cultural orientation refers to "how individuals, communities, and organizations find their direction both within and by way of culture."

- Myths refer to a culture's collective way of thinking about something and help people make sense of their lives.
- Ideology can be understood as a specific social platform—propositions, policies, proposals, and practices—designed to put myths to work in everyday life.
- Rituals, including rock concerts, television watching, and film going, work to assure us of the fulfillment of the promise of the myth.
- Narratives are an important part of the cultural orientation process because they facilitate communication of myths, ideologies, cultural ideals, beliefs, and values.

Discussion Questions

1. What kinds of things (upbringing, church, events, books, experiences, others) have shaped the development of your cultural orientation?
2. Discuss reasons why people of a common faith might have different views on social, political, economic, or aesthetic issues in life.
3. Consider other films that adhere to the same rags-to-riches formula as *Rocky* and *Erin Brockovich*. How are they different and yet the same (e.g., character and setting)?
4. While this will be treated in later chapters, give some thought to how a Christian perspective might contribute to your engagement with popular art—both in terms of production and criticism.
5. What are some prominent American ideals, beliefs, and values? Can you find them represented in popular artworks?

PART
TWO

4

CLOSE ENCOUNTERS
OF THE HIGH, LOW,
AND DIVINE KIND

REIMAGINING THE POPULAR ARTS

The transcendent ecstasy of a rock gig easily translates into a religious experience.

Details Magazine

Movies, like religion, have an uncanny ability to make people believe things that are directly contradicted by their everyday experience. And that ability sometimes enables movies to, in a weird way, replace religion. *Star Wars*, anyone?

Premiere Magazine

My friend Paul loves action films like *The Last of the Mohicans* (1992), *Braveheart* (1995), and *The Matrix* (1999). He arranged for "the boys" to go to a late-night showing of *Gladiator* (2000). During the trailers, however, several teenage girls sat right behind us; their whispering and giggling was too much for Paul, so he moved several rows in front of us to watch the movie. At the end of the film, when the hero lies dead in the arena and the Roman senator asks, "Who will carry this soldier?" Paul raised his hand. The next night he called me and wanted to go back again to "that world" of the Roman coliseum.

Has that ever happened to you? The movie ends, and you just sit there not wanting to leave that world—the characters you've gotten to know and the events you have experienced with them. How is it that when we enter into the world of a film we can become emotionally engaged, even moved profoundly, while fully aware at the same time that what is being presented to us never actually happened and is not happening now, that the characters and events we're seeing exist only as a product of imagination? Perhaps this is what is meant by "movie magic."

Under normal circumstances people go to the movies fully aware that they are allowing themselves to be drawn into the world of the film. Participation in the popular arts involves *a willing suspension of disbelief*. When we watch a film, we put aside for a time the fact that we are sitting in seats, popcorn and drink in hand, staring at images projected on a screen, and we allow the projections to take us to another world. We can have a range of physiological responses. Our palms sweat during a suspenseful scene. We get an upset stomach during a car chase through the streets of San Francisco. We cover our eyes when things get scary. We cheer wildly when the heroine prevails. We laugh out loud, cry, or jolt when we're frightened, all the while reminding ourselves, "It's only a movie."

In *Last Action Hero* (1993), a boy is given a magic ticket that transports him and, as the result of a misadventure, other fictitious movie characters between the cinematic and real worlds. But as the cliché goes, this can only happen in the movies. One film theorist described the screen on which the world of a film is projected as a kind of barrier.[1] The screen separates us from the world the film portrays, making us invisible in that world; characters don't seem to be aware that we're watching their every move closely. The screen also screens the movie world from the audience. We might find ourselves in the middle of an intergalactic battle to the finish with the Death Star, but we never have to worry about actually being hit by a Blaster, or that the evil Darth Vader might turn and come after us. The cinema experience allows for anonymity and safety; you feel no responsibility for what takes place in that world, although you may be affected emotionally and have opinions about it.

In another sense, the screen is not a surface but a space. The cinema transports its audience elsewhere, making us travelers, adventurers, and even voyeurs—a theme Alfred Hitchcock treated in many of his films. Movies can take us shark hunting, dirty dancing, exploring the globe, and can admit us into the privacy of people's lives, letting us listen to boardroom and bedroom conversations. For these reasons and more, the movies are talked about as being magical and dreamlike.

Christian ideas about popular art have a long history and are grounded in beliefs and assumptions about life in God's world. So it is worthwhile to examine two important historical developments that have had an impact on our thinking about the popular arts: the similar and competing nature of the church and the arts, and the division between high and popular cultures. How have these cultural patterns affected the role and character of popular art and also influenced Christian attitudes?

Religion and Popular Art

Playwrights in Elizabethan England tried to fend off religious criticism by arguing that their productions affirmed the moral lessons of the church, or at least were not in opposition to them, but a clergyman put them straight. He wrote, "God requireth no such thing at their hands, that they should take it upon them. . . . God gave authority to instruct and preach, to correct and anathematize, only to the Apostles and to their successors, and not to players; for it is unlawful to cast pearls before swine."[2] Is that any way to talk about William Shakespeare and company?

There were many reasons for the disdain that some church leaders had for the theater. The playhouses drew audiences away from church services; critics thought theater attendance was a frivolous waste of time and money that fostered idleness. In addition, they believed that "drama was based upon the principles of lying, pretence, and deception, and, which was worse, it elevated these sins into a commercially rewarding practice." Elizabethan dramatist Thomas Heywood wrote about the power of an actor to blur the distinction between truth and illusion for some audience members and even suggested that "the presentation of the supernatural on stage still had a peculiar power. Devils were a special threat, since even their pretended presence was in danger of summoning the real thing."[3] And so it is no surprise that church leaders denounced theater in the harshest terms as the "devil's workshop."

The conflict with the theater reveals an historic passion in the church that gives us an insight into attitudes about popular art today. At the crux of the church's concern about the nineteenth-century theater was an intense rivalry "derived from the similar—and competing—nature of their appeal," historian Harry Stout explained.

Both encouraged a suspension of belief in the experience of the everyday to introduce their viewers to different worlds. Theater, in its capacity to combine the pageantry of art, the intensity of poetry, the enchantment of fiction, and the movement of dance, represented a religious-like amalgam of art and energy that, as one contemporary put it, had the power to "get Possession of the heart." Not surprisingly, many clerics accorded the contemporary stage the status of a church: the church of Satan.[4]

The theater was not only wildly entertaining, but also played an important role in shaping people's perceptions and informing attitudes and opinions by offering maps of reality that clergy perceived as rivaling the church's vision of life.

Such attitudes continued in the twentieth century. One historian even compared the cinema to the church: "Complete with stars and even gods and goddesses, housed in palaces that (even down to the massive organ) resemble huge cathedrals, motion pictures became for thousands a new religion."[5] The contest for people's hearts and minds exists in our media-saturated society. "You may think that Billy Graham is the leading evangelist in America, but he's not," Reverend Donald Wildmon of the American Family Association said. "The leading evangelists in America are those people who make the TV programs."[6]

Popular Art and Spirituality

Understanding the similar and competing nature of the institutions of art and religion helps us understand the tendency of some to invest popular art with a spiritual capacity to "get possession of the heart." After previewing *The Prince of Egypt* (1998) an evangelical journalist reportedly said, "That was like an act of worship."[7] Another evangelical writer likened seeing the movie to a spiritual experience that could somehow effect religious conversion. "Maybe *The Prince of Egypt* can attract seeking hearts through the flickering silver screen that would never approach the worn wooden altar," she wrote, hoping that this Hollywood film might perhaps "lead a few people to the Prince of Peace."[8]

The Passion of the Christ (2004) was also heralded as an extraordinary evangelistic opportunity. Some churches bought blocks of tickets; ministers encouraged members of their congregations to bring their "unsaved" friends to screenings. "I don't know of anything since the Billy Graham crusades that has had the potential of touching so many lives," one denominational leader said. "It's like the Lord somehow laid in our lap something that could be a great catalyst for spiritual awakening in this nation."[9] And Mel Gibson reportedly said, "The Holy Ghost was working through me on this film, and I was just directing traffic. I hope the film has the power to evangelize."[10] Likewise, the release of *The*

Chronicles of Narnia: The Lion, the Witch and the Wardrobe (2005) was hailed as "truly a unique opportunity that God has created. By clearly conveying the message of Christ and the cross, it can serve as a powerful evangelistic tool."[11]

A chorus of evangelical musicians have claimed spiritual import for their songs. The late Keith Green reportedly said, "As for me, I repent of ever having made a record or ever having sung a song unless it's provoked people to follow Jesus, to lay down their whole life before him, to give him everything."[12] Can a song really do that, "provoke people to follow Jesus," or is that the work of the Holy Spirit? Likewise, Carman explained, "I don't just want to spend my time on social commentary because there's too much of it going on and *it doesn't deliver anyone from sin*." And the members of a Christian rock group said, "Issues are great, but there's no *transforming or cleansing power* in them."[13]

Does that mean that these songs are inspired by the Holy Spirit ("the Lord gave me this song") and that they have some sort of divine authority? Considering that one study found contemporary Christian music "to be almost devoid of doctrinal content in any direction," I think it's safe to say that we are talking about human creations that are marred with sin.[14] Many praise and worship songs, for example, can be criticized for privatizing faith and promoting values associated with American notions of individualism. Some of these songs encourage world flight instead of Christian cultural engagement and can undermine community and accountability beyond one's self.

When someone says, "That song ministers to me," I think they are trying to explain an artistic experience as a spiritual one. What they are describing is the experience of popular art communicating in a way that resonates with their life by affirming their beliefs and values or by presenting something in a way they never quite thought of it before. "The line between a *spiritual* experience and an *aesthetic* one is very fine, and the two are easily confused," scholars pointed out. "The very feelings of tranquility and delight that art gives us can lull us into thinking that we are right with God." As they observed, "Art can create a longing for God or an awareness of God, but it cannot give us a life lived under God . . . [which] is about our relationships and our work, about what we do with our lives alongside and through the experience of art."[15]

Divine Encounter

Consider this description of a U2 concert at Madison Square Garden by a *New York Times* reporter:

First, the entire arena went dark, and then, in a cone of white light through which innumerable bits of confetti fluttered and danced, Bono materialized, twirling slowly, ecstatically, his arms raised to the light as if asking to be drawn up to the heavens. It was a gesture with intimations of the messianic. And yet what you felt, throughout the evening, as Bono pranced and hopped along the catwalk that extended out into the crowd in the pit, inviting girls up to dance with him, was that he was beckoning his fans to join him in the ecstatic place where the music came from. Even his political appeals, which he generally kept in check, felt like an invitation to the transcendent.[16]

Again, it is not uncommon for people to draw comparisons between artistic experiences and religious ones. The finest rock music "has always pushed beyond the mundane, has always believed in a better life to come, and that in the ecstasy of the greatest musical moments we catch a glimpse of heaven," one British writer explained. "It's not heaven itself, but momentarily we feel enlarged and, in this state, aware of the grandeur of our God-likeness."[17] Similarly, one theologian wrote about a "divine encounter" with the cinema: "Movies have, at times, a sacramental capacity to provide the viewer an experience of transcendence."[18]

I understand a religious experience to mean one that deepens our awareness of God's presence in the world and the ways that humans bear God's image. That this can occur through a film or song can legitimate going to movies and listening to popular music for some people of faith. Such a religious experience is not something peculiar to popular art itself but can occur anywhere in life. It goes to reason that the same rationale can be employed to justify Christian participation in every aspect of life. I don't mean to deny people's experiences, only to point out that such a broad justification can hardly be identified as a unique and specific feature of the popular art experience or used as the basis of a faith-informed aesthetic.

The relation between an aesthetic and religious experience seems to hinge on the nature of the willing suspension of disbelief; to some extent both kinds of experience call for active imaginative engagement. It is not uncommon under normal circumstances for people to experience a sense of losing themselves for a time, of being swept away by the story and images projected on the screen in the darkened theater, for example. And most people go to the theater anticipating such an experience.

I witnessed the power of suspended disbelief while watching the 3-D movie *Honey, I Shrunk the Audience* (1995) at a Disney theme park. In the movie, when Wayne Szalinski (Rick Moranis) arrives at the Inventor of the Year Award ceremony in his latest flying invention—a hovercraft—it goes haywire. He crashes through a glass sign and the 3-D effect sends particles of shattered glass at the audience. People ducked and put up their arms to shield themselves. Then the inventor hovers there in the air. And what did people in the audience do? Young and old alike reached up and tried to touch the hovercraft. They had to know this was just an image—not physically there to be touched—and yet they tried to grab it. This shows the power of suspended disbelief; people want to cross over that threshold and enter into the world of the film.

For many people an aesthetic experience may be like a religious one to the extent that artworks provide stories through which they might make discoveries about transcendent reality or find epiphanies, revelations, wisdom, insight, and critique. Despite possible similarities between these two experiences, one theologian at least offers a qualification: the filmic experience was perhaps not "a specifically religious experience" but nonetheless could still "make us think profoundly about issues of religion, ethics, and human rights."[19]

Ordained by God as part of human life, the aesthetic experience is a legitimate one that is enriched with creativity, deepening aesthetic features, and solid critical evaluation. For this reason, Christians do not have to make popular art into a spiritual event in order to properly enjoy and delight in it. This is not only unnecessary but misconstrues its meaning, value, and purpose. Understanding the experience for what it is—primarily an aesthetic one and not a spiritual one—calls us to consider specific and distinct ways that Christians should be involved not as minister and congregation but as artist and audience. In other words, we should understand our participation in popular art not as a worship service but as an artistic venue for critical engagement.

Spiritualizing popular art can make it into something more than a human cultural activity in God's world that requires hard work, inventiveness, and critical perspective. As we have already seen, the institutions of art and religion share a similar nature, but that still doesn't infuse celluloid and CDs with a supernatural power to "get possession of the heart."

In sum, efforts to make the movie theater or concert hall into a revival tent invest the popular arts with powers they do not really possess. According to a George Barna survey, among those who accepted Christ as their Savior, the most important factors in their decision were family conversations or upbringing (mentioned by 38 percent), response to a sermon (14 percent), and a conversation about Christ with a friend (10 percent).[20] A mere 3 percent cited evangelistic television programs. There was no mention of movies or Christian music, and even if we were to include Christian concerts in "attended an evangelistic event," only 5 percent named this as an important factor in their coming to Christ. Communication scholar Quentin Schultze explained, "Research clearly documents the ineffectiveness of electronic media as agents of religious conversion, yet the popular mythology holds that spiritual battles can be won technologically."[21] Despite a nationwide grassroots campaign and all the evangelistic hype for *The Passion*, a survey by the Barna Research Group showed that less than one-tenth of one percent of those who saw the movie accepted Jesus Christ as their Savior as a result of seeing the film. Not much of a yield.[22]

Nevertheless, while the media cannot substitute for personal evangelism, popular art has been instrumental in bringing at least some people to the faith. The task for Christians, however, is to discover and employ the most effective roles and purposes for popular art, a topic we will explore further in the next chapter. For now, suffice it to say that we can all benefit from artworks that provide a means of personal self-reflection, entertainment, cultural insight, or social critique, as examples.

Partakers of the Divine Nature

"Movies are *not* art," an evangelical film critic argued. "Rather, they are a form of *entertainment* which employs artistic and communicative elements."[23] Most people use the term *art* to refer to high culture or the traditional fine arts: painting and sculpture, drama, the symphony and opera, poetry and certain types of literature. If you want to discuss movies, popular music, television, or romance and detective novels, we more often use the term *entertainment*. Beethoven and Bach, Shakespeare and Dickens, Rembrandt, Renoir, and Picasso—that's art. Bob Dylan and the Beatles, Lucas, Spielberg, Tarantino, Sorkin, Spelling, and Lear (Norman, not the king)—that's entertainment.

This distinction implies that there are considerable differences between high and popular art forms. For many, the high arts are just that: higher or more valuable than popular art based on distinct roles and purposes.

But high and popular art actually have much in common as social practices. For example, although he is now an icon of high culture, Shakespeare was actually a popular artist in his time (and not immune to political pressure and religious criticism). People from different classes and social backgrounds all attended his plays, which were shaped not only by the interests of artistry but by profit making and business management. *Hamlet*, *Macbeth*, and *The Winter's Tale* gave artistic treatment to issues of the day—from familial concerns and political corruption to the divine right of the monarchs—while also being extremely entertaining.

Similarly, going to a movie premiere may be a social outing with friends, but the experience at the cinema is also an artistic one requiring critical understanding and interpretation. This is also true of a concert performance by a rock, country, gospel, or rap artist. Afterward, people are usually engaged at one level or another in trying to interpret what they've just experienced and to evaluate it according to some set of criteria.

It has also become increasingly difficult to distinguish the high and popular arts based on artistic value. Films can be both beautiful and perceptive, songs can be instructive and enjoyable. A good deal of popular art is mediocre, overly formulaic, and lacking artistry, but this is also true of high art forms. As one scholar observed, "There are bad sculptures, inelegant and clumsy poems, ugly paintings, and trivial choreography."[24] And as the exhibition of Manet's paintings *Olympia* and *Lunch on the Grass* (both 1863) showed, elements that some people find offensive in popular art—nudity, in this case—can also be found in high art.

Now, as I hinted when mentioning Shakespeare's plays, the commercial character of popular art can be used to judge it inferior to high art. The assumption is that popular art is "not primarily produced in order to gratify the creative urge of its maker but primarily intended to meet the requirements of a patron or a buying public," one scholar explained.[25] But the arts always have a commercial base, whether patronage, public funding, or the consumer marketplace.

High and low are not simply categories for different art forms, but a way of thinking about the arts that is inseparable from its historical origins. Like their British and European counterparts, the wealthy, educated, and prominent Anglo-Saxon Protestants in the United States wanted to legitimate their privileged social status, so they staked a claim for the superiority of their cultural tradition as a way to distinguish themselves from the mass of immigrants arriving around the turn of the twentieth century.

It should be obvious that highbrow-lowbrow distinctions have as much, if not perhaps more, to do with class than the actual art in question. The high arts have long been used as a way to show off, appear important, and display wealth. Those who attended a Beethoven concert in the late eighteenth century not only heard the composer's latest work, but the event itself was associated with social status and class. By praising the "greatness" of the symphonic and chamber works of the composers that they patronized, Vienna's social aristocrats maintained their cultural superiority. Likewise, in the nineteenth century, wealthy theater patrons who sat in the boxes not only had the best seats for the night's performance at the opera house in New York, but they could also be seen by all as they sported the latest fashions and showed off their distinguished guests.[26] Nearer to our day, the social elite funded and patronized the "legitimate" theater, opera, symphony, museums, and art galleries, while (at least initially) the working and middle classes frequented vaudeville theaters, dance halls, and motion picture theaters. These cultural venues represented class distinctions and even hostilities, which on occasion broke out into violence and bloodshed.

"Culture" became the exclusive domain of the privileged class, who thought of it as the "pursuit of our total perfection by means of getting to know, on all the matters which most concern us, the best which has been thought and said in the world" (in the words of high culture theorist Matthew Arnold). The pursuit of Culture (pronounced "Culchah" with a capital C) became a religion for many, a "faith in the progress of humanity towards perfection" that culminated in the refinement of nineteenth-century British and European high culture.[27]

Comparable attitudes and beliefs still exist in our own time. In *The Closing of the American Mind*, for example, the late Allan Bloom wrote of culture in flowery language as though it were a golden calf, "something high, profound, respectable—a thing before which we bow." Bloom could see "no relation between popular culture and high culture," insisting, for example, that classical music is "probably the only regularly recognizable class distinction between educated and uneducated in America . . . a class distinction between high and low."[28]

The idea of high culture as a path to salvation is thoroughly humanistic; it assumes that the pursuit of high culture will enable us to be "partakers of the divine nature."[29] Culture, in this sense, is not our universal human task as God's image bearers but another version of the irresistible temptation to "be like God." But culture ("high" or "low") cannot save us, as though by developing refined aesthetic and intellectual sensibilities we can escape sin.

As you can see, the ideals, beliefs, and values associated with high culture were entangled with class antagonism and a human-centered desire for perfection. These are serious considerations that should serve as warnings against any uninformed commitment to high culture itself as an alternative to popular art and culture—let alone Christian faith.

Even so, there were some Christians who wanted to draw a spiritual line, making it seem that high culture was godly and popular culture was evil. More than one writer, for example, has thought that classical music is "inspired by the Spirit of God," and that popular music "in its crazy rhythm, its sensual swing, and hideous tunes, reflects the spirit of hell."[30] One Christian anti-rock critic wrote, "Any serious Christian young person can see that rock music in particular lures us from true Christian living," adding that "It should also be obvious to Christian young people that 'The Hallelujah Chorus' might indeed welcome us into God's presence."[31]

Even Christians who have written thoughtfully about the subject tend to condemn the popular arts based on an uncritical assumption that high culture is somehow morally or aesthetically superior, or both. Critics made statements like, "there is more that is true, good, and beautiful in high culture than a mass popular culture can ever yield."[32] But there are plenty of popular artworks that honestly explore life and exhibit a high level of aesthetic excellence, just as there is much about high culture that deserves criticism. Why such a blanket condemnation of popular art? And why the uncritical glorification of high culture?

To Understand and Reimagine

In their pursuit of human perfection, cultural elitists in the late nineteenth century wanted to turn an aesthetic event into a spiritual experience. Orchestral performances were framed as sacred rituals, and the distance between artist and audience was strengthened by avoiding the work of living artists, darkening the concert hall during performances, and developing a proper concert etiquette. Some of these features obviously characterize the cinema experience, enhancing the élan of larger-than-life stars on the screen. And popular musicians have appropriated these same elements in addition to elaborate theatrical stage productions that give today's concerts the appearance of a kind of religious ritual for youth.

The cultural elite also talked about the symphonic musician as a "high priest in the temple of the beautiful" who could lift his audience to a "plane of spiritual aesthetic gratification."[33] The authors of *Art and Soul* pointed out that various scholars have described Mozart as "only a visitor on this earth," "not only reaching heaven with his works but also coming from there," "more than earthly," "not of this world," and even "divine."[34] Artists became worship leaders in the humanistic urge to replace religion with the pursuit of culture.

Contemporary Christian artists often express the same attitude when they claim a sacredness for their work—as though it is something to be set apart from everyday experience and immune to criticism. The authors of *Apostles of Rock* recounted an experience at a CCM concert. "I have this vision," the musician said on stage, "the vision that we are surrounded by people bowing, bowing to the gods of money or other worldly 'gods.' But while everyone else is bowing, this is what we're doing," she said, referring to worshiping and praising God at the concert. At the intermission, however, the crowd flocked to the merchandise table in the lobby to purchase the artist's tapes, CDs, posters, and T-shirts.[35]

Christians often promote popular art and music as ministry, but then market and merchandise it as a commercial product no different from athletic shoes, baseball caps, or blue jeans. Should artistic and consumer practices like attending a Christian concert or listening to a CD qualify as the same experience as worshiping with a local congregation of believers? Synthesizing religious and consumer values in this way, are we responsibly cultivating popular art and culture or, however inadvertently, just advancing the goals and beliefs of the consumer culture—a way of life that can be, and often is, antithetical to religious traditions?

Let's look more deeply at the effects of confusing art with religion and separating art from everyday life. High art was distinguished by a unique and single purpose—aesthetic contemplation. In other words, the only reason for an artwork to exist was for people to reflect on its aesthetic features and potential meanings. High art, in principle at least, became devoid of social functions. It was produced solely for its own sake. In this view, the popular arts may not qualify as art at all, because they fulfill other purposes—whether social, cultural, or commercial—that elitists think somehow denigrate art. However, even though popular art is not created for disinterested contemplation, that particular artworks can be provocative and make people think shows that their cultural value need not be limited to mere entertainment.

Such exaltation of the fine arts rendered them the exclusive property of an educated elite composed of virtuosos and connoisseurs who thought they alone could understand and properly appreciate art. But this had the untoward effect of divorcing the traditional high arts from any meaningful purpose in the everyday lives of the general public; the majority of people lost interest in the traditional arts, finding them irrelevant, pretentious, and boring.

Not surprisingly, while the high arts increasingly grew out of touch with most people, the popular arts assumed roles and functions historically associated with art. They may not have been considered art by many, but the popular arts provided different and equally valid artistic experiences for people. They not only entertained but also played an important role in shaping perceptions and informing attitudes and opinions. They provided a sense of belonging to a larger community for most people by addressing widespread concerns and nurturing common aspirations, fears, and prejudices. In other words, the popular arts became a unique phenomenon that required a new understanding of art, entertainment, and leisure in the burgeoning mass society of the twentieth century.

Conclusion

Many people still regard the popular arts as "lowbrow" entertainment and not something to be thought about or evaluated as art. Popular art is often considered more a product to be marketed or a vehicle to be used to accomplish some goal other than to create and experience good works of art. The aesthetic that emerged for popular art is primarily a commercial one based on profit making; cultural and artistic roles and qualities all too often are given secondary status. All of these circumstances worked together to prohibit deeper artistic development of popular art and understanding of its artistic and cultural roles. Undermining the status of popular art has not led to education of the audience to heighten appreciation; for most people, evaluation of a popular artwork is left almost completely to personal taste and whim. Much of the popular art that is produced is geared to market forces; success and achievement are gauged solely in terms of commercial viability, which translates into "popular." There can be little doubt that these factors have led to some of the degeneracy we see in popular art today.

In short, there are enough problems with the concept of high art that we should not rely on it too much in trying to understand and reimagine the popular arts. We do not have to depend on the high culture of an era gone by to understand how to invent and transform contemporary art forms and new technologies for service in God's kingdom. What "art" or an "artist" is depends on the institutions and culture in which it is produced and consumed. Simply trying to turn popular art into high art also overlooks the reality that today's popular art is produced in different social, cultural, and industrial contexts than the traditional high arts. How do these different contexts affect the popular arts today? And how have people of faith responded?

Summary

- The institutions of religion and popular art are both concerned—if for different reasons—with values, meaning, and visions of life.
- A religious experience is one that deepens our awareness of God's presence in the world and the ways that humans bear God's image.
- The aesthetic experience is a legitimate part of life in God's world and one that is enriched with creativity and solid critical evaluation.
- The relationship between an aesthetic and religious experience hinges on the nature of the willing suspension of disbelief; to some extent both kinds of experience call for active imaginative engagement.
- High and low are not simply categories for different art forms, but a way of thinking about the arts that is inseparable from their historical origins.

- The ideals, beliefs, and values associated with high culture are entangled with class antagonism and human-centered desire for perfection.
- High and popular art have much in common as social practices, and it is difficult to distinguish them based on artistic value.
- While the high arts increasingly grew out of touch with most people, the popular arts assumed roles and functions historically associated with art by providing different but equally valid artistic experiences for people.
- There are enough problems with the concept of high art that we should not rely on it too much in trying to understand and reimagine the popular arts.

Discussion Questions

1. Can you think of a movie, television program, or musical recording that transported you "elsewhere"? Discuss how and why you think this happened.
2. What are some of the problems with "a strictly evangelistic understanding of art"?
3. The author suggests, "When someone says, 'That song ministers to me,' I think they are trying to explain an artistic experience as a spiritual one." Discuss this and consider ways that Christians might learn to think differently about engaging popular art based on the understanding of culture presented in earlier chapters.
4. Why are distinctions between high and popular art problematic and unhelpful for approaching popular art and culture?
5. Discuss ways the division between high and low culture and the "spiritualizing" of art have affected Christian attitudes and also the roles and character of popular art.

5

MAPPING REALITY

POPULAR ART AND CULTURE

The invention of the arts, and other things which serve the common use and convenience of life, is a gift of God by no means to be despised, and a faculty worthy of commendation.

John Calvin, *Commentary on Genesis*

The bard, the artist, the creator of theater, the poet, the teller of tales, have all been seen as the creators of culture, the refiners of social life, the conscience of humanity that exposes its foibles, clarifies its virtues, and celebrates its approximations to them.

Max L. Stackhouse, Princeton Theological Seminary

The movie *Tea with Mussolini* (1999) is set in Italy before World War II. The young boy Luca's mother has died and he is being cared for by a group of English women. One of them, Arabella (Judi Dench), takes Luca to the Accademia in Florence. Showing him a room full of Italian sculptures, she inspires him to be an artist. "The human form divine; the body beautiful," she says. "And you, yes, you could be part of that world. To make, to create, to live as those old artists did is to share a part in the divine plan."

Every culture has its own distinctive arts. They show us how people in past civilizations lived, loved, worshiped, waged war, and died. Beginning with the most primitive peoples, humans have always used some form of art to express themselves and to represent their understanding of the world. Cave paintings at Lascaux, for example, show how important hunting and food were to this prehistoric people. The significance of the pharaohs cannot be missed in the pyramids of the ancient Egyptians. The polished black granite of the Vietnam Veterans Memorial in Washington, D.C., inscribed with the names of Americans who never returned home, is a national reminder of personal loss and the cost of war.

All this is true of the popular arts in our own day. While there is much in popular culture that is mindless and trivial, the popular arts do have the capacity to provoke serious reflection on our lives and our society. Popular music, movies, and television programs often address important issues and communal concerns, offering accessible artistic interpretations of our lives and times.

Rock and roll represented the voice of the youth subculture that emerged after World War II. Soul music was an expression of the African-American self-identity of the 1960s, while much of today's rap is a display of urban anger and discontent. Set in the McCarthy Era of 1950s, the film *Good Night, and Good Luck* (2005) probed the role of news media in keeping those in political power accountable to the people and questioned present-day conditions of American journalism, while *Syriana* (2005) gave an intriguing look at geopolitics and America's dependence on foreign oil. *Crash* (2005) dealt with racism. Class differences were the source of much of the humor in the ribald comedy *Caddyshack* (1980), which was a cutting satire of the country-club set. And NBC's *ER* gave us glimpses of this nation's perplexities over emergency medical care and disenfranchised people, as well as the everyday struggles of human relationships. These forms of media are both forceful and controversial; they educate while they entertain.

The value of art has almost always been related to its roles and not limited to aesthetic or "disinterested" contemplation. Writing about the emergence of "art" as such, one scholar showed that "ancient writers and thinkers, though confronted with excellent works of art and quite susceptible to their charm, were neither able nor eager to detach the aesthetic quality of these works of art from their intellectual, moral, religious and practical function or content."[1] Understanding the roles contemporary popular art plays in our lives, culture, and society is central to the development of a critical approach. The arts acquire their status in a society by the way they function and are used, and in terms of the social institutions within which works are produced, distributed, and consumed—the patron-funded art museum or symphony, advertising-sponsored television programming, concert and movie box-office venues. And so one way we can talk about the arts is in terms of their functions. "Art plays and is meant to play an enormous diversity of roles in human life," observed philosopher Nicholas Wolterstorff, who considered analysis of these roles "fundamental in any full-fledged attempt to understand works of arts."[2] The arts, he argued, equip us for acting in the world. Let's look more closely at popular art and its potential for helping us understand our lives and culture.

A Mishmash of Good and Bad

Popular art has a long history. We know, for example, that Greek drama and Elizabethan theater were popular art in their own time. The popular arts I am concerned with in this book are products of the mass culture that emerged in the twentieth century. While in some respects these electronic forms of popular art share characteristics of earlier ones, they are also distinguished from earlier forms by (1) mass technology, (2) scale of distribution, (3) audience demographics, and (4) a consumer commercial base. I use the term *popular art* because it better represents the purpose of these artworks than the more common term *entertainment*. The latter suggests that the popular arts are somehow not really art or that they do not serve the same roles and purposes of art. I want to challenge such attitudes.

Prior to the age of mass media, art forms like the theater, opera, symphony, and even some literature were limited to a more sophisticated and educated audience, primarily from the upper classes. In contrast, mass technology dramatically increased the distribution scale of art; popular artworks are intended to reach mass audiences that cross national, class, religious, political, ethnic, racial, and gender boundaries. Indeed, movies, recordings, and television shows produced in the United States are presented to audiences around the world.

And the commercial stakes are high. I understand that a nonfiction book can sell 100,000 copies and make the *New York Times* bestseller list. But a successful CD might sell 500,000 to one million units or more. And the "average" film today (in terms of production and marketing costs) has to sell over 30 million tickets (at an average price) in order to break even. According to the Motion Picture Association of America, a "frequent" moviegoer is someone who goes to the theater at least once a month. That's twelve or more movies a year. But even if they go two or three times a month, that still does not generate enough of an audience to financially support the more than 400 movies that Hollywood studios release each year.

The media hype over the final episode of *Seinfeld* exposed the fragmentation of the television-viewing audience along racial lines.

For commercial reasons, then, producers like to cast a wide net to reach and satisfy a large "popular" audience. In reality, however, this audience is not a homogenous or monolithic one, but a collection of many different audiences in the United States and other countries around the world. Audiences differ according to gender, age, class, race, and other factors, including religious beliefs.

This was clear during the hype over the final television episode of *Seinfeld* in 1998. Every newsstand magazine made it seem the entire population of the United States would be united in grief, but the overwhelming majority of the 76 million viewers who watched the final episode were apparently white "yuppies." The show was never popular with older viewers, African Americans, and Hispanics. "Many of my white friends think they'll never laugh again," one journalist wrote. "Most of my black friends thought, You mean that show set in New York City but where you only see a person of color every forty-fifth episode?"[3] Surveys showed that while *Seinfeld* ranked second in popularity among whites, the sitcom was only fifty-fourth with black audiences.

To secure common ground among audience members, producers tend to seek a lowest common denominator in productions. As one film scholar put it, the popular arts "promise accessibility with minimum effort, virtually on first contact, for the largest number of untutored (or relatively untutored) audiences."[4] On the one hand, this accessibility democratizes the popular arts, that is, makes them available to large numbers of people—not just to the richest and most highly educated. But the effects of mass culture and commercialism also tend to restrict artistic possibilities; popular artworks tend to be formulaic and repetitive to ensure that a wide range of people will be able to understand them immediately.

Popular artists will often deal with "nearly universal emotions" and such "widespread human interests as love, sex, violence, mystery, heroism, and wealth" to communicate easily with a broad audience.[5] As this implies, producers are more interested in catering to what audiences find appealing than treating themes or ideas that might challenge the dominant myths and beliefs. And so to be "popular," artworks regularly exploit those basic themes, stereotypes, and resolutions that have already been proven successful with audiences: boy gets girl, one superhero after another defeats an arch villain bent on world domination. However, the sameness of popular art—basic themes, stock characters, and predictable stories—is driven not only by goals to maximize audience size and profits but also the nature of popularity.

There is a relationship between life perspective and the degree to which someone finds satisfaction with a particular artwork. Popular culture scholars even assert a formula: "the popularity of a given cultural element (object, person, or event) is directly proportional to the degree to which that element is reflective of audience beliefs and values. . . . The formula assumes that audiences *choose* a specific cultural element over other alternatives because they find it attractive in its reassuring reflection of their beliefs, values and desires."[6] A survey by the Barna Research Group confirmed the basic assumption of this formula. Most of the respondents who had seen a movie that made them reflect on their own faith were "already most inclined to think about faith matters."[7] Typically, then, the popular arts do not introduce new beliefs, but reinforce already existing ones; people generally want to be entertained while also being affirmed in what they already believe. As one reporter observed, "most American motion pictures—made by committee and marketed by corporations—aren't designed to begin trends but to cash in on them, not to build consensus but reflect it."[8]

That producers seek to maximize their profits by reaching as large an audience as possible has created many of the problems that we have with the popular arts today. The commercialization of popular art can also work against pluralistic developments. In other words, to cash in on the largest possible audience, popular productions reflect widely dominant myths, offering a limited range of perspectives. Marginalizing specific perspectives—whether religious or ideological—in order to reach broad audiences also limits the popular arts as a marketplace for ideas and, as critics have been pointing out for some time, distort the media as a mirror of society. Mass art can give an undifferentiated audience exposure to material that some believe should be restricted to more mature audiences, so there is constant haggling over ratings and parental advisories. Media watchdogs rightly denounce marketing campaigns that target younger audiences for adult-oriented fare. And some religious groups mount boycotts of programs they find offensive, on the grounds that they are protecting impressionable children from harm.

A mishmash of good and bad, the popular arts are at once an affirmation of their value and a distorted version of something that God intended to be good. Particular artworks can be profound and intriguing, captivating and exciting, dull and mediocre, shoddy and exploitative, or even bizarre combinations of these. Freely mixing artistic functions with crass commercialization has produced works that can be disturbing or delightful, both artistically and morally. Driven by an entanglement of concerns, artistic, commercial, cultural, and religious matters are inseparable in any discussion of popular art. However commercialized they have become, the popular arts cannot be adequately described in terms of production and consumption, for they serve as cultural representations. They are part of the active process of generating and circulating meanings among people. It is important that people of faith understand this broader, complex context as we attempt to responsibly engage popular art.

Roles for Popular Art

Having seen how culture can be both a comforting affirmation and a contentious argument, let's look more closely at how the popular arts convey culture. Artists use common language, symbols, sounds, and images to represent human thought, emotion, and experience. The popular artworks they create show us what people believe and value—their attitudes, questions, and preoccupations; their hopes and dreams, fears and anxieties, heroes and villains. In the popular arts we can see what people find humorous, frightening, captivating, or intriguing, and can discover what tensions and contradictions exist in their world. For these reasons, the arts are said to embody the spirit of an age.

By treating ordinary life and problems—love and romance, family joys and conflicts, business and politics, wealth and economic hardship, failure and forgiveness, faith and disbelief—as well as historical and contemporary events, the arts give us insight into the human condition and our place in the cosmos. In this sense, the popular arts can be understood as "imaginative orderings of experience."[9] Popular artworks transform the real world into an imaginary one by representing experience along the lines and contours of a cultural landscape. Artists draw on the constellation of cultural ideals, beliefs, values, and attitudes to make symbolic or artistic maps of the world in which we live, work, and play.

That's why I find the phrase *maps of reality* useful in discussing popular art; it suggests imagery associated with navigation, journey, seeking direction, and finding one's way. Mapping reality refers to the way people make sense of life and the world in which they live, that is, the shaping and transmitting of meanings. In this process people embrace, develop, and contest ideas and beliefs about human nature, behavior, and society. These beliefs involve assumptions and judgments about the nature of good and evil, truth, justice, stewardship, social order, and so forth. As maps of reality, the popular arts play a basic role in the process of cultural orientation.

We all know that a map is not the reality it depicts, but is instead a representation of roads, rivers, landmarks, and distances that can give us directions, point out the sights along the way, and help us reach our destination. So popular art provides stories, symbols, images, metaphors, and melodies that depict cultural values and assumptions, behavioral norms, social roles, and gender roles. In this way, the popular arts mediate between culture and life, that is, our cultural conceptions and our social and environmental realities.

In this sense, the popular arts can provide us with "equipment for living," as one literary theorist put it, equipment that can help (or hinder) us as we try to navigate through the issues and complexities of life.[10] The popular arts can *enlighten* us in the sense that they furnish knowledge and offer insight into our lives and culture.

We have already been discussing how the popular arts are a vital and important means of *cultural communication*. They are one way that we convey and examine common cultural ideals, beliefs, values, and assumptions. For example, by showing that love can conquer anything, movies represent democratic values and ideals associated with a classless society. The love between Jack and Rose transcends the class barriers denoted by the upper and lower decks of the ship in *Titanic* (1997). Racial barriers are erased in *The Bodyguard* (1992). In *Notting Hill* (1999), a common British bookstore owner falls in love and eventually marries a gorgeous American movie star. In Billy Joel's catchy song and music video "Uptown Girl" (1983) a beautiful, rich woman falls for a "downtown man," a gas station attendant, when her chauffeur pulls in to refuel her Rolls Royce. Secluded in her "uptown world" for "As long as anyone with hot blood can / And now she's looking for a downtown man," he sings. "That's what I

A conventional tale of princess and pauper, the forbidden romance between Rose and Jack levels class differences in *Titanic*.

am." In this classic fantasy, the working-class guy liberates the well-heeled woman (from her life of luxury?) and satisfies her sexual longings.

Likewise, the "ideal" platoon in World War II movies, like the John Wayne vehicle *Sands of Iwo Jima* (1949), represented the American Dream: a group of men from different racial and ethnic groups bound together in a common goal to defeat an external enemy (even though the armed forces were actually not desegregated until after the war). The much later *Platoon* (1986), however, employed this same structure, but showed an American platoon at war with itself as a metaphor for America's struggle to understand the meaning of the war in Vietnam.

By revealing argument and unrest over the Vietnam War, *Platoon* is also a good illustration of how popular artworks perform the second cultural role, *social and cultural criticism*. There are any number of films that treat dilemmas and contentious issues of contemporary life. *Philadelphia* (1993) dealt with homosexuality and AIDS. *When a Man Loves a Woman* (1994) explored a family's struggle with alcohol addiction and marital stress. *Sleeping with the Enemy* (1991) revealed the physical pain and psychological distress of domestic abuse. *North Country* (2005) tackled sexual harassment. *Million Dollar Baby* (2005) sparked debate about euthanasia. Racism was the principal concern in movies like *Do the Right Thing* (1989), *Boyz N the Hood* (1991), *Remember the Titans* (2000), and the music of Tracy Chapman. Television programs like *CSI* and *Law &*

Soldiers at war with themselves in *Platoon* serve as a metaphor for America's struggle in Vietnam.

Order told stories that raise questions about crime, public safety, and the legal system, while also exploring human nature and the meaning of justice. Songs by U2 ("Bullet the Blue Sky") and Bruce Cockburn ("If I Had a Rocket Launcher") angrily denounced armed conflicts in Central America and the principle that might makes right.

The popular arts also provide us with a kind of *social unity* through both our ritualistic common experiences as well as the cultural system artworks represent. Almost one-third of America's ninety-seven million television households owned a videocassette copy of Disney's animated feature film *The Lion King* (1994). An estimated 76 million viewers tuned in to watch the final episode of *Seinfeld* in 1998. And while these may be pseudo-events that superficially bind people together, they are nevertheless common experiences with the popular arts that inform people's communal identity. "Popular culture is the very oxygen of our collective life," sociologist Todd Gitlin wrote. "It circulates the materials with which people splice together identities."[11] That Mel Gibson's *The Passion* and Michael Moore's *Fahrenheit 9/11* symbolized opposing socio-political groups captured much press attention during the 2004 election year.

Finally, the popular arts contribute to our *collective memory*, our "recollections of the past that are determined and shaped by the group."[12] Just as our personal past is stored in individual memories and belongings, so we find our collective memory in cultural forms and especially stories of past events, traditions, and social practices. In this sense, popular arts "serve the function of remembering for the human race."[13]

The television series *Roots* (1977), based on the novel and ancestral history of author Alex Haley, gave Americans an entirely different way of thinking about antebellum slavery and African-American history. Bruce Springsteen's "Born in the USA" was a poignant reminder of the uncertainty that remained after the Vietnam War and the difficulties it presented to the traditional American Dream. *Schindler's List* (1993)—filmed in a black-and-white documentary style—became a painful and moving treatment of the Holocaust, one of the most horrific events of the twentieth century. *Saving Private Ryan* (1998) recalled the dedication, fear, and sacrifice of those who served in World War II. And however fanciful a journey through the second half of the twentieth century, *Forrest Gump* (1994) stirred our memories with historical footage and a musical soundtrack that merged popular songs with the spirit of the times.

Because collective memory is determined by the group, it "presumes activities of sharing, discussion, negotiation, and, often, contestation," as one communication scholar observed.[14] That is why popular artworks that represent the past can be so controversial. Just as personal memories can shape our individual identities and lives, so collective memory informs our understanding of ourselves and our actions as a group of people or a nation.

The Academy Award–winning film *Dances with Wolves* (1990), for example, portrayed the Sioux not as savages but as a tribe of people with their own culture—beliefs, values, ideals, language, rituals, artifacts, and traditions. In doing so, this film countered depictions of the frontier in hundreds of American westerns that dehumanized Native Americans by portraying them as vicious savages. Like most sagas of the wild, wild west, *Dances with Wolves* tended to romanticize too, but this representation of the past rendered Anglo-American acts of violence and conquest indefensible.

Perhaps no film in recent history has generated more controversy for its depiction of a past event than Oliver Stone's *JFK* (1991). Even before this film reached theaters, journalists attacked it as propaganda and a distortion of history. Stone thought *JFK* was a "countermyth" to the Warren Commission's lone-gunman theory; the film showed several gunmen firing at the president in Dealey Plaza that day. Regardless of whether you accept Stone's conspiracy theory, *JFK* is brilliant filmmaking—a seamless montage in the quick-editing style of MTV videos that blends fact and fiction, evidence and speculation, into a gripping drama. But the scope of the conspiracy presented in *JFK* inferred CIA involvement in a plot to murder the president and subsequently cover it up. This "meaning" of the event raised stabbing questions about American democracy, and some critics thought the film would foster a general cynicism and distrust of American institutions. So much so that, amidst the spirited public debate the film provoked, federal legislation was passed to open more of the files in the assassination case.

As we have seen, by virtue of the similar nature of the institutions of art and religion, popular artworks provide us with maps of reality that can act as guides for getting around in the world, establishing a cultural orientation. In this sense, they can be understood as models both of and for life in the form of stories and songs. The popular arts facilitate our cultural conversation by aiding us in our communication, social criticism, social unity, and collective memory—four important roles historically associated with art. These are good purposes, valuable ways that humans employ popular arts to aid them in the search for meaning and truth. And Christians cannot ignore these purposes if they want popular art and music to serve God, the church, and the larger human community. That movies, music, and television can serve in these capacities requires an evaluation of them along these lines.

The World behind a Work of Art

A popular artwork invites us into an imaginative world that is an artistic invention. Think about the universe in *Star Wars* (1977), for example. Jawas, droids, Wookies, and Jedi Knights make the jump to hyperspace to travel between galaxies; all of the characters' actions and destinies are entangled with a dualistic benevolent/evil Force that filmmaker George Lucas imagined as "an energy field . . . an aura that at once controls and obeys."[15] The New Zealand film *Whale Rider* (2002) presents viewers with an entirely different kind of world in which human desires and actions interact with the mystical power of the people's Maori Ancestors.

Artists can imaginatively create worlds of the past, present, or future. *Shakespeare in Love* (1998) captures the ambience of the Globe Theater in Elizabethan England. The television series *Desperate Housewives* is a racy soap opera that's been described as "a razor-sharp satire of suburbia."[16] The creators of *The Matrix* invented a futuristic world where people are computer-simulated clones unaware that they are managed by super-intelligent humanoid machines. The world of music videos featured on MTV is a highly sexualized environment largely informed by male adolescent fantasies. How does an artist go about constructing these imaginative worlds?

Every artist has a life vision that to one extent or another permeates his creative work as an imaginative model both of and for reality. Wolterstorff captured this idea with *"the world behind* a work of art, that complex of the artist's beliefs and goals, convictions and concerns, which play a role in accounting for the existence and character of the work."[17] The "world behind a work of art" is a useful avenue into thinking about the perspectival nature of popular art. It suggests that artworks represent a belief system and contemporary values—a faith perspective and cultural orientation.

Consider depictions of the crucifixion of Jesus, for example. Calvin Seerveld's comparison of two fifteenth-century paintings by Mathias Grünewald and Pietro Perugino revealed dramatically different interpretations of the meaning of this event.[18] Likewise, Gibson's *The Passion of the Christ* can be discussed as imaginative reality. We might consider, for example, different kinds of justifications (or lack of) for the amount of violence in the film. Was the film anti-Semitic? As co-screenwriter, Gibson said that he relied not only on the New Testament but also the writings of two nuns, Mary of Agreda, a seventeenth-century aristocrat, and Anne Catherine Emmerich, an early nineteenth-century stigmatic.[19] To what extent, then, was this rendering of events historical or fictive? Why include certain flashbacks from Jesus's life and not others? How did director Mel Gibson's traditionalist Catholic beliefs inform his dramatic representation of these events? Is there a relationship between his Catholicism and the painterly quality of the film, which Gibson described as "a moving Caravaggio," referring to the Italian Baroque painter?[20] More specifically, we might ask who (if anyone) sent the blackbird to pluck the eye out of the disbelieving thief on the cross next to Jesus? Why did the director have Jesus stand up to invite more scourging by the Roman soldiers? Is this historically accurate, a reflection of Gibson's theology, or does it disclose a contemporary attitude? What place does this film have in the filmmaker's repertoire? Do common themes exist that reveal the artist's preoccupations and cultural orientation?[21] These are the kinds of questions we can ask in trying to understand, interpret, and evaluate the perspective in this or other films and popular artworks.

This is all to show that artworks can reveal in whose service the artist stands. "Art is a symbolically significant expression of what drives a human heart, with what vision the artist views the world, how the artist adores whom," Seerveld wrote. "Art itself is always a consecrated offering, a disconcertingly undogmatic yet terribly moving attempt to bring honor and glory and power to something."[22] And insofar as popular artworks affirm the beliefs and values of patrons, they can also reveal in whose service members of the audience stand. A community can see itself and its concerns represented in the popular arts.

Perspective and Entertainment

Let me emphasize that what we are hearing and seeing in popular artworks is not reality but an artistic vision of reality—imaginative reality—that is most often informed and molded by a community of creative people who work together on a production. These people may have competing goals and concerns, deadlines and budget restraints, pressures for high ratings and strong box-office attendance or sales, or worries about critical reception. Even as they live within a common cultural environment, the attitudes and convictions of a scriptwriter, producer, director, actors, cinematographer, and others might contribute to the character of a film or television program; composer, singer, musicians, and record producer may shape a recording. When we speak of the "artist" in the world of popular art, we are not really talking about an alienated individual working in solitude to please only himself or herself (a nineteenth-century high-culture notion). There is a collaborative aspect to the creation of popular art, and my use of the term *artist* is meant to encompass that reality.

Even so, popular artworks should not be understood as being somehow "natural" or neutral depictions of the way things really are. Instead, we should understand that the concerns and life perspectives of those involved will inform these productions; what we see and hear is that version of reality shaped by the contours of the artist's perspective. Focusing on the vision of the artwork heightens our awareness of the existence of that vision and how the artist presents it to the audience. It leads us to questions about both the nature of that vision and the artistic qualities that enhance communication.

As we engage and experience an artwork, we learn to see things from the artist's perspective, whether notions about love and romance, heroic ideals, the purpose of life, the cause and effects of war, or the value of faith. By offering a vision, a popular artwork sets up the possibility for our accepting or criticizing that vision, and an insightful and honest Christian response will often mean affirming certain aspects while rejecting others.

Our critical guard sometimes goes down because we expect to be entertained by movies, music, and television. And they certainly can be entertaining. This observation points to something very important about the character of popular art. Perhaps it seems too obvious to say that people choose to watch TV programs and movies or listen to music because they enjoy them, but that fact gives us a simple and straightforward connection between the popular arts and the rest of life. Humans have a legitimate need for pleasure and entertainment. People take delight in songs and stories that can provide diversion from cares and concerns and even satisfy desires unfulfilled in our everyday lives.

The entertaining quality of popular artworks coexists with their potential to enlighten. As Margaret Miles observed, "the cultural message is coated or masked by pleasure, so that the greater the pleasure, the less one notices and examines the cultural message."[23] As I showed earlier, an artistic vision usually does not appear in an artwork in the form of direct statements or contemplation about culture. Rather, artists present a vision for life in their work by communicating cultural ideals, beliefs, values, and assumptions. These aspects of culture inform the story, characterization, themes, images, and even artistic style.

No matter how "heavy" the cultural message, the most successful popular artworks connect with people first at a very visceral and immediate level. Recognizing this can enrich both our experience and our evaluation of the artwork. With some effort, we can also understand why and how the music, movies, and television shows we enjoy affirm, challenge, or contradict our faith-informed perspectives.

Summary

- Contemporary popular art is distinguished by: (1) mass technology, (2) scale of distribution, (3) audience demographics, and (4) a consumer commercial base.
- The term *popular art* better represents the purpose of these artworks than the more common term *entertainment*.
- To be "popular" (and commercially successful) the popular arts typically do not introduce new beliefs, but reinforce already-existing ones.
- Four important roles for popular art as "maps of reality" are:
  - Communicating culture
  - Playing the role of social and cultural critic
  - Providing social unity
  - Contributing to our collective memory.
- Every artist has a life vision (artist's goals, beliefs, concerns, convictions) that permeates his or her creative work. As a result, artworks represent belief systems and contemporary values.
- An artistic vision usually does not appear in an artwork in the form of direct statements, but cultural ideals, beliefs, values, attitudes, and assumptions inform the story, characterization, themes, images, and even artistic style.

Discussion Questions

1. Using the four roles for popular art considered in this chapter, create a list of movies, television programs, or popular songs/videos that serve in each of these categories. Looking at this list, what does it reveal about our culture (e.g., cherished ideals and values, key beliefs and attitudes, basic assumptions about life, purpose, social and gender roles, and so forth)?

2. "By offering a vision, a popular artwork sets up the possibility for our accepting or criticizing that vision, and an insightful and honest Christian response will often mean affirming certain aspects while rejecting others," the author argues. "Our critical guard sometimes goes down because we expect popular art to entertain us." How can we learn to balance being entertained with maintaining a critical posture?

3. In a conversation, a friend argues that all movies are purely for entertainment reasons. How would you respond?

4. Why is the distinction between *popular art* and *entertainment* important for developing a Christian approach?

6

MEASURING CHRISTIAN DISTINCTION

MORAL, IDEOLOGICAL, AND THEOLOGICAL APPROACHES

The filmmaker is an artist who presents a vision of reality in his work, a vision that can enrich our own, *whether or not we share it*.

James M. Wall, *Church and Cinema: A Way of Viewing Film*

... it is difficult to imagine participants in Western culture who could mistake Darth Vader as generous.

Noël Carroll, *Philosophy of Mass Art*

Michael Moore's brazen election-year film, *Fahrenheit 9/11* (2004), won all kinds of awards and set a new box-office record for a documentary. Moore, a Michigan native, organized the Traverse City Film Festival with a program of films billed as "nonpartisan and motivated only by appreciation for artistically superior filmmaking," according to press reports.[1] None of Moore's own films were scheduled for viewing; the lineup included thirty-one films, among them traditional Hollywood fare like *Jaws*, *The Princess Bride*, and *Casablanca*, and a U.S. premiere of *Broken Flowers*, the 2005 grand prize winner at the Cannes Film

Festival. There were a number of movies like *Enron: The Smartest Guys in the Room* (2005), *The Assassination of Richard Nixon* (2004), and *Gunner Palace* (a 2004 documentary on the soldier's experience in Iraq) that addressed "political issues such as unemployment, globalization and corporate corruption," as one news report put it.[2]

Sixty percent of the residents of Traverse County, however, voted for George W. Bush in the 2004 election. When a local conservative activist, Genie Aldrich, could not dissuade the city commission from letting Moore's festival use a municipal waterfront park, she contacted the Texas-based American Film Renaissance and together they organized their own counter Traverse Bay Freedom Film Festival and scheduled it to overlap with Moore's during the last week in July 2005. Jim Hubbard, AFR's president and founder, said some of the local townspeople were "just a little bit nervous" about Moore's festival. "They don't really share Michael Moore's worldview."[3]

That was putting it mildly. "People are fed up and tired with the extreme left-wing radical fringe—America haters, family haters, Christian haters," Aldrich told the press. The movies in Moore's festival "represent the minority, extreme, radical left view," she said. Her festival would "show the world that this is Heartland region, and we are pro-family, pro-faith and pro-freedom."[4] Based on the themes "faith, freedom and patriotism" the Traverse Bay Freedom Film Festival screened about a dozen films, including Hollywood favorites *Top Gun*, *On the Waterfront*, *Charlotte's Web*, *Raiders of the Lost Ark*, and the Disney documentary *America's Heart and Soul*. But the lineup also included *In the Face of Evil* (a pro–Ronald Reagan documentary), *Confronting Iraq* (a pro–Iraq War documentary), and *Michael Moore Hates America* (all 2004). In response, Moore said his festival featured "highly acclaimed films" while his competitor's films were "works of political propaganda."[5]

The film festival wars in northern Michigan showed how much the discussion about popular art is informed by social, political, and other factors. At one level this dispute centered on conflicting views of the world and their cultural representations. But it was also about different ways of thinking about popular art: its nature, purposes, functions, and effects.

Those who write about popular art often reveal different emphases. Concerned with plot and character, for example, a *Rolling Stone* critic thought, "At the risk of understatement, *The Matrix Revolutions* sucks," while an evangelical dismissed such negative reviews and was thrilled that the main protagonist Neo was "a Jesus Christ parallel."[6] A critic concerned with morality denounced *Kill Bill* as "a degenerate movie," while another praised it as "a virtuoso piece of filmmaking."[7]

In this chapter we will look at three established means of criticism that have been employed by people of faith: moral, ideological, and theological. Each approach is qualified or characterized by a specific locus, a key motif that animates this sort of criticism (or production) in both explicit and implicit ways, whether moral propositions, ideological arguments, or theological precepts. Though employed in various ways, some more sophisticated than others, these approaches highlight different ways that people have claimed a measure of Christian distinction in thinking about popular art.

This is not meant to be an exhaustive treatment, but a charting of salient characteristics and tendencies. These categories should not be thought of as representative groupings of people, but rather as illuminating observable vantage points from which artists, critics, and patrons work. Nor do I think of them as hard and fast categories; because they are all avenues into the meaning-making process, individuals often employ them in varying combinations depending on the situation. Each has commendable strengths but also inevitable shortcomings. As one would expect, individual artworks will sometimes lend themselves better to one kind of approach over another.

Nevertheless, these three methods are useful in sorting out and making sense of the ways in which people of faith have criticized popular artworks. This examination can help us better understand situations like the film festival in northern Michigan by revealing how complicated the relationship between a critical perspective and popular art can be. My own approach is not something altogether different from those treated in this chapter; affinities do exist. Nevertheless, looking at some influential existing approaches will set the context for and help distinguish the approach I put forth later in this book.

Moralist Approaches

Chicago's Cardinal Francis George found *The Da Vinci Code* "a very, very enjoyable read, as page turners go." But he also thought Dan Brown's novel played on popular biases and cast suspicion on the Catholic Church. For that reason, he said, "I resent the book, because it does undermine people's faith."[8] These attitudes were only amplified when SONY announced production of a film version of the novel. There would be no long-term damage done to the church by the novel and movie, "But in the short run, a number of people will be confused," the communications director for the United States Conference of Catholic Bishops said. "And if only one person were to come away with a distorted impression of Jesus Christ or his church, our concern would be for that person as if he or she were the whole world."[9]

Moralists worry that popular art is a source of false beliefs and immoral values and practices that threaten the social fabric. It follows that they commend art affirming their moral position on the assumption that these works will encourage morally right behavior. As expected, they condemn artworks that do not, arguing that people will identify with characters made to appear attractive and adopt whatever immoral views, ideas, and practices these characters display.

The use of a set of assigned moral values as the sole calibration of a popular artwork's value might make such criticism appear "Christian" easily enough. But this can also be a very superficial kind of criticism when it does not get much beyond identifying incidents of (im)morality; it can even cloud artistic judgments, leading to distorted interpretations.

A British scholar, for example, observed this in evangelical reviews that found Steven Spielberg's award-winning film on the Holocaust, *Schindler's List* (1993), "very offensive from a Christian perspective" because of "extensive nudity in concentration camp scenes . . . graphic sex scenes between unmarried individuals . . . [and] 19 obscenities, 8 profanities and several vulgarities." He remarked that "Faced with one of the great moral evils of our century, these reviewers could do little more than tot up the number of swear words."[10] Apparently, these evangelical reviewers were gauging moral appropriateness in terms of suitability for the family market. We should certainly be concerned with questions about how much a film ought to reveal of the horrors of humanity, but the standard for appropriateness need not reside only in the capabilities and sensitivities of twelve-year-olds.

In contrast, film critic Roger Ebert thought *Schindler's List* showed us "the Holocaust in a vivid and terrible way." He noted the extent to which everything in the film served the meaning Spielberg rendered of these events. "The movie is brilliantly acted, written, directed and seen," Ebert wrote. "Individual scenes are masterpieces of art direction, cinematography, special effects, crowd control."[11] But even that was not enough for someone with a personal connection to the historical events. After hearing his father's experience of starvation and brutality in a Nazi concentration camp, one film critic, who identified himself as the son of a "Schindler Jew," thought that Spielberg's movie did not so much contribute to "an understanding of the Holocaust as cloak its horrors." He wrote that "the Holocaust deserves to be rendered truthfully in all its detail because it challenges and contradicts any advances made by human beings."[12] Can you imagine what he might have thought of the "Christian" review cited above?

Don't misunderstand me. We ought to be critical of the gratuitous inclusion of sex, profanity, or violence in motion pictures. But are there not appropriate uses of these elements in art?

To use one example, war consists of excessive and unnecessary violence. How does a filmmaker honestly and realistically depict the horrors of war? Reviewers have found incidents worth considering in this regard, where depictions of violence were justified by a perspective that showed fighting as horrific and dehumanizing. A *Books & Culture* critic observed that while *Hotel Rwanda* (2005) revealed "the most horrible realism about human sin," the film managed to create a viewpoint amidst the fear and suffering it depicted so that audiences were "buoyed by the heroic acts of Paul Rusesabagina, the hotel manager who saves the lives of hundreds of Tutsi refugees during the Hutu massacres of the 1980s."[13] Roger Ebert found the opening sequence in *Saving Private Ryan* (1998) "as graphic as any war footage I've ever seen." But the depiction of violence was justifiable given the film's perspective on war: "In fierce dread and energy it's on a par with Oliver Stone's *Platoon*, and in scope surpasses it—because in the bloody early stages the landing forces and the enemy never meet eye to eye, but are simply faceless masses of men who have been ordered to shoot at one another until one side is destroyed."[14] One college student told me that after seeing *Saving Private Ryan* he was both grateful for the sacrifices that generation had made and also glad that he's never had to fight in a war. That seemed an appropriate response to this film, which was remarkably different in attitude than the jingoistic military films of the 1980s, like *Top Gun* (1986) and the Rambo series (1982, 1985, 1988).

Reducing evaluations to a moral legalism can make faith-based criticism seem largely irrelevant to a public eager for fresh interpretive strategies and insightful discussion of the movies, music, and TV shows they patronize. I do not mean to imply, however, that people of faith should not assess a popular artwork in terms of the moral universe it represents. But this kind of critical engagement is as necessary for country and rap genres as it is for contemporary Christian music; for HBO productions like *Sex and the City* or *The Sopranos* as well as family sitcoms; for movies like *Traffic* (2000) or *Pulp Fiction* (1994) along with PG-rated pictures that make it seem all issues are plain and simple, based on a moral polarization. For while some artworks might offer a moral vision that dwells on darkness with little room for goodness or redemption, others perhaps bask in the light depicting the battle between good and evil in sharp and contrasting terms that become superficial by making it all too easy—evildoers are destroyed, and the virtuous are rewarded.

After a presentation at a university campus, I responded to a question about *The Passion of the Christ*. In my estimation, it is difficult to provide dramatic justification for some of the violence in the film. A young man countered that if it happened (by which he meant if it was historically accurate), it should be shown on the screen. He made this assertion, I gathered, as a Christian defending a film that affirmed his convictions. On the drive home I wondered if he would be just as quick to support a

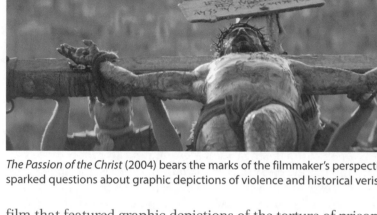

The Passion of the Christ (2004) bears the marks of the filmmaker's perspective and sparked questions about graphic depictions of violence and historical verisimilitude.

film that featured graphic depictions of the torture of prisoners in Abu Ghraib, for example. It happened. And for all the conservative evangelical protestations that the violence in *The Passion* was justified "because it happened," it is worth noting where Gibson starkly avoided historical verisimilitude: namely the nakedness of the crucified. Here is a film in Aramaic, going to excruciating lengths to show the horror of Christ's dying, but quite carefully keeping loinwraps in place at all times. How would those so patient with the violence "because it happened" have responded to an equally historically accurate depiction of reality?

Most of us, I think, would prescribe limits in terms of onscreen representations. Good moral criticism has to wrestle with questions about portrayals in the popular arts, pointing out their significance (or lack thereof), and rendering judgments about the artist's manner of treatment. But as often as not what might satisfy one viewer can offend another. Sometimes this has to do with their ideological positions.

Ideological Approaches

Ten days before the United States invaded Iraq in 2002, a member of the Dixie Chicks criticized President George W. Bush onstage during a London concert. Her comment was widely reported in the press and led to an angry partisan backlash with country fans and conservative commentators branding one of the top-selling country groups in the early 2000s as unpatriotic. Listeners demanded that radio stations drop the Dixie Chicks from playlists and within days the group's CD *Home* (2002) vanished from the airwaves and stalled on the sales charts. Protestors appeared at their concerts and members of the group received death threats.[15] Popular artists and particular artworks can serve as symbolic representations of the ideological solidarities and conflicts that exist in life.

"Politics is a part of life and art is about life," Canadian musician Bruce Cockburn maintained. "It doesn't mean that all the art has to be about politics—in fact, heaven forbid. But politics is a totally legitimate area of focus for any art, whether it's painting or songwriting or anything else, as much as sex is, as much as spirituality is, as much as any other behavior of people is."[16]

As many scholars have shown, narrative is a good vehicle for ideology. Songwriters and storytellers fashion representations of the world informed by social, political, and economic assumptions. These stories can be understood as a kind of ideological argument. *The Life of David Gale* (2003), for example, tells the tale of a man famous for his opposition to the death penalty who finds himself on Death Row for the rape and murder of a co-activist. With a surprise twist ending, the narrative itself can be read as an argument against capital punishment.

The locus of ideological criticism, then, is concern with popular cultural expressions as they represent the structure of power relationships in a society. When people make judgments about popular art that center on social, economic, political, or gender-based power struggles, they are employing an ideological approach.

Critical response to the controversial *Cider House Rules* (1999) is an apt illustration. Catholic and evangelical reviewers dubbed the film "abortion propaganda," "an extended meditation on abortion," and a statement that "women should have the right to kill their unborn children."[17] One reviewer pointed out that Homer's (Tobey Maguire) one exception to his opposition to abortion was in the case of incest. "But in the moral terms of the movie itself, there is no reason why we should find incest any more objectionable than abortion," he argued.[18]

There were contrary voices as well (though I'm unaware of their faith persuasions). A *Village Voice* critic thought the film's "implicit position is that abortion is wrong except in cases of rape or incest. Worse still, it makes men the arbiters of what happens to a woman's body and the abortion debate a defining factor of manhood," she wrote. "The mind boggles at the plethora of patriarchal assumptions."[19] Yet another reviewer thought having main characters on both sides of the issue gave a "real sense of fairness to the film's approach." He found it offered "a reasonably balanced perspective" without "short-changing the anti-abortion side."[20]

As an avenue into the meaning-making process, ideology affirms the social construction of reality; as a critical approach it stresses the perspective of popular artists. But artists who emphasize ideology tend to be dogmatic and risk turning their work into propaganda. For some, this is the point of message-oriented media. "I would say that we are propaganda," one evangelical filmmaker said. "But all film is propaganda. Ours just happens to be trying to move you into a direction of who God is."[21] Critics stressing ideology will often evaluate a popular artwork positively to the extent that its content adheres to the critic's own ideological agenda. Arguably, a popular artwork can still be "good," that is, artistically excellent and a viable representation of the world, even if it doesn't affirm the viewer's ideological position. The larger, perhaps more important issue to consider is the extent to which popular art should be used (i.e., made to serve) as a vehicle for ideology. In other words, when does didacticism diminish the quality of a popular artwork as art?

Questions about art and ideology were central to the response to Ang Lee's *Brokeback Mountain* (2005), lauded as "groundbreaking" and a "landmark" film for its tragic tale of forbidden homosexual love.[22] Mainstream and Christian reviewers alike were nearly unanimous on the artistic mastery of the film, lavishing praise on the story, directing, acting, and cinematography. While some Christian critics dismissed the film as propaganda, most found it evenhanded. *Brokeback* "creates vast plains of space for the audience to interpret Jack and Ennis' actions and the hope and fears that motivate them," a *Christianity Today* reviewer observed. "It's quite possible that no matter what the viewer believes about homosexuality, he or she will be able to read their own stance on the issue into this story."[23]

Questions about art and ideology were central to the critical response to *Brokeback Mountain* (2005).

As many critics observed, *Brokeback Mountain* is an artistically excellent film with a perspective—characteristics of good art. Instead of delivering a "message," *Brokeback*, despite being facetiously tagged the "gay cowboy movie," invited viewers into the world of Ennis Del Mar (Heath Ledger) and Jake Twist (Jake Gyllenhaal). An assumption in that world is that the homoerotic feelings Ennis and Jack have for each other are real and even "natural," genuinely human, however much these characters experience them as mysterious in origin and spend their lives in a painful struggle to understand and deal with them.

Accepting the terms of the film, mainstream reviewers wrote about it as a tragic story of forbidden love that was "universal," a film "ultimately not about sex . . . but about love," and an "epic, complicated love story" in which "The two lovers here just happen to be men."[24] A *Christian Century* critic drew a comparison with *Wuthering Heights*: "As a movie about the ways that love can both define and destroy lives, *Brokeback Mountain* is a stunning piece of work."[25] And in a review praising the film's artistry, a writer for the *Catholic News Service* concluded, "While the actions taken by Ennis and Jack cannot be endorsed, the universal themes of love and loss ring true."[26]

A writer in the *New York Review of Books*, however, argued that by casting *Brokeback* as a universal love story, these reviewers were diminishing the "specifically gay element" of the film and consequently misconstruing the story. "Both narratively and visually, *Brokeback Mountain* is a tragedy about the specifically gay phenomenon of the 'closet'—about the disastrous emotional and moral consequences of erotic self-repression and of the social intolerance that first causes and then exacerbates it," he explained. "If Jack and Ennis are tainted, it's not because they're gay, but because they pretend not to be; it's the lie that poisons everyone they touch." He concluded, "The real achievement of *Brokeback Mountain* is not that it tells a universal love story that happens to have gay characters in it, but that it tells a distinctively gay story that happens to be so well told that any feeling person can be moved by it."[27]

Christian critics not accepting the film's basic assumption interpreted the film not as a love story at all, but as a tale of infidelity and lust. Jeffrey Overstreet, to cite one example, wrote about the main characters' relationship as "an unhealthy sexual obsession rather than a flourishing friendship and love—they become enslaved to their lust, and it disrupts the rest of their lives." He understood their homoerotic feelings as an addiction comparable to "the junkies of *Requiem for a Dream* or the alcoholic played by Nic Cage in *Leaving Las Vegas*," and concluded: "Essentially, the story of *Brokeback Mountain* is the same as most stories of infidelity—two people who 'can't control' their desire for each other end up hurting others, telling lies, and excusing themselves of responsibility for their actions."[28]

As these dramatically different readings of the film show, ideological assumptions weigh heavily in how critics and viewers understand, interpret, and evaluate a film or popular artwork. We can learn even more about this aspect of popular art criticism by looking closely at two reviews that reveal the difficulties we all face when encountering viewpoints different from our own.

Steven D. Greydanus, a Catholic critic at the online Decent Films Guide, went some length to argue that *Brokeback Mountain* was not "propaganda, a tract," but "a work of art, more concerned with telling a story about characters than with making sure that the viewer feels a certain way about a moral issue." The film "doesn't commit the artistic fraud of shaping every single element in its story to move the viewer's sympathies in one and only one direction," he noted approvingly. "That sort of one-sidedness is increasingly the single thing that I find most quickly sabotages a film's persuasiveness; nothing else so glaringly announces that the filmmaker himself hasn't really put his own point of view to the test, and doesn't trust the audience to see things his way unless he stacks the deck in his own favor."[29]

Greydanus found *Brokeback* to be an artistic film, persuasive in its appeal without becoming a one-sided tract, but he judged the film's perspective to be "a profoundly problematic one, one that makes it potentially far more insidious than mere propaganda." Compared to *Brokeback*, he wrote that "the euthanasia advocacy of *Million Dollar Baby*, the anti-Catholicism of *The Magdalene Sisters* and the abortion activism of *The Cider House Rules* are practically child's play."[30] Greydanus defined *Brokeback* as art but then treated it as propaganda, if only because the film harbors a perspective in conflict with his own. He seems to have drawn too firm a distinction between art and propaganda, not realizing perhaps the extent to which all popular artworks are representative of cultural ideals, beliefs, values, and assumptions. Does he mean to imply that he would prefer propaganda to a film that is artful but does not accord with his own beliefs? Is he suggesting that popular artworks should simply entertain by reinforcing popular beliefs instead of probing important but contentious issues?

In the review referred to above, Overstreet gave *Brokeback* a grade of C- ("Its flaws outweigh its virtues") because in his judgment the film was about "dishonest, unfaithful men who mistake lust for love, serving only themselves without regard for anyone else." By comparison, he gave Ridley Scott's *Kingdom of Heaven* a "B" ("Its virtues far outweigh its faults") even though "it falls short of being profound, due to its glorification of godlessness over faith."[31] Why does Scott's film—deemed to glorify godlessness—rate higher than Ang Lee's? Overstreet applauded *Kingdom of Heaven* for its inclusion of "some old-fashioned, red-blooded drama and romance," "vast, intense, massive battles" (that many other reviewers criticized as being overly violent), with the director filling "the cast with strong, masculine actors who command our attention." But he also made the point that "almost any Christian character with any degree of authority in the film is portrayed as some combination of liar, buffoon, idiot, hypocrite, or coward" while Muslims are treated "as people of honor and respect, for the most part." The main character makes a "quick jump into the sheets with a married princess." Overstreet nevertheless recommended the film: "It gives us a context rich with provocation that will spur viewers to investigate all kinds of questions . . . and we should focus on those questions."

Good art invites discussion and provokes questions, and both *Kingdom of Heaven* and *Brokeback Mountain* did just that. Both films contained (even glorified?) behavior that Christians might variously consider to be sinful. On what basis did Overstreet evaluate the one film more positively than the other? As is often the case, this critic's evaluations were largely informed by his own ideological position that led him to favor a certain treatment of subject matter (violence or heterosexuality, for example) over another (homosexuality). Ultimately, it would seem artistic excellence counted for much less with both of these critics when the basic assumptions at work in the world of the film conflicted with their own.

Perhaps we should consider that there is a difference between how a critic/viewer *actually* responds and how she believes she *should* respond to a particular movie, especially in this case given the contentious subject matter of *Brokeback Mountain*. The United States Council of Catholic Bishops changed the classification of the film from "L" (limited adult audience) to "O" (morally offensive) in response to reader protests of the positive review in the *Catholic News Service*.[32] *Christianity Today* received "an avalanche" of letters from readers with many complaining about the magazine's three-star review of the film, even though an editorial note made it clear the rating was not to be construed as a recommendation for readers to see the film and referred only to "the quality of the filmmaking," not the "moral acceptability" of the film's subject matter.[33] That reviews of movies like *Kingdom of Heaven* did not warrant such editorial qualification shows further the influence of social, political, and commercial contexts in popular art criticism.

Theological Approaches

The term *theology* is generally understood to refer to talk about God or "in the broadest sense, to describe any reflection on religion and the divine."[34] However, as one theologian explained, "Because human beings do not invent God, and because God is held to be a reality independent of human experience, then theology cannot comprise merely human conceptualizing."[35] Theological study also entails talk "from God," so to speak, with such study nested in a particular theological tradition (Jewish, Christian, Muslim) and relying in various ways on sacred texts. Theologian Robert Johnston used the term theology in two senses, having to do, first, with "a way of knowing God and what God reveals," and second, as a discipline aimed at developing "an integrated knowledge about God."[36]

Theology should not be understood as static or arcane, but an aspect of the ongoing human search for truth. All of us, regardless of our faith convictions, face questions about God, the meaning of life and particular events, guilt, suffering, injustice, and more. People of faith can often find such situations more perplexing than others; trying to reconcile deep-seated beliefs with the personal or social turmoil of real-life experiences can create doubt or spark inquiry about one's assumptions.

As we have seen, church leaders have always been uneasy about commercial entertainment media doing the work of theology. That overtly theological movies—from *The Last Temptation of Christ* (1988) to *Dogma* (1999) to *The Passion*—always seem to generate controversy aptly makes the point. But some theologians observed that much theological debate seemed to be taking place outside the church. They realized that discussions in pizza parlors and coffee shops over movies, TV shows, and rock concerts were "abounding with the search for transcendence."[37]

In response, they began to appropriate the popular art and culture that was previously disregarded for reasons of spiritual corruption or aesthetic inferiority to the traditional high arts as an important site for theological discourse. Considering a popular artwork "a vehicle for theological speculation," they related biblical texts or classic theological themes to popular art, often treating artworks as parables or allegories.[38] Robert Johnston's *Useless Beauty*, for example, drew comparisons between Ecclesiastes and contemporary films.[39]

As I noted earlier, not all artworks benefit equally from a specific kind of analysis; a critic will often look for what suits best the salient features of his approach. There is nothing unusual about this. *Pretty Woman* (1990) lends itself easily enough to ideological interpretations, while movies like *The Mission* (1986) or *Babette's Feast* (1987) are enriched by theological ones. And so critics using this approach tend to privilege artworks lending themselves to theological consideration or risk making exaggerated claims about their theological significance. Theologians generally concede that not all movies benefit equally from theological interpretation. As Joel Martin put it, "We have no desire to squeeze blood from turnips."[40] But according to Martin and Conrad Ostwalt, theological criticism "hinges upon the notion that the critic, director, screenplay writer, or some other creative force behind the film develops a certain theological agenda or concept, and the distinctive goal of the theological critic is to uncover that concept."[41] This points to a significant shortcoming of theological approaches. How are these critics to take an artwork on its own terms considering, as one theologian noted, that most films "would never be conceived of in themselves as theological or even religious"?[42] Given this situation, how is a theological approach to be applied while still guarding the integrity of the film? And how "theologically" reflective, then, are these "secular" films of the culture at large? Some theologians have argued that since Judeo-Christian themes have had "a tremendous impact upon Western culture and all its art forms, theological scholars are positioned to make many valuable insights about the modern Western art of Hollywood film."[43] But to what extent does the artist's intention create boundaries for possible interpretations? And on what basis are Christians to think about those films that do not address theological issues?

The best theological analyses give us unique insights into individual artworks. Roy Anker's investigation of *The Godfather* (1972) revealed differences between Vito and Michael Corleone that showed a relationship between their respective temperaments and moral visions.[44] Ostwalt showed that by investing humans with complete control over time and the destiny of humankind, Hollywood films have secularized the apocalyptic literature tradition.[45] Gordon Lynch analyzed an episode of *The Simpsons* as a popular cultural text that broadly supported a notion of American civil religion.[46] Writers have illuminated Catholic symbolism in the music of Bruce Springsteen, dialogued with Canadian musician Bruce Cockburn, and critically evaluated images of God in popular culture.[47]

There are occasions, however, when theological criticism seems more like an imposition on a text than a deepening of our insight. For example, after the famous shower scene in Alfred Hitchcock's psychological thriller *Psycho* (1960), Norman Bates disposes of Marion's body and her car by sinking them in a swamp. Using a Christian theological framework, one scholar suggested, "One can hope, as the car is pulled from the swamp, that the dead shall be raised incorruptible."[48] Such an interpretation is possible, I suppose, but even considering Hitchcock's Catholic upbringing, how viable is it? Or other writers proposed that *Austin Powers: International Man of Mystery* (1997) "resolves one apparent contradiction that has dogged our understanding of the Bible. Are we to relish the freedom Paul emphasizes in Galatians or adopt the restraint evident in Corinthians?"[49] Such a reading of the James Bond movie parody seems like a well-meaning but strained effort to find evidence of theology in popular culture.

The concerns outlined in this section raise questions about the viability of a theological approach as a full-fledged Christian criticism. Isolating popular artworks for theological analysis largely ignores the reality that movies, music, and television programming are all products of a profit-driven commercial enterprise, made in a crucible of entangled concerns—aesthetic, moral, political, social, and economic, among others. Cultural discourse involves many partners, theology being one—but one with a limited horizon. And why privilege the theological over ideological, social, or cultural functions for film? Christians can also benefit from the cinema as a means of self-reflection, entertainment, cultural insight, or social critique, as examples.

Representatives of all three of these approaches tend to make comprehensive claims that make theological, ideological, or moral conjectures the sum total of interpretation of a work, even if it means diminishing the significance of other dimensions. One writer, for example, claimed that movies are "finally, centrally, crucially, primarily, *mostly* about redemption," and more specifically about "a person's redemption—or lack thereof."[50] Many American popular stories can be thought about in terms of redemption; *Titanic* (1997), for example, has a clear and even overt redemption motif. But such a broad generalization as this writer makes does little to help us understand the nature of redemption in Hollywood films where characters are more likely to redeem themselves through a journey of self-realization or find romantic love, perhaps, than to seek salvation in God. And what about films like *Gentlemen Prefer Blondes* (1953), *Rear Window* (1954), *Bonnie and Clyde* (1967), *Chinatown* (1974), *Taxi Driver* (1976), *Memento* (2000), *Million Dollar Baby* (2004), or many others that are mostly about something other than redemption? That these films are better understood in terms other than the theological or redemptive suggests a serious limitation to this kind of criticism.

Mobilizing Popular Art

Adherents of these approaches are inclined to mobilize popular art in service of some education-related goal, like teaching moral values, affirming social or political positions, or advancing theological discussion. Concerned about the effect *Cider House Rules* might have on impressionable youth, one reviewer wrote, "High school freshmen, who require no 'parental guidance' to see this film, have probably never heard a cogent argument against abortion. For them, what a movie like this presents as credible serves as a truth claim."[51] Likewise, concerning *The Da Vinci*

Code, a Vatican spokesperson said, "There is a very real risk that many people who read it will believe that the fables it contains are true."[52] The same kind of argument was made earlier along ideological lines about Oliver Stone's film *JFK* (1991); many feared this dramatization of a conspiracy to assassinate the president would become the accepted version of events and foster a cynicism toward American government.[53]

These critics respond as they do in part because they fear popular art will negatively influence people by promoting false beliefs and immoral values. Film philosopher Noël Carroll, however, argued persuasively that rather than being taught to us by art, "most of the beliefs that we might be said to acquire from art are things we already know and which, in fact, we must bring to the text in order to understand it."[54] In other words, a common moral framework is a condition for comprehending an artwork. And in order to be accessible to audiences across cultures, producers generally subscribe to a widely shared moral understanding.

Even before the film begins, for example, most of us root for Indiana Jones because we arrive at the theater already believing the Nazis are despicable. Likewise, people will endorse those characters that demonstrate moral values and behavior they already approve of. In *Titanic*, for example, Rose's fiancé, Cal Hockley, does not need to twist the corners of an oily black moustache to be recognized as the villain. Concerned only with the approval of his social set, Cal equates wealth and social status with worth and character. Aware of the limited lifeboat capacity, Rose says, "Half the people on this ship are going to die." The snobbish Cal responds, "Not the better half." These attitudes run against the grain of American values associated with freedom and equality. Even though he is handsome and extremely wealthy, no one in the movie theater wants him to touch Rose, let alone marry her. In opposition to Cal, free-spirited artist Jack is the ultimate expression of pure freedom. His character traits, luck, talent, and good looks easily identify him as the hero.

Our reactions to popular artworks, then, are better understood in terms of the moral values that inform our engagement with the work than those values displayed in the artworks themselves. In that regard, it is less a matter of acquisition of new knowledge than a deepening of our understanding of our moral values, emotions, and the issues of life. The popular arts manage to do this by encouraging us to apply our moral vision to the specific situations artworks represent. Most patrons of the movie *Crash* (2005), for example, went to the theater knowing that racism is bad; seeing the harmful and destructive experiences the characters had as a result of racist attitudes and behavior only reinforced this belief.

Academy Award–winner *Crash* (2005) depicts personal and social harm and the complexity of racism.

Much the same is true of spectator identification with characters. Viewers construct an understanding of a character based on how much we know about that character through their actions or our access to their thoughts and feelings. Our "allegiance" to a character, film scholar Murray Smith explained, "depends upon the spectator having what she takes to be reliable access to the character's state of mind, on understanding the context of the character's actions, and having morally evaluated the character on the basis of this knowledge."[55] As Smith showed, identification with characters is complex and depends on a variety of factors that might include viewer beliefs and attitudes about class, nationality, age, ethnicity, and gender. How a viewer responds emotionally, whether or not a viewer is sympathetic with a character, involves rendering a judgment about the character based on the viewer's already-existing beliefs, values, and attitudes. While any popular artwork that fosters a change in moral or theological views should "not be dismissed lightly," according to a Barna Group survey only five percent of *Da Vinci Code* readers altered their "beliefs or religious perspectives" as a result of reading the novel. (Of course we don't know from the survey results what kind of changes occurred, whether skepticism or renewed interest in one's faith as examples.) "Upon reading the book, many people encountered information that confirmed what they already believed. Many readers found information that served to connect some of their beliefs in new ways," George Barna explained. "But few people changed their pre-existing beliefs because of what they read in the novel. And even fewer people approached the book with a truly open mind regarding the controversial matters in question, and emerged with a new theological perspective. The book generates controversy and discussions, but it has not revolutionized the way that Americans think about Jesus, the Church or the

Bible."[56] This further supports the proposition introduced earlier that popular artworks typically affirm audience beliefs instead of introducing new ones, and again this shows the importance of patrons being conscious of their own perspective in their critical engagement with the popular arts.

Complexity of Criticism

Critics employing the three approaches considered in this chapter tend to treat a popular artwork as an isolated text that they interpret along moral, ideological, or theological lines. The effect is to fragment the popular art phenomenon, as if this one aspect is unrelated to other dimensions. This is most obvious in discourse related to the connection between a critical perspective and artistic presentation; it is not uncommon for a specific agenda to conflict with artistic worth. Of course this is not the case with all critics. Reacting against the use of theological accord as the barometer of value, for example, some theologians proposed a kind of "dialogue" between theology and popular culture.

Nevertheless, sometimes the inclusion of perceived immoral elements was enough reason for moralists to dismiss a work. "We can find a few movies that perhaps have some positive values but those are negated by throwing in partial nudity, sexual references, and profanity," a representative of the Michigan American Family Association said. "True Christians don't want the negatives, regardless of how small the amount."[57] But others accepted artworks that did not explicitly or directly oppose their values. For example, there is a scene in the "family friendly" hit film, *My Big Fat Greek Wedding* (2002), when Ian (John Corbett) invites Toula (Nia Vardalos) "up to his apartment and she jumps him," as one evangelical reviewer put it. But while noting that "some language and sexual situations are disappointing," this critic still considered the movie "one of the sweetest romantic comedies to come along in some time."[58]

It can also be the case that an artwork affirms a viewer's moral or ideological position, but is not very effective artistically. A reviewer for the national gay and lesbian newsmagazine *The Advocate* noted that even though Oliver Stone's *Alexander* (2004) didn't "shy away from the story's queer content," it was still an artistic "mess." "While it's worth applauding *Alexander* for not making its legendary hero 100% hetero, there's nothing else to recommend about this stilted, tedious epic," the critic wrote. "Instead of asking 'Will it be gay enough?' perhaps the gay media should have been asking 'Will it be any good?'"[59] Of course, the reverse is just as likely. Even though the Academy Award–winner *American Beauty* (1999) received worldwide praise, an evangelical critic withheld recommending the film on moral grounds: "While *American Beauty* is technically exceptional, its offensive material outweighs any redeeming values."[60]

It is also possible to emphasize the aesthetic to an extent that devalues discussion of social, moral, or theological aspects as inconsequential. It is as if art transcends these or other dimensions. Such an approach may be attractive to those who recognize the problems with criticism that demands an artwork's adherence to a specific moral, ideological, or theological agenda. Even so, a focus on formal aesthetic features can also be myopic, leading to a kind of high-art "disinterested contemplation" that renders evaluation of content according to one's perspective as having little, if any, significance. As I have already shown, perspectives are critical to our engagement with popular art.

All of this demonstrates the complexity of popular art criticism. Democratic values associated with freedom of expression conflict with fears about the potentially negative impact of the media. Those who desire to evangelize or present a social perspective have to acknowledge that people with different cultural orientations also want to express themselves in like manner. "Complicated it is." That's how Yoda might describe the multifaceted world of popular art.

Summary

- Moral, ideological, and theological are three established kinds of criticism that have been employed by people of faith.
- Moralists might issue warnings against artworks in terms of levels of profanity, explicit sex, or violence, but this critical approach does not get much beyond the most superficial level of analysis and can even lead to distorted interpretations.
- Ideological criticism is concerned with popular artworks' representation of power relations in society. Ideological criticism runs the risk of evaluating art solely on the degree of its adherence to the critic's own ideological agenda.
- Theological critics seek to relate popular artworks to biblical texts or classic theological themes, but an emphasis on the transcendent and theological concepts limits the scope of this approach.
- Critics employing these approaches tend to treat a popular artwork as an isolated text that they interpret along moral, ideological, or theological lines.
- To be accessible to audiences across cultures, popular art tends to affirm widely held beliefs and a shared moral understanding.

- How viewers respond to stories and characters is based largely on the viewer's pre-existing beliefs, values, and attitudes.

Discussion Questions

1. Find examples of music, movie, or TV criticism that represent the moralistic, ideological, and theological approaches described in this chapter. Discuss the merits of these reviews.
2. What are the benefits of these approaches to criticism? What are the limitations?
3. "A Christian critique of popular art will criticize the gratuitous inclusion of profanity, sex, or violence," the author asserts, while also asking, "But are there not appropriate uses of these elements in popular art?" Respond to this question.
4. Where do you get your information about popular art? How do these sources typically evaluate art?

7

POPULAR ART AS ART

MARKING THE AESTHETIC

[*A History of Violence*] has a simplicity, such a transparency that you can
see through it into something else that is underneath.

David Cronenberg, Film Director

We imagine differently.

Andrew M. Greeley, *The Catholic Myth:
The Behavior and Belief of American Catholics*

Los Angeles Magazine once called the City of the Angels Film Festival
(CAFF) "One of the top 10 coolest things to do in L.A."[1] CAFF found a
niche showing retrospectives of feature films followed by panel discussions on their "cultural capital and spiritual significance." I participated
in a session that centered on advancing the conversation between Catholics and evangelicals regarding film and the media. During the discussion
an audience member pointed out that there are a number of prominent
Catholic filmmakers—John Ford, Frank Capra, Alfred Hitchcock, Francis
Ford Coppola, Martin Scorsese. "Why are there no notable evangelical
filmmakers to speak of?" he asked.

The Billy Graham organization's Worldwide Pictures made modest
independent films to evangelize youth—*The Restless Ones* (1965), about

teenage pregnancy; *A Thief in the Night* (1972), an end-times thriller; and the Nicky Cruz biopic *The Cross and the Switchblade* (1970). A reporter dubbed them "religious tracts first, entertainment second."[2] More recently, evangelicals made news producing sci-fi films about the apocalypse, like *The Omega Code* (1999, 2001) and *Left Behind* movies (2000, 2002, 2005), that were profitable but artistically flawed. These are hardly the kind of creative and provocative movies that attain critical acclaim.

In contrast to evangelical productions, however, the depiction of faith in films by Catholic directors is so implicit as to be "undetected even by the filmmakers themselves," according to Catholic film scholar Richard Blake. Blake still maintained that although they "achieved renown not as Catholics but as secular filmmakers," they continued "to see the world through a Catholic optic." He attributed this to an involuntary phenomenon called an *afterimage*, a term that refers to "an image or sensation that remains or returns after the external stimulus has been withdrawn."[3] It is something like when the light from a camera flash remains even after you close your eyelids, and it temporarily alters your vision.

Hitchcock and others might have displayed a "characteristically Catholic view of the world," even if they were not conscious of it, but their films also exhibited an uneasy mixture of Catholic and American secular beliefs. Frank Capra created inspirational works, but as Blake observed, "the moral 'message' stems from a frankly materialistic brand of American egalitarianism rather than religious belief." Likewise, "Ford used an idealized version of American history to enshrine a noble humanism, and Coppola idealizes the family."[4]

The creative impulse is deeply complex. Blake's use of afterimage implies an almost inadvertent role for faith convictions; it works better as a descriptive model than prescriptive one. My contention has been that people can be, and often are, conscious of their beliefs in their experiences with popular art, whether as creators, critics, or consumers, and this can enrich the effort.

The issue I want to address is this: How can people engage popular art in imaginative ways that are mindful of and consistent with a faith perspective? Furthermore, how does perspective figure into engagement with popular art as art, that is, an experience qualified foremost by the aesthetic? These are difficult and complex questions that do not lend themselves to simple answers.

The popular arts factor into the meaning-making process and for that reason ought to be taken seriously to the extent that they contribute to the ongoing process of cultural orientation. Part of the dilemma is that our experience with popular art is multifaceted, and focusing on one aspect has an isolating effect that tends to discount others that factor significantly into the experience. We should not lose sight of the many and various functions the popular arts serve in our lives and society, including personal reflection, social activity, entertainment, cultural insight, or social critique, as examples. And so I argue for a contextual and functional approach to analysis of popular art as art. Such an approach should focus our attention on the artwork itself, the formal artistic qualities and perspective it represents, while also factoring in the various contexts in which the popular arts are experienced.

The Aesthetic Dimension

There is a fundamental aesthetic dimension that includes not just the creation and interpretation of artworks but also the stuff of ordinary life. Telling a joke, decorating a room, presenting a meal for guests, or dressing for a particular occasion all have an observable aesthetic quality. Actually, as one scholar noted, the term *aesthetic* initially referred to "everyday perceptual experience and only later became specialized to art."[5] Proposals marking the aesthetic realm abound.

Calvin Seerveld defined *art* as "an object or event conceived and structured by human design to be perceived by our senses, and characterized by an imaginative and allusive finish that affords the piece its own independent identity." Art is qualified by the aesthetic. It can and should be discussed in terms of formal properties: symbolic suggestiveness, imagination, craftsmanship, and complexity. But there's more. "Properly conceived and crafted, artworks are allusive objects which tickle your imagination with nuances of knowledge, giving you insights especially into the hidden crevices of human deeds and the wonderful recesses of God's world at large."[6] Art, as we have seen, is imaginative activity that contributes to the meaning-making process. That is why much of the discourse about popular art includes what some might consider non-aesthetic matters. Storytelling, for example, is central to the narrative popular art forms we have been considering here. Interpreting and rendering judgments about these stories are critical to the aesthetic process. In other words, there is an interpretative discourse that exists beyond the story itself that is a crucial aspect of the artistic experience. Artists harness the conventions of their medium to create a narrative, to tell a story that asks to be understood in terms of that medium.

Popular artworks are often intended to represent a life vision and invite dialogue about the matters they address. Engaging artworks in terms of their veracity to our real-life experience is an important benefit of the arts. And even though most people understand that popular art is highly commercialized, they still expect artworks to be consistent with an artist's own experience or perspective. Since the intent of these narrative artworks is for them to be understood, appreciated, contemplated, talked about, judged in some sense as dramatic, comedic, interesting, and so forth, these features belong as part of the aesthetic dimension.

The opening drum roll and musical introduction to Bruce Springsteen's "Hungry Heart," for example, brings a shout of recognition at a concert. Springsteen points the microphone at the crowd and they sing together the memorable opening refrain: "Got a wife and kids in Baltimore, Jack. I went out for a ride and I never went back." We can be delighted with the song's artistic craftsmanship, the rhyming lyrics, for example, the appealing melody in the chorus: "Everybody's got a hungry heart." But we can also find satisfaction in our sense that the lyrical content is truthful to actuality or gives us insight into something beyond our own experience. People do have a "hungry heart," a thirst for a satisfying and complete life. But even if we sometimes fail, "Ain't nobody like to be alone," the narrator reminds us with a pounding rock beat behind his vocals and wailing sax interlude. Sometimes we can find enjoyment in a song's manner of treatment, that relationship between artistic style and the subject that evokes a certain emotional response.

The nexus of an approach to popular art (where it all comes together) lies in the *exploration*, *interpretation*, and *presentation* that characterize the aesthetic process not only for artists but also critics and patrons.[7] Artistic experiences encourage us to explore life and the world, interpret events and representations, and present these discoveries in the form of artworks, discourse, or reviews.

Let's consider this in some detail. An artist imaginatively explores, interpreting events and situations from her perspective. She then re-presents these in a creative artwork, using story, imagery, sounds, lighting, and so forth in ways that best express her interpretation and make it communicable. A person who engages this artwork also explores those events and situations by discovering the artist's vision, and as is bound to happen, thinks about these things in terms of his own perspective. He interprets the artist's vision, gives it thought, discusses it with others, or writes a review. Through this artistic encounter, he gains an understanding of the issues of life presented in the artwork, but not without some appraisal based on his own life vision.

Interpretation, however, is not boundless and has to be grounded in the text itself. This requires an understanding of the unique capacities of the medium—in the case of film, for example, not just story, character, dialogue, and imagery, but lighting, production design, costuming, sound, music, editing, and so forth. Critics comb the artwork itself for insights into the artist's vision, asking what relationship exists between the formal or technical aspects of the artwork (cinematography, characterization, narrative moments, and so forth) and interpretive strategies.

An artwork presents a world to us with more or less reliability. How we understand and draw conclusions about that world is through the artwork's disclosure, that is, what it reveals to us through its treatment of events, portrayal of characters, prominent features of the story's setting, visual imagery, sounds, lighting, and costumes.

Such an analysis begins with the artwork itself. The function of criticism is to make the work intelligible, giving due consideration to its cultural orientation, highlighting its significant symbolic representations—the meaning given and manner of subject treatment—drawing attention to artistic style and its relation to content, so that we gain deeper insight into the artwork.

Artistic Representations

The arts all share common principles, while each exhibits its own uniqueness. Good criticism requires us to take the time to figure out a specific art form and learn to work within its parameters while exploring its possibilities. How do artistic or textual elements work together to create representations of life, people, and events? How do they play with our emotions and thoughts and get us to transfer interpretations to the real world?

Let's consider an array of illustrations to see how we come to understand an artwork's meaning through artistic elements and style.

To appeal to its target demographic, the world of MTV videos is largely a male adolescent "dreamworld."[8] More than a few videos are representations of male fantasies. Many of the shots in music videos pan over a woman's body or fragment her into images of body parts. Instead of showing them as whole people, these portrayals work to objectify women, robbing them of their humanness by reducing their identity to sexualized objects. Also, MTV videos dispose of a conventional linear narrative and use a quick-editing style to tell three-minute stories that are based more on mood and emotion than substance. Music videos provide viewers with a certain feeling, not knowledge based on plot and continuity. The very style of music videos relates to the content, representations, intended audience, and viewing habits.

Narrative features themselves can provoke moral judgments. Suspense, for example, involves uncertainty; it puts us on the edge of our seats because we are not sure what will happen next. But suspense also generates concern for what is morally right. We want and expect a certain resolution based on a system of ethical beliefs. When the serial killer stalks FBI agent Starling (Jodie Foster) in the blackened basement, our desire is that she (and justice) will prevail in *The Silence of the Lambs* (1991).

Will James J. Braddock (Russell Crowe) survive in a boxing match for the heavyweight championship of the world with the bigheaded Max Baer, who has already killed two men in the ring? We want Braddock—the down-and-out underdog—to beat the odds and win, even if it means beating his opponent to a pulp in *Cinderella Man* (2005).

In a sequence in *Bonnie and Clyde* (1967), it is pouring rain and the fated couple is sitting in a car, which has come to symbolize their life on the run. Bonnie is reading to Clyde a poem she's written about them and the media coverage of their crime escapades. It's an intimate moment. Clyde asks Bonnie, "You think if I sent that to the newspapers they'd publish it?" In a voiceover, Bonnie continues to read through a shot dissolve that takes us into the office of the Texas Ranger in pursuit of the couple. He's reading the poem printed on a newspaper page. Bonnie's voiceover continues through another dissolve back to the couple sitting now on a blanket in an open field (suggesting a kind of freedom); Bonnie's holding a newspaper, reading the final lines of her poem. The use of a voiceover and dissolves aurally and visually suggests the passage of time while also associating Bonnie, Clyde, and the Texas Ranger; we know from this sequence that their destinies are irrevocably connected.

Editing for Effect

A common narrative device in movies is called parallel editing or crosscutting. Two or more lines of action taking place in different locations are woven together, suggesting that they are occurring simultaneously. Crosscutting is often used to build suspense. In *Back to the Future* (1985), Doc Brown (Christopher Lloyd) struggles to connect the cable to the clock tower. Cut to Marty McFly (Michael J. Fox) trying to start the plutonium-charged DeLorean. Cut back to Doc sliding down the cable. The pace of the editing quickens as we get closer to the fated time—four minutes past ten. Cut back to Marty accelerating to eighty-eight miles per hour. Then back to the clock tower as lightning strikes, sending an electric charge along the cable and into the flux capacitor, sending Marty back to the future.

In *The Godfather* (1972), Francis Ford Coppola used parallel editing to expose the hypocrisy of society. In the opening scene, Connie's (Talia Shire) wedding reception is juxtaposed with the backroom dealings and underworld activities of her father, Don Corleone (Marlon Brando). The use of parallel editing shows viewers that beneath the surface of marriage, family, and tradition is an underworld of crime that is ruled by threat and the force of violence.

The climactic moment in *The Godfather* is a montage sequence, a scene that achieves its emotional impact and meaning by compressing a passage of time or events into brief shots or images. Coppola used this technique to suggest the meaning of being godfather. While Michael Corleone (Al Pacino) attends a baptism, he is simultaneously taking his place as the new head of the family "business." As he becomes godfather to his sister Connie's child, his henchmen carry out his orders to murder the men who were involved in an assassination attempt on his father. The baptism scene is intercut with shots of the brutal murders of rival gang leaders, murders ordered by Michael. Contrasting images of life and death, light and darkness, peace and violence highlight the disparity. At the most violent moments, Michael baptismally pledges to "renounce Satan and all his works." The juxtaposition of the baptism and gangland killings also gives a religious dimension to the godfather, a man who controls life and death, making offers you can't refuse. As the title God-Father suggests, he is a larger-than-life figure to be feared and respected.

There is a scene in the film *Priest* (1994) in which parallel editing is used to suggest that, while a young clergyman is praying for help, God is already at work responding to the priest's appeal. During confession, a man revealed to the suspecting priest that he was involved in an incestuous relationship with his daughter. He confessed not to repent and seek forgiveness but to silence the priest in order to prevent him from exposing his sinful behavior. Torn between the sanctity of the confessional and his desire to help the family, the priest yells and pleads with God for a way out of this dilemma. In the meantime, the wife's church meeting is inexplicably cut short; she returns home early and catches her husband in the act of molesting their child.

The camera work on NBC's award-winning *The West Wing* gives home viewers a sense of being right there in the midst of all that's going on at the center of political power. The camera often follows characters around—down hallways, through doors and into rooms—as if the viewer were walking right behind them, peering over their shoulders. We might see a White House aide watching a breaking event on a television news program. A shot of the news anchor on the television screen fills our TV picture. Then the camera pulls away from the television screen to show the president watching the same program in the Oval Office. The camera pans from a close-up of the president's face to the news anchor on the television screen, to a White House staff person in a hotel lobby watching the same news report. The shot of each character registers an emotional response to the event (suggesting how viewers should feel). Home viewers sense the simultaneity in the communication of world events while feeling like they are smack dab in the middle of it all.

Relating Style and Content

Music critic Jon Pareles demonstrated the important relationship between musical style and lyrical content. He pointed out "the personal, political and spiritual merge" in the title song of Bruce Springsteen's *Devils & Dust* CD (2005), which Springsteen wrote after the United States invaded Iraq in 2003. As Pareles observed, it was Springsteen's choice of a "subdued" musical arrangement and "gentle" vocals that made the narrator "sound so alone" and not "heroic." The effect was not just a confluence of musical style and lyrical content but also to artistically connect personal and publicly felt emotions. "I got my finger on the trigger / But I don't know who to trust," the narrator sings. "I got God on my side / I'm just trying to survive." Then he wonders, "What if what you do to survive / Kills the things you love." In one sense, it is a private feeling of uncertainty that is expressed, and Springsteen said, "Most of the songs on the record, you're listening to someone think." But the narrator's musings have a universal quality suggesting he "could be a soldier in Iraq or America itself," as Pareles observed.[9]

Style can be used to communicate ideals and attitudes. We can recognize immediately the traditional cowboy hero in western movies. But the narrative in John Ford's *The Searchers* (1956) juxtaposes Ethan Edwards (John Wayne) with other characters to rework the traditional western gunslinger image by revealing flaws in Ethan's moral character. The pairing of Ethan with his brother, Aaron, sets up Ethan as the lone western hero who is not at home in the civilized world. By pairing Ethan with the renegade Sioux, Scar, however, Ford suggests that both the hero and antagonist are driven by the same racist passions.

In *Eternal Sunshine of the Spotless Mind* (2004) the story is structured on two levels, one moving forward in time (covering approximately one night) and the other in reverse chronology as Joel (Jim Carrey) has two years of his memories of Clementine (Kate Winslet) erased. Running in opposite directions, the narrative generates questions about meaningful relationships. "When you break up with somebody you tend to surround yourself with the worst memories to protect yourself from regret," director Michel Gondry said. "But when the pain starts to ease, you begin to remember the good memories—and actually it becomes more painful."[10] When the opening scene with Joel and Clementine meeting on a train is replayed for us, we see the characters differently now. Aware that they are not meeting for the first time, we wonder: Are they are destined to repeat the past? Or with their slate of memories wiped clean, can they pursue a different course in life and love? What factors might make a difference one way or another?

The creative story and narrative structure of *Eternal Sunshine of the Spotless Mind* (2004) works to raise questions about personal identity and meaningful relationships.

As all these illustrations show, the best popular artworks exhibit a confluence of style and content. There ought to be *fittingness*, as Wolterstorff put it, between the character of an artist's work, its presentation, and its subject matter.[11] In other words, the artist's convictions, perspective, attitudes, and emotions should inform her art in ways that affect style, composition, and approach. "At bottom," C. S. Lewis wrote, "every ideal of style dictates not only how we should say things but what sort of things we may say."[12] The Irish rock band U2, for example, brought a certain slant or attitude to their musical style that made it distinct, while still fitting in with existing contemporary styles. Their music—characteristically raw, highly emotive, and energetic with no frills—to a degree sounds like their life perspective and experience. In other words, there is a "fittingness" between their musical style and lyrical content.

Of course most criticism tends to stress content over form and style. *Los Angeles Times* reviewer Manohla Dargis said that film critics, for example, often "pay very little if any attention to the specifics of the medium, to how a film makes meaning with images—with framing, editing, *mise en scène*, with the way an actor moves his body in front of the camera."[13] Nevertheless, understanding both how a popular artwork communicates and the perspective expressed are central to good criticism because it is through artistic elements that popular artworks transform the external world in ways that engage our reason, memory, emotions, and imagination.

Popular Art in Context

We also benefit from an understanding of popular art *in context*. Popular art is animated in various interactive contexts—social, cultural, religious, aesthetic, industrial, and technological. Taken together this makes for a complex system of production, consumption, and evaluation. A helpful way to understand this is to think of the popular arts as encapsulated in what one scholar called an art world. An *art world* is an institutionalized social network with established conventions, rationales, and philosophical justifications that serve to identify roles for art and standards for production and evaluation.[14] As I noted earlier, the arts in any society have an institutional context. The popular arts we are considering here are products of huge entertainment conglomerates dependent on mass and computer technologies that are consumed in an increasingly global consumer capitalist economy.

And so, along with aesthetic and social dimensions, the popular arts also have economic, political, moral, juridical, and technological dimensions as well. For example, advertising dollars can influence the content of TV programs. A TV sitcom has to adhere to a strict time limit with breaks in the narrative to accommodate commercials; the action is centered in the frame to fit into the space of a television screen. Reaching a potential audience demographic may mean that a director will re-edit her film to attain a certain MPAA rating. Costuming, narrative, editing, and camera angles work together to present women in music videos in ways that will appeal to largely male adolescent record buyers. Because Hollywood films are designed to attract the largest possible audience, the major studios tend to shy away from overt social criticism, creating

The lifelike appearance of Gollum in *The Lord of the Rings* (2001, 2002, 2003) was the result of a creative synthesis of actor performance and computer-generated digital animation.

instead an ideological mix that might appeal to viewers' different positions on issues. The character Forrest Gump, for example, was both a Vietnam war hero and antiwar hero. Finally, technological advances like CGI (computer-generated imagery) made cinematic renderings of fantasy and science fiction stories like *The Lord of the Rings* (2001, 2002, 2003) and *War of the Worlds* (2005) more captivating.

Exploring the Art in Art

Popular artworks call upon us to think about characters, images, and stories in terms of what we believe; it is no surprise that we like to discuss and make judgments about them along those lines. But as Margaret Miles pointed out, "One can choose to accept, reject, or adopt in part a film's proposed values only when the question of how to live is consciously brought to watching and thinking about a film."[15] Viewers can engage an artwork on its own terms while also thinking about it from the vantage of their own perspective.

As we have seen, however, those perspectives vary greatly, as do attitudes about the popular arts and how people of faith should engage them. This can lead to all kinds of misunderstandings, disagreements, and even conflicts. For example, mainline Protestants who look for creative artistic expression and authentic portrayals of the human situation often fault evangelicals for their moralistic criticism and propagandist art. For many evangelicals a focus on artistic expression of the human situation looks like cultural accommodation; they want to see a clear moral or theological message in an artwork.

An exchange in *Commonweal* aptly illustrated such conflicting approaches to film. It is worth quoting at length. A reader (John Hagen) blasted the Catholic journal's film critic, Richard Alleva, for his reviews of Oliver Stone's *Natural Born Killers* and Quentin Tarantino's *Pulp Fiction* (both 1994). Regarding Stone's film, he charged that Alleva "critiques this hateful film exclusively from an aesthetic standpoint: he faults it for a lack of style." Likewise, the review of Tarantino's film was "all about style, without the least tincture of moral critique. And *Pulp Fiction* cries out for moral denunciation, if ever a movie did."[16] Hagen expected more from a Catholic reviewer. "*Commonweal* offers a forceful Christian moral witness on issues of politics, economics, the rights of the disadvantaged, and international justice," he asserted.

> But it treats the arts from an absolutely secular and (generally speaking) completely amoral perspective. *Commonweal's* reviews are erudite, witty, clever, diverting—but for the most part they are sophisticated persiflage

of the sort one finds in magazines like *Harper's* and the *New Yorker*. They treat the arts as a sort of intellectual parlor game, without any social or moral ramifications or points of reference in the gospel.

Alleva responded with a question: "How can you get at the moral sickness or health of a movie without examining its art or lack of art? That would be like a doctor trying to determine a patient's vitality without examining his or her body." In his own defense, he explained the affinity between the moral and aesthetic in film criticism.

> Sooner or later, a movie's or novel's moral delinquency betrays itself through aesthetic delinquency. Plot illogic may signal unconcern with human motive. Mindlessly obscene dialogue betrays indifference to the substance of human speech, a moral as well as an aesthetic failing. Mindless editing choices or camera set-ups may reveal a basic lack of interest in the humanity of the situation posited by the script. Someone (maybe Truffaut?) once said that a well-timed close-up was a moral choice. That's true. Planning the sequence of events in a story can also show moral choice.[17]

Alleva exposed the superficiality of much criticism by showing how isolating specific moments in a movie can lead to a distorted understanding of the film's vision. "*Pulp Fiction* is an adolescent, ultraviolent, foulmouthed romanticization of the gangster milieu. But it is also exhilarating, mind-teasing, breathtakingly well-made—and fundamentally moral," he maintained. Hagen refused "to see this because aesthetic matters like plot development are beneath him. He can see the isolated incidents of immorality that dot the landscape of *Pulp Fiction*, but he can't connect the dots to see the pattern. But without the pattern—no morality!" Alleva concluded, "I will persist in recognizing the morality in art by exploring the art in art."

Critical approaches are attempts to make sense of the popular arts by explaining their nature, how they function, how people should think about them. We evaluate a critical approach on the kinds of questions it asks and answers it provides, how well it helps explain situations, and can predict what will happen. A good critical approach should be useful and provide helpful and reliable insights. Does it open up possibilities for artistic creation and criticism or restrict them? A critical approach can yield better or worse results, sometimes offering imaginative insight, sometimes ridiculously distorting an artwork's meaning. It can and should foster the development of a certain kind of imagination, a way of thinking and acting, not just about the arts but, ideally, in life also.

Summary

- Art should be discussed in terms of its formal aesthetic properties (e.g., plot, character, dialogue, lighting, sound, editing, costuming, narrative structure, and point of view) and how these properties work together to create representations of life, people, and events.
- The nexus of an approach to popular art lies in the *exploration*, *interpretation*, and *presentation* that characterize the aesthetic process.
- A critical approach needs to account for both *how* and *what* a popular artwork communicates, for it is through artistic elements that popular artworks transform the external world in ways that engage our reason, memory, emotions, and imagination.
- Christians should direct their energies to developing a critique of the value and perspective that artists give to the issues of life, the significance and quality of their endeavors, and the way that various popular artworks can be used to deepen our understanding of God's world.
- Popular art is influenced by the interplay of social, cultural, and industrial forces.

Discussion Questions

1. Name and discuss elements that are crucial to a Christian criticism of the popular arts.
2. The author shows that "it is through artistic elements that popular artworks transform the external world in ways that engage our reason, memory, emotions, and imagination." Consider ways that you can become more "media literate."
3. Give a repeat viewing of a favorite film or television episode and pay attention to one artistic aspect (e.g., story, characterization, dialogue, cinematography, lighting, sound, editing, costuming, use of rhetoric, and narrative structure). Or listen to the songs on a CD while paying attention to vocal style, instrumentation, metaphors and symbols, and the relationship between musical style and lyrical content. Does this change your appreciation of the work? If so, in what ways?

PART
THREE

8

Cultural Landscape

Toward a Christian Framework

The popular arts are not ineffectual; they color consciousness and teach us how to act.

> David G. Myers, *The American Paradox:*
> *Spiritual Hunger in an Age of Plenty*

Individuals differ in their capacity to handle challenges to their faith, but each of us in our own way should endeavour to be both distinctive and culturally engaged.

> John Coffey, University College, London

In 1985, I went with some friends to a Bruce Springsteen show during the *Born in the USA* tour. It was one of the most memorable concert experiences I have ever had. There were 65,000 people at Three Rivers Stadium in Pittsburgh yelling "Brrrooooouuuuce." Springsteen and the E Street Band performed for over three hours. "The Boss" was really on that night, and Clarence Clemens was hitting on the sax.

"I generally try to write songs that are about real life, not fantasy," Springsteen said in an interview. He continued,

I try to reflect people's lives back to them in some fashion. And if the show is really good, your life should flash before your eyes in some way. . . . I think on a night when we're really good you can come and hopefully you can see your relationships with your parents, brothers, sisters, your town, your country, your friends, everything—sexual, political, the whole social thing. It should be a combination of a circus, a political thing and a spiritual event.[1]

And that is exactly what happened. The energy of Springsteen's rock music and the folk poetry of his lyrics (in the tradition of Woody Guthrie and Bob Dylan) made for a performance that was fun, captivating, and sparkling with artistic insights.

Springsteen writes and sings about "pure American stuff," as one fan put it.[2] His songs are like brushstrokes that create a portrait of a "runaway American dream." Images of rivers, cars, streets, and highways suggest "people in transition," Springsteen explained. "They've left and they haven't arrived anywhere."[3] Most of Springsteen's songs are about ordinary people trying to keep their hopes and dreams alive in spite of disappointments and frustrations in life. A constant theme is refusing to surrender, never giving up hope, but finding new dreams to replace lost or damaged ones ("You've gotta learn to live with what you can't rise above"). Ultimately, survival is a matter of believing in the human spirit and community.

Writer Andrew Greeley detects a spirituality in Bruce Springsteen's music that he calls "profoundly Catholic."

Springsteen's vision is laced with social critique; in the world of his music, war exists and racial and class tensions are real ("Some folks are born into a good life; other folks get it anyway anyhow"). He sings about loneliness and the need for personal relationships, sensual desire, and the urge to move on and press the horizon ("It's a town full of losers, and I'm pulling out of here to win"). Characters in these songs work and play hard. They can have "a bad desire," suffer loss, and need a respite from life ("This old world is rough; it's just getting rougher"). They can be caught in their own guilt, unsure who to blame when things don't work out, and so desperate that she "cried till she prayed." They are not always in control of their destiny; auto plants, textile mills, and hometowns shut down, throwing people's lives into disarray. Sometimes these folks do the right thing and sometimes they make the wrong choice.

These are experiences colored by ideals, beliefs, and values that most people can relate to in one way or another, and that's what makes these songs popular and significant. "Instead of offering an escape from the mundane by creating a fantasy world of flash and glitz, Bruce glorifies the ordinariness of life," one writer explained.[4] As a fan put it, "It's like he's your best friend, and you could sit down and talk to him and know everything he's talkin' about."[5]

I'm not certain of Springsteen's faith convictions, but his songs reveal a way of seeing that resonates with a Christian vision. "Everybody's got a hungry heart," the whole crowd sings while Springsteen explores the human condition ("You're born into this life paying for the sins of somebody else's past"). Commenting on his *Devils & Dust* recording (2005), Springsteen said, "I like to write about people whose souls are in danger, who are at risk." He added, "In every song on this record, somebody's in some spiritual struggle between the worst of themselves and the best of themselves, and everybody comes out in a slightly different place. That thread runs through the record, and it's what gives the record its grounding in the spirit."[6] Music critic Jon Pareles observed, "Thoughts of redemption, moral choices and invocations of God have been part of Springsteen songs throughout his career, but they have grown stronger and more explicitly Christian on his 21st-century albums."[7]

Andrew Greeley had earlier detected a spirituality in Springsteen's work that he found "profoundly Catholic." He wrote, "Springsteen sings of religious realities—sin, temptation, forgiveness, life, death, hope—in images that come (implicitly perhaps) from his Catholic childhood."[8] Greeley showed how this rock artist grapples with original sin and Paul's lament about having the desire to do what is good but not being able to carry it out (Rom. 7:18). The singer explores guilt, failure, desperation, and disillusionment of freedom, but he does not leave us in despair. His songs are laced with "light and water as symbols of rebirth" that constantly suggest renewal of love and life. Greeley concluded that if "you assume that the church exists to serve people by bringing a message of hope and renewal, of light and water and rebirth, to a world steeped in tragedy and sin, you rejoice that such a troubadour sings stories that maybe even he does not know are Catholic."[9]

Apparently, Springsteen has become more aware of how much his Catholic upbringing has impacted his life vision. "You're indoctrinated," he said of Catholic schooling. "It's a none-too subtle form of brainwashing, and of course, it works very well. I'm not a churchgoer, but I realized as time passed that my music is filled with Catholic imagery. It's not a negative thing. There was a powerful world of potent imagery that became alive and vital and vibrant and was both very frightening and held out the promise of ecstasies and paradise. There was this incredible internal landscape that they created in you."[10]

Along with Greeley, I want to be careful about imposing a Christian tradition on Springsteen. Nevertheless, there is something right about the way he creates popular music. The word *aesthetic* comes from the Greek, meaning "sensitive." Artists make us stop, look, and listen—they make us aware, sensitive. The artworks they produce explore the human condition by offering images and stories that can resonate with our lives by entertaining widespread concerns and interests.

So now I want to suggest that we unfold a biblical vision into a cultural landscape, a map of reality that artists, critics, and patrons alike might use in their engagement with popular art. These fundamental faith beliefs provide a framework for a Christian cultural landscape. They shape the contours of this landscape, the cultural meanings that represent what it is like for people to live in God's good but fallen world. The basic features are:

- God is at work in the world, and an invisible spiritual realm exists.
- Believing people inhabit this landscape, and faith is integral to all of life.
- Human sin is real, and evil exists.
- God offers forgiveness and the possibility of redemption.

This list is obviously not meant to be complete or exhaustive, but illustrative and exploratory—to set up some landmarks and signposts that offer a sense of direction toward developing a faith-informed cultural orientation for thinking about popular artworks.

God Is at Work in the World

Popular artists have found many ways to depict God and the supernatural realm. Amy Grant sings about "angels watching over me," and we've seen all kinds of celestial beings in movies (*It's a Wonderful Life* [1946], *Michael* [1996], *The Preacher's Wife* [1996], *City of Angels* [1998]) and television shows (*Touched by an Angel*). Bette Midler croons, "God is watching us from a distance," and Joan Osborne wonders what if God were "just a slob like one of us." God takes on human form in films like *Oh God!* (1977) and *Dogma* (1999), with George Burns and Alanis Morissette respectively playing the Almighty. In Cecil B. DeMille's biblical epic *The Ten Commandments* (1956), dark clouds form and dive into the Red Sea, holding back the waters while the Israelites cross. "Behold the power of God," Moses tells us. Ghostlike creatures consume the villainous Nazis with fire when they open the Ark of the Covenant in *Raiders of the Lost Ark* (1981). *Constantine* (2005) featured characters who could see spiritual beings working among humans in the earthly realm, and in *The Sixth Sense* (1999) a young boy could "see dead people."

Artists can fashion allegorical worlds that give symbolic existence to the unseen—think of C. S. Lewis's Narnia, Tolkien's Middle-earth, or J. K. Rowling's magical London, home to Harry Potter. Or look at the "world" in *Star Wars*. While most characters have at least heard of the Force, they exhibit a variety of beliefs about it. Obi Wan Kenobi and Yoda serve the good side of the Force, while Darth Vader has turned to the dark side. Han Solo thinks the Force is pure superstition. The audience, however, is convinced that the Force exists in this fictional world because we see evidence of it: the spectral presence of Obi Wan Kenobi, Yoda lifting Luke Skywalker's X-wing spaceship out of the swamp. And so when Luke, at the prompting of Obi Wan's voiceover, turns off his computer and then makes the extraordinary shot that blows up the Death Star, spectators attribute it to the Force being strong in young Skywalker.

By inventing imaginative worlds, artists can affirm that there is more to reality than what we experience with our senses, even though these portrayals may not match our real-life experience. Movies as diverse as *American Beauty* (1999), *Gladiator* (2000), *Places in the Heart* (1984), *Dead Man Walking* (1995), and many others demonstrate that just living in God's world bears witness to the existence of unseen dimensions of the universe that we experience in ordinary life.

Just before the film's opening battle in *Gladiator*, Maximus (Russell Crowe) tells his men: "What we do in life echoes in eternity." Maximus believes he will join his family in an afterlife; that hope motivates his heroics. The audience is persuaded to accept this belief as legitimate by the director's inclusion of repeated shots of a disembodied hand brushing across stalks of wheat. The man (presumably Maximus) walking through a field of grain serves as a metaphor for the hereafter—not a Christian redemption, but a belief in an existence beyond death. Likewise, in *American Beauty* Ricky is convinced there is more to existence than the material world. He tells Jane, "That's the day I realized there was this entire life behind things, and this incredibly benevolent force that wanted me to know there was no reason to be afraid. Ever."

It is not easy to demonstrate the existence of all there is—seen and unseen—in popular artworks, especially those supposed to be based in reality, at least reality as we understand and experience it. The adage, "Coincidence is God's way of remaining anonymous," captures something of the difficulty of identifying a spiritual influence as being God's handiwork. Perhaps that explains why some Christian artists are attracted to fantasy and science fiction genres.

I've only seen the waters parted at Universal Studios Theme Park in Los Angeles, and the Force has never lifted my car out of a snowbank. God and the spiritual realm remain invisible to us. Even so, the Bible does give us a picture of reality that accounts for human experience in God's world as "but a poor reflection as in a mirror" (1 Cor. 13:12). The insights we can take from this verse help shape the contours of our cultural landscape.

We know, for example, that even though God remains invisible, the creation testifies to God's existence, "his eternal power and divine nature" (Rom. 1:20); God's law is written on the human heart (Rom. 2:14–15). In other words, the creation order—everything from the environment to powers, authorities, social relations, and the whole realm of ideas, emotions, and imagination—reveals God's glory as Creator and Lord. Christian artists are called upon to take notice and bring these glories in the world into focus, so that we too see them with eyes of faith, understanding what God's good intentions are for life and recognizing the dreadful ways that sin corrupts and wreaks havoc in the world.

It follows that popular artworks affirming creational principles—love, justice, stewardship, truthfulness, courage, and responsibility to one's neighbor—can attest to the existence of a world created by God. The Academy Award–winning film *As Good as It Gets* (1997) applies the principle of loving your neighbor in a contemporary context. Jack Nicholson plays Melvin Udall, a very successful writer of women's romance novels. Melvin is as crude and crusty as he is obsessive-compulsive. But when his favorite waitress, Carol (Helen Hunt), is unable to work because her son is ill, Melvin sends his own doctor to help and foots the bill. Down the hall from Melvin lives Simon (Greg Kinnear), an acclaimed gay artist who suffers regularly from Melvin's verbal abuse. Simon is badly beaten during a robbery in his apartment. He is financially broken by the medical bills. When Simon's parents offer no help, Melvin provides for his neighbor in distress. These characters are all presented as broken people in need of love and companionship. They carry on in life by sharing their struggles and caring for one another.

Popular art can also affirm that humans share a sense of a loss of innocence, a desire to understand the nature of evil, a yearning for redemption, and the hope of living in a world without pain and anguish. All this testifies to the account of the human condition and circumstances as revealed in the biblical narrative.

We also know that God is not limited by human merit and that our thoughts and ways are not God's thoughts and ways (Isa. 55:8–9). People have only limited control over circumstances and their own destiny. We are unable to see the whole picture and have to act on the information available to us; our understanding of events is largely a matter of perspective. Popular artworks reflecting Christian assumptions will show that actions have consequences, even when entirely unintended, that actions and events can take on a life of their own, and that no one can foretell the consequences.

The film *Magnolia* (1999), for example, traces the lives of eight interconnected characters as they make their way through a single day in the San Fernando Valley. The narrative style itself suggests a different kind of human portrayal, and one that contrasts with the self-reliant humanism that dominates mainstream Hollywood productions (a point we'll take up in the next chapter). The story is advanced not so much as a result of characters' actions; the way that plot threads are interwoven shows that characters are not entirely aware of all that's happening around them or even to them. Each has pursued his or her own dreams and ambitions "as if their best-laid plans were not vulnerable to the chaotic interruptions of the universe," as one film critic observed.[11] A sudden, unexpected, and inexplicable event breaks into the action near the end of the film. Out of nowhere frogs begin to fall from the sky. References to the Book of Exodus sprinkled throughout *Magnolia* mark the shower of frogs as a divine intervention. Whether it is a warning, a punishment, or a sign of redemption, the frog shower is of biblical proportion, showing the existence of a supernatural presence concerned with people's ordinary lives. It reminds us of the Proverb: "Many are the plans in a man's heart, but it is the Lord's purpose that prevails" (Prov. 19:21).

Most films, however, depict a world in which God is absent or nonexistent. For example, there is nothing in the film *Titanic* (1997) to suggest that God is even interested in the fate of those on board the ship. Real-life Titanic survivor Eva Hart said that her mother refused to go to sleep while aboard the ship, "because she had this premonition, solely based on the fact that she said to declare a vessel unsinkable was flying in the face of God."[12] There is hardly a trace of this attitude in the film. The extreme long shots that make the gigantic ship seem infinitely small while cruising alone in the vast darkness of the ocean suggest that if God is watching it is only as a distant observer. Whether uncaring or impotent, God is irrelevant in the world of this film, and our foreknowledge of the impending disaster makes singing hymns about God's protection seem ironic at best and the prayers of those on board futile. As people race to the highest point of the ship to escape the rising water, a passenger reads from the Bible: "Yea, though I walk through the valley of the shadow of death, I will fear no evil." To which Jack sarcastically remarks, "You want to walk a little faster through that valley?" Whatever outward appearances of belief dot the landscape of *Titanic*, they have little bearing on the faith of the main characters, especially when compared to the film's glorification of the human will and spirit.

However, popular artworks need not contain overt references to God or the supernatural to represent a cultural landscape that resonates with Christian beliefs. Actually, explicit suggestions can sometimes be misleading. *The Matrix* (1999), described as a "high-octane blend of comic-book action and lofty metaphysics," is a useful illustration.[13] Despite numerous and sometimes obvious "Christian" allusions, the film can hardly be said to represent a Christian cultural landscape, at least as I am describing it here. There is no evidence that God exists in the fictional world of this film. The basic problem, then, is not alienation from God as a consequence of human sin, but "ignorance and illusion," as Gregory Bassham observed, "an understanding of the human predicament more consistent with Eastern mysticism or Gnosticism than it is with Christianity."[14] The ultimate source of evil in the world of this film is the Matrix itself. Neo's training to defeat the Agents is a quest for self-mastery. As I will show in chapter 9, this journey to self-discovery is typical of Hollywood narratives; it represents a faith in one's self (and not God) as having salvific potential for the individual and community.

It is not easy to understand and portray convincingly the mysterious entanglement of God's will and human scheming. The important issue is this: What does it matter that God might exist in the world of the artwork, or that characters believe God exists? In *Million Dollar Baby* (2004) Frankie Dunn (Clint Eastwood) trains boxers. His own life has been one long bout with God, Frankie believes. Whether or not viewers are sympathetic with this character or agree with his actions, there is no doubt that he makes his decisions knowing he is accountable to God.

There are many different ways that people of faith account for God's presence in the world, and artistic wrestling with these difficulties can make for interesting characters and stories that might offer insight into the ordinary and extraordinary in life.

Frankie Dunn's life is one long bout with God in *Million Dollar Baby* (2005).

Irony and the Unreliable Narrator

This understanding of God's presence in the world points to two avenues for artistic presentations: irony and the unreliable narrator. One way biblical stories show God's handiwork in human affairs is through the use of irony, a narrative device that works to conceal or hide what is actually the case. By highlighting the incongruity between people's expectations and what actually occurs, biblical accounts intimate that, despite careful human planning, it is God's intentions that are realized. There are many accounts in scripture of people acting in ways that are inappropriate to the circumstances or experiencing an outcome that is not at all what they intended or anticipated: "A man's steps are directed by the LORD. How then can anyone understand his own way?" (Prov. 20:24).

One of the most intriguing uses of irony in the Bible is in the Book of Esther, in which God is never mentioned. But God is in the details, working to preserve his people. Esther—a Jewish woman going incognito in the Persian king's harem—wins a beauty contest and becomes queen. Mordecai, scheduled for an early execution at the hands of his enemy Haman, is dressed royally and paraded through the streets instead—according to a suggestion the king solicits from Haman. While begging Esther for his life, Haman accidentally falls on the couch where Esther is reclining just as the king enters the room: "Will he even molest the queen while she is with me in the house?" the king asks. Haman, the king's first minister, ends up hanging on the seventy-five-foot-high gallows he constructed for Mordecai; Esther is given Haman's estate, and the Hebrews are spared.

The story of Joseph (Gen. 37–50) shows that the results of sin are often ironic. In jealousy, Joseph's brothers sell him into slavery, but Joseph's rise to power in Pharaoh's court puts him in a position to save his family—and the starving nation of Israel—years later during a famine.

The unreliable narrator can contribute to an ironic style of storytelling while also demonstrating the perspectival nature of life. Instead of an omniscient narrator who knows everything, telling stories through the eyes of participants can make characters more human and reveal how we have different faith convictions and perceptions of reality. Narrators and characters all have a specific vision of the world and certain perspectives on the matter at hand. Any one of them—or all of them to one degree or another—may be unreliable. We see this in movies like *Citizen Kane* (1941), *Courage under Fire* (1996), and *JFK* (1991). Carrie's (Sarah Jessica Parker) voiceover establishes her point of view in the HBO series *Sex and the City*, as does Cher's (Alicia Silverstone) in *Clueless* (1995), a remake of Jane Austen's *Emma* set in contemporary Los Angeles.

Remember that the popular arts are cultural texts and artistic constructions. Artists interpret reality and invite audiences to share their vision of life—to see and respond to things the way they do—and so popular artworks are designed to elicit emotional responses and deeply felt value judgments. This occurs by guiding a spectator's pattern of responses by depicting ideals, values, and attitudes and suggesting approval and disapproval, directing point of view, creating an allegiance with a particular character, and so forth. Stories present events in ways that invite us to think about why they occur, how they affect characters, or how we might respond.

In the movie *The End of the Affair* (1991) based on Graham Greene's novel, a woman's adulterous lover is thrown down a flight of stairs in a bomb blast during World War II. When she cannot revive him, she kneels beside a bed and prays fervently, pledging to end the illicit affair if God will restore the life of this man she loves. Unaccountably, her lover revives and walks into the bedroom where she is praying. She believes that God has answered her prayer and, keeping her promise, ends the affair.

The story then becomes "an agonizing tug of war between religious faith and carnal love," as one critic put it.[15] Through this experience, the woman rediscovers Roman Catholicism: "I've fallen into belief like I fell in love," she writes in her diary. But her lover is embittered by the breakup, and after discovering the reason for it, he becomes jealous, as though God were a rival lover. His hatred ironically makes God real to him. He cries, "I hate you, God, I hate you as though you existed." The film shows us the same events from the differing perspectives of the characters and leaves us to contemplate love, desire, jealousy, commitment, and the nature of God. Did God answer her prayer and miraculously revive her lover? Or did she panic and overreact, only thinking him dead when he was really just unconscious? How does God hold us to our promises?

The End of the Affair is "an agonizing tug of war between religious faith and carnal love."

Believing People

It comes as no surprise that a Christian landscape would be populated with "believing" people, men and women who are meant to worship and serve God. Faith is a natural dimension of this world, and a faith orientation matters for all of life; understanding the role of faith can give us insight into a character and her choices. It is a matter of giving "characters a sense of something deeper than themselves and their environment, a sense which culminates in the decisive action," filmmaker Paul Schrader explained.[16]

As we have already seen, the fall into sin does not take away our urge to worship God as living sacrifices but misdirects it; in a fallen world, people can serve selfish and idolatrous purposes. There are myriad life situations that call us to act and think deeply in terms of what we believe. How might this play itself out in everyday life and in our cultural landscape?

We know from scripture that people tend to conform to the "pattern of this world" and to the "likeness" of their (often idolatrous) god (Rom. 8:29; 12:2). That people conform to the image of the god they serve shapes their ideals, values, attitudes, and beliefs, and also justifies their actions. Characters can be identified and motivated in various ways by what they believe and how they perceive life. This approach contrasts with a more humanistic one, in which characters are guided by some mystical inner moral compass that lets a man know "what a man's got to do."

In art as in life, a wide range of beliefs exist and faith convictions can be entangled with many different cultural patterns. Characters might be tempted to fashion a god after their own imagination, one who votes like them, shares their opinions, thinks and has ideas like them (cf. Isa. 55:8). Artists might explore the tension of being in the world but not of it by showing the difficulty of living according to established principles in a world that values immediate gratification, for example, or by showing how easy it is to find certainty in the power and status that comes from material wealth. Gordon Gekko (Michael Douglas) in the movie *Wall Street* (1987), for example, gives self-interest and the pursuit of materialism the highest priorities in life and surrounds himself with wealth, fame, and power while living an illusion of invulnerability. Ways of life can lead to peace, justice, and freedom, but also to madness, tragedy, and death.

Like people in real life, characters in songs and stories should be wonderfully complicated and believably flawed. They can be happy and fulfilled but also selfish, angry, bitter, and disappointed, fallible and not free from doubt and uncertainty. While some are content, others have a "hungry heart." Character traits are not always clear and unchanging, for in reality, people's motivations are mixed and not entirely pure (Rom. 7:18–20). Life experiences inform our perspectives, and the interaction of faith and culture can create interesting characterizations.

Is there any doubt that our lives are influenced by social, political, cultural, economic, and even spiritual forces beyond our control? Popular artworks can grapple with the complexities of life that result from economic recessions, factory closings, natural disasters, disease, accidents, and so forth. They can demonstrate how decision making is a mixture of genetics and social upbringing, deeply held ideals, beliefs and assumptions, past experiences, and current circumstances. And it is important to understand that race, class, sex, gender, and other factors also inform our identity and approach to life.

The popular arts can explore these human dynamics that motivate people in complicated and interesting ways, opening windows and exposing even the most private acts, wishes, and thoughts to the light. Fame, envy, greed, talent, sex, and money are powerful forces in life, and issues related to love and hate, sex and power, and success and tragedy have solid dramatic potential for all artists.

The strength of the characterizations in *Schindler's List*, for example, comes from their complex mix of motivations. Oscar Schindler (Liam Neeson) is a Nazi sympathizer who profits from the cheap labor of Jewish prisoners while also saving the lives of several hundred. He is an unlikely savior. During the course of the film his attitudes and desires are altered as he comes to see the humanity of his Jewish workers and their suffering under the shameful cruelty of the Nazis. Amon Goeth (Ralph Fiennes), the concentration camp commander, is also depicted as psychologically complex—torn by ideological convictions, emotional instability, and conflicted affection for his Jewish servant. These kinds of human characterizations intensify the inhumanity of the Holocaust. Only the most calloused spectator could miss the indignity of malnourished Jews trying to look healthy while they are paraded naked in public before German officials. Goeth indifferently shoots Jewish workers for sport from his balcony, demonstrating the blatant disregard for human life that results from a racist worldview.

By exploring the conflicting emotions and actions of these characters, the heights of humanity and the depths of depravity, *Schindler's List* raises important questions about the nature of evil and heroism and the complexity of the human soul.

Fallen World

Film director Martin Scorsese, who has a Catholic background, once said that his films explore "what it is to be a human being—that is, a human being is made up of both good and bad. And in some people, one takes over the other."[17] Indeed, as one writer explained, the "vision of humanity as the flawed pinnacle of creation has driven art, literature, religion, and philosophy for the past three millennia, inspiring, provoking, disturbing, and directing the development of culture."[18]

If popular artists are going to be honest, their work will reveal the complexities of the human heart. Because of the nature of sin, characters can be both confused and confusing. As I have said, people are a complicated mix of social and cultural influences and inherited personality traits. Sometimes their perspectives can turn them into villains. From Shakespeare's *Macbeth* to movies like *The Silence of the Lambs* (1991) and *Basic Instinct* (1992), popular artworks have shown that, however degrading and destructive, evil has a certain appeal and attractiveness to some. Portrayals representing a Christian faith perspective have to be honest about sin but should not glorify it. Popular artworks will have to go into the shadows to bring our fallenness into the light.

Cultural Landscape

Robert Duvall's *The Apostle* (1997) introduces us to a fiery southern Pentecostal preacher whose deep passion—clearly a gift from God—is both a virtue and a vice. Sonny (Duvall) is at once honest and supremely devoted to serving God but also a womanizing, ill-tempered, and violent man. The filmmaker's treatment of Sonny's struggle with "the evil I do not want to do" (Rom. 7:19) captured the imagination of audiences and garnered critical acclaim. Film critic Roger Ebert praised the film for dealing "honestly with a subject both spiritual and complex," and in the process giving us all "a lesson in how movies can escape from convention and penetrate the hearts of rare characters."[19] David Denby considered *The Apostle* "the best movie ever made about a man of God—which is to say, the most honest and morally the most ambiguous."[20]

On the television show *House*, the doctor's brilliant medical diagnoses and respect for human life clash with his alienating and cantankerous behavior. But that's what makes him such an interesting and edgy character. House remains dedicated to his work and patients even while he endures constant pain from a leg injury and struggles with an addiction to prescribed painkillers. Aware of both his talent and brokenness, House chooses a self-imposed loneliness and keeps people at a distance as a way to continue with life even as he continually struggles with needs for love and companionship.

People are sinful by nature and inclined to do evil, regardless of how much money, talent, social status, or education they have. The world portrayed in *Traffic* (2000), a movie about the drug trade and addiction, suggests that people are such an ambivalent mixture of good and evil that it is difficult to see where one begins and the other leaves off. This is also true of the world in the film *Munich* (2005), an espionage thriller about a secret Israeli hit squad that tracks down and assassinates Palestinians responsible for the killing of Israeli athletes at the 1972 Munich Olympics. This plot of vengeance becomes devastatingly personal for the secret assassins involved. "What begins as an act of patriotic fervor ends in a quagmire of moral ambiguity," critic James Berardinelli observed. As they track down and kill their targets, the central character Avner (Eric Bana) "doesn't know what to believe any more, and he has lost the capacity to differentiate right from wrong, necessary from gratuitous."[21] The film's probing of these uncertainties increases as the destructive cycle of violence spirals beyond the assassins' and even the state's control.

An honest artistic representation of God's world in popular art will include images and metaphors of chaos, injustice, pain, suffering, and alienation, for they are all part of living in a fallen world. It should confront the greed and materialism, sexism, racism, and homophobia, hedonism and extreme individualism of our time and address human rights abuses—forced religious conversions, human slavery, torture, rape, murder—that continue in countries around the world.

Christians need not shy away from the reality of evil in favor of sentimentalism, but a difficulty for artists is to treat the ugliness, brutality, vice, and meanness of sinful humanity without falling into the kind of gratuitous and exploitative depictions that characterize many productions. And yet, popular art should not be simpler than the reality it attempts to represent. The critical issues are how the artist depicts sin and the perspective the artist gives to the events.

There are popular artists who revel in sin and exploit it, some who present the world as though it needs no salvation, and others who find salvation in human achievements. These are different ways of approaching life in a fallen world that deserve consideration and critical appraisal. We might ask: If we live in a fallen world, how are artists to make the conflict between good and evil real? What is the artist's attitude toward the characters she has created, their actions, and the issues they deal with? Does the artist approve? Disapprove? Remain ambiguous? How do we know? The way an artist establishes this attitude is not just through things that characters say and do, but also the reaction of other characters, imagery, and so forth.

Christian insights on the nature of good and evil and the workings of the human mind can give a spiritual dimension to popular artworks. Characters can exhibit a variety of attitudes toward life, from bitterness and despair to a posture of gratitude. How do these come about? What forces and events in life shape people's life perspectives? These insights into human nature can impact the story and characterization in ways that affirm Christian beliefs and assumptions.

The Breakfast Club (1985) has become a classic teenpic. In the film, a group of teenagers from different social groups in their high school get to know each other while serving detention on a Saturday morning. The reason Andy (Emilio Estevez), a star wrestler, is doing detention is because he "taped Larry Lester's buns together." Removing the tape was extremely painful. When "they pulled the tape off most of his hair came off and some skin too." Andy admits that he "tortured this poor kid" because he wanted his own father to think he was cool. "Andrew, you've got to be Number One," Andy yells, imitating his father. "I won't tolerate any losers in this family. Win, win, win!"

Afterward, while sitting in the principal's office, all Andy could think about was "Larry having to go home and explain what happened to him and the humiliation he must have felt. . . . How do you apologize for something like that?" he asks. For a moment at least, Andy realizes he is driven by conflicting attitudes and desires, and experiences guilt and shame over his actions.

Forgiveness and Redemption

Recognizing the potential for evil within all humans can lead to a situation of desperation, but as one writer explained, "while it is true that human beings cannot reverse their situation, or in any way create their own redemption, the very helplessness of their position evokes a search for the grace which alone can solve their predicament."[22] The film *Chinatown* (1974), for example, depicts city agencies and social institutions (including the family) as thoroughly corrupted by the greed, lust, and desire for power that resides in the human heart. So great is this corruption that not even the detective-hero can redeem the situation, in part because he too is fallen. The film suggests, however unintentionally, that salvation has to come from outside sinful human beings.

In movies as in life, the power of forgiveness and redemption is both moving and compelling. Many Hollywood films—*Schindler's List*, *The Shawshank Redemption* (1994), *Tender Mercies* (1983), *Dead Man Walking*, and even the controversial *Pulp Fiction* (1994)—show the redemptive power of the human spirit, a spirit that is made in the image of God.

Forgiveness and reconciliation are central themes in *Magnolia*. Earl Partridge (Jason Robards) abandoned his first wife and son as she died of cancer. On his deathbed, the same disease, and now also guilt and remorse, are consuming him. His second wife (Julianne Moore), who made a lifestyle of unfaithfulness, is tortured now by the realization that she loves him. Partridge's abandoned son, T. J. Mackey (Tom Cruise), has grown up to become a misogynist. He markets a Seduce and Destroy program to help men sexually conquer women. A TV whiz kid (Jeremy Blackman) and former one (William H. Macy) seem destined to share the same fate—a betrayal by manipulative parents. The TV game show host (Philip Baker Hall), weakened by bone cancer, reaches out to his drug-addicted daughter, Claudia (Melora Walters). But she wants nothing to do with him because of a childhood of sexual abuse. A divorced, Catholic policeman (John C. Reilly) meets Claudia, is immediately attracted to her, and wants to pursue a relationship.

Redemption does not come easily for these people. They are broken and fallen, struggling with past hurts and regrets, and trying to come to terms with the choices they've made and the pain they've inflicted on others. As one critic observed, "*Magnolia* finally calls attention to the unfathomable mystery of why people love and forgive each other."[23]

Too often, however, redemption is portrayed in humanistic terms as part of human progress. When this happens, there is little need for repentance, as people simply shake free of some limiting past and are renewed by the possibility of new life.

This widely publicized image from the film represents Rose's desire for the freedom Jack has in *Titanic*.

This is a central theme in *Titanic*. In a memorable line from the film, Rose declares that Jack "saved me in every way that a person can be saved." This is a testimony to love's redeeming power, which can overcome even the stern barriers that divide the Titanic along the lines of social classes. Salvation for Rose, however, is really a matter of self-fulfillment. Her desire is for what Jack has—the freedom to pursue the American Dream. In one scene, as they stand on the deck of the ship, Rose says, "Why can't I be like you, Jack? Just head out into the horizon whenever I like it?"

In a much-publicized image from the film, Jack supports Rose with her arms outstretched at the bow rail as though she were flying. It is a symbolic moment of freedom that Rose desperately desires and is later realized as she stands beneath the Statue of Liberty. Now, renaming herself Rose Dawson (Jack's last name), she is a survivor of the Titanic and freed from family and social obligations to pursue her own American Dream. Love conquers all in *Titanic*, including death. Just before she dies Rose dreams of heaven, symbolized by a white light. She and Jack are reunited for eternity on the grand staircase of the Titanic. As one writer observed, "The ship's dome has become the celestial sphere, while the grand staircase to the first-class dining room has become the stairway to paradise. Heaven is the upper deck."[24] Here romantic love substitutes for salvation in Christ and secures one's place in a Titanic heaven where everyone travels first-class.

In a fallen world there is need for a source of redemption that, by necessity, cannot come from within the sinful individual. This does not mean there has to be a Christ figure in every popular artwork, but the Bible is clear that "by grace you have been saved, through faith—and this not from yourselves, it is the gift of God—not by works, so that no one can boast" (Eph. 2:8–9). Redemption comes from experiences that make us aware of our own human brokenness and insufficiency. Paul Schrader once said that movies should contain enough plot so that the audience does not lose interest, but not enough to distract them from the "incremental movement of a soul."[25]

As we see in the Bible, redemption can come in the darkest places and through the most unlikely people: "But where sin increased, grace increased all the more" (Rom. 5:20). Redemption is disruptive, and grace is an intrusion. Redemption breaks the flow and direction of a person's life. It can alter character traits and give people a different outlook. Characters have a change of heart, an altered perspective, as they begin to see themselves, others, and life in a new way that causes them to repent. We know we belong to Christ if we obey his commands (1 John 2:3–6). What does Jesus command? That we love our neighbors as ourselves, hunger and thirst for righteousness, give to Caesar the things that are Caesar's, and to God the things that are God's, love our enemies, make laws that are just, forgive those who sin against us, and do justice, love kindness, and walk humbly with our God. Characters who act in these ways demonstrate ideals, values, and attitudes that are in harmony with a Christian vision.

Happily Ever After

A final factor deserves attention as we seek to bring a deeply Christian perspective to making and partaking of popular art. Does a Christian perspective demand that all endings be happy?

There is much pressure on popular artists (of all stripes—and not just Christians) to create happy endings, however manufactured they might be. Healthy sales and box-office receipts are connected with stories in which people "live happily ever after," as numerous accounts of movies being edited and re-edited based on market research and the response of test audiences attest. The blockbuster hit *Pretty Woman* (1990) was originally a dark story with a grim ending. Producer Laura Ziskin reasoned that if they left the film that way "it probably would be a *really* good movie" but "it wouldn't make the same kind of money."[26]

Commercial success may be an indicator that a popular artwork has connected with an audience by somehow capturing the spirit of the times or by affirming a popular mythology. But commercial success alone should not be used as the mark of good popular art. Christian artists will always have to struggle with pressures between what the audience wants—as indicated by sales and ratings, for example—and creating challenging programming that represents some kind of Christian perspective. (It would be good for Christian patrons to keep that struggle in mind too.)

Let me assure you that I do not mean to imply that artists can never employ happy endings or that audience members should find happy endings repulsive. But all too often, happy endings are contrived and fabricated, if only because they are not sufficiently justified by the course of events in the narrative. When this occurs, we should be critical of these artworks—artistically and in terms of the perspective they represent—for they tend to trivialize human experience instead of enlarging it. The answers they provide have less value because they come too easily.

The happy ending assumes that all things work out for the best for "good" people. They fall in love, marry the right person, and live happily ever after. Wrongdoers are always punished, and justice is secured for the innocent. Scripture does tell us that "in all things God works for the good of those who love him, who have been called according to his purpose" (Rom. 8:28). But in real life, love does not conquer all, and even the best intentions can go awry: "There is a way that seems right to a man, but in the end it leads to death" (Prov. 16:25). And the writer of Hebrews gives us a sober reminder of what happened to some of God's people (Heb. 11:35–39).

There is no doubt that we can derive a sense of satisfaction from happy resolutions, and many things in life do seem to work out just fine. Happy endings do affirm the ultimate triumph of truth and justice and, in that sense, have roots in Christian hope. Christians eagerly await the final and real happy ending, when God "will wipe away every tear from their eyes. There will be no more death or mourning or crying or pain, for the old order of things has passed away" (Rev. 21:4). In the meantime, however, life is filled with loose ends, unanswered questions, unresolved mysteries, and times when the ultimate victory does not seem sure. As the writers of *Art and Soul* point out, "And if life is like this, then our art had better reflect it too. God does not need us as his spin-doctors."[27]

If we believe that salvation is by God's grace, we should expect to find all kinds of failings among us. For example, God describes David as "a man after my own heart; he will do everything I want him to do" (Acts 13:22). After a successful career in the military (launched by his slingshot victory over the giant Goliath), David becomes king. But he is guilty of voyeurism and adultery, and he plots and carries out the murder of Bathsheba's husband. Awareness of his guilt makes him weak as a leader and father. One son shamefully rapes his sister and is killed by his brother. David remains the leader of a nation divided and torn over conflicts, threatened by foreign enemies and disease. As he nears death, looking back over his life, even this man after God's heart seems unsure of his status before the Lord (2 Sam. 23:5).

Rev. Elward Ellis heads an evangelical ministry that calls African-American churches to full involvement in the mission of Christ in the United States and around the world. I heard him speak to over one thousand college students at the Jubilee Conference in Pittsburgh, Pennsylvania. He was talking about how Christians don't have to be perfect before they can serve Christ. "Let me tell you about the virtue in our 'mess,'" he said, referring to the array of problems that trouble our lives. "Everybody in the world got 'mess,' except Christians act as if we ain't got no mess. And that's why half the world can't relate to us," he explained with some sarcasm. "We got ourselves so together we can't talk to them about our struggles. Hello? We can't identify with them," he continued, building to a crucial point. "The funky reality is that you witness best to Jesus Christ when you are witnessing horizontal about your journey with Him, and the ups and the downs, the highs and the lows of the truth of your experience in God. And when you can be as human as you are then folk can relate to you." The college students burst into applause, showing their affirmation of Ellis's assertion.

I sat there wondering why popular art and criticism labeled "Christian" can't also affirm that principle. Many Christians want to at least give the appearance of being holy and righteous and free from at least the serious kinds of sin. They seem to believe that a trouble-free life is somehow a better testimony for God, a better witness to their neighbors. This is a kind of Christianity that "blinds itself to pain and thereby makes a falsehood of its praise," as one writer put it.[28] Minimizing the depth of sin minimizes the height of God's boundless grace.

Try This Perspective On for Size

The popular arts can show us the meaning of things, or their purpose in God's kingdom, by helping us to articulate our experiences or by offering a deeper understanding of our own lives and the lives of others. Popular artworks can explore the heights and depths of human experience, illuminate our mundane lives, and get us to transfer artistic interpretations to the real world. They can help us to enjoy, examine, and make sense of life; good art encourages an audience to engage what is happening in the world.

The best popular artworks communicate not by stating so much as displaying ideals, beliefs, values, attitudes, and assumptions—not by telling so much as showing. Artists and critics wanting to find ways to represent their faith perspective should not adopt an attitude of "This is what we believe and it's true. Take it or leave it." But something more like, "This is what life looks like from our perspective. What do you make of it?" There is empathy in the latter approach, with an artist or interpreter suggesting that the audience try this perspective on for size.

Now that I've outlined some of the contours of a Christian cultural landscape, I want to turn our attention to sorting out some of the dominant features in American popular culture.

Summary

- The contours of a Christian cultural landscape are made up of cultural meanings: ideals, beliefs, values, attitudes, and assumptions that represent what it is like for people to live in God's good but fallen world. The basic features are:
  - God is at work in the world and there exists an invisible spiritual realm.
  - Believing people inhabit this landscape and faith is integral to all of life.
  - Human sin is real and evil exists.
  - God offers forgiveness and the possibility of redemption.
- This understanding of God's presence in the world points to two avenues for artistic presentations: irony and the unreliable narrator.
- Christian popular art will affirm that a wide range of beliefs exists and that faith convictions can be entangled with many different cultural patterns.
- When happy endings are contrived and fabricated, Christians should be critical of them—artistically and in terms of the worldview they represent—for they tend to trivialize human experience instead of enlarging it.
- The best popular artworks communicate not by explicitly stating so much as displaying ideals, beliefs, values, attitudes, and assumptions.

Discussion Questions

1. Discuss ways the Christian cultural landscape mapped out in this chapter can be used to evaluate popular artworks.
2. As Christians, can we take spiritual implications out of "spiritual" depictions—like the Force in *Star Wars*, for example—as being a kind of reference to Christianity? Are we justified in doing so?

3. What makes movies with strong villains, like *The Silence of the Lambs* or *Basic Instinct*, so appealing—even to Christians?
4. The author argues, "An honest artistic representation of God's world in popular art will include images and metaphors of chaos, injustice, pain, suffering, and alienation, for they are all part of living in a fallen world." But many Christians tend to avoid and even criticize such depictions in popular art. If we live in a fallen world, how are we to make the conflict between good and evil real?
5. Why do people—Christians included—want, even demand, happy endings? What should we make of our cultural obsession with living happily ever after?

9

THE AMERICAN MELODRAMATIC WAY

INDIVIDUALISM, RELIGION, AND MATERIALISM

Far more than any other influence, more than school, more even than home—my attitudes, dreams, preconceptions and pre-conditions for life had been irreversibly shaped five and a half thousand miles away in a place called Hollywood.

David Puttnam, Producer of *Chariots of Fire*

American culture, through the movies, television, and the Internet, pervades the world, but with what message? The idea of affluence and self-indulgence as the meaning of life would not seem to be a firm basis for the dissemination of democracy.

Robert N. Bellah, Sociologist

Americans are sentimental, and at least since the nineteenth century, melodrama has been a favored form in art, music, theater, film, and television—from *Dallas* and *Dynasty* to *Desperate Housewives* on TV, from *Gone with the Wind* (1939) and *The Sound of Music* (1965) to *Signs* (2002) and *Cinderella Man* (2005) in movies. To be honest, most of us are suckers for melodrama (even if we're embarrassed by the fact). We root for the underdog and shout approval when the good guy violently destroys the bad guy. When boy meets girl and then loses girl, we find it heartwarming when they get back together to live happily ever after. *Titanic* (1997) might have been pure old-fashioned melodrama, but a *Variety* reviewer rightly projected that the love story, which was "as effective as it is corny," would "definitely help put the picture over with the largest possible public."[1] What is it about these kinds of stories that captures the collective imagination?

This chapter begins our analysis of the key themes that pervade American popular culture. With limited space, I will focus on what scholars call the classical Hollywood film as a case study, an avenue into the popular arts. Mainstream Hollywood films reveal persistent themes that can also be identified in other popular art forms. While certainly not monolithic, Hollywood films represent a general cultural orientation, a system of meanings and values related to the individual hero, religion, gender roles, sex, violence, and materialism. I will take up each of these in this and the next two chapters. The topics in this chapter coalesce around ideals, beliefs, and assumptions associated with self-reliant individualism. Let's begin by looking at the melodramatic world behind mainstream Hollywood productions.

The Melodramatic World

Melodrama is characterized by strong emotionalism and excessive expression. It features extreme situations and actions, Pollyannaish heroes and heroines, and dastardly villains (who always get "foiled again"). The world it portrays is black and white; all issues are plain and simple, based on a moral polarization. The battle between good and evil is depicted in sharp and contrasting terms; evildoers are destroyed, and the virtuous are rewarded. *The Legend of Zorro* (2005) is just one of many melodramas that could be described as "a hiss-the-villain, cheer-the-hero kind of movie."[2]

While making it all too easy, melodrama aligns the audience with the good that always triumphs over evil. And this is a primary reason why melodrama is so popular: it represents the way people want the world to be and, to a certain extent, believe that it is. In their optimism and belief in progress, Americans tend to overlook the persistence of evil in human history; Christians can also be susceptible to thinking the advance of civilization means the erosion of sin. Eighty-three percent of Americans maintain that people are basically good; 77 percent of born-again Christians agree.[3] Moreover, as theologian Carl Henry observed, it is a widespread belief "that the American people are essentially good at heart in a world whose inhabitants are more prone to evil."[4] These pervasive beliefs are evidence of Christian cultural assimilation.

Melodrama is also utopian, in that it puts forward a hopeful vision of a world in which everything is made right—a kind of new heavens and new earth. As a mythic vision, melodrama does not critique culture but only affirms it by representing its inevitable triumph. In that sense, it assures us of the rightness of our cause and offers certainty about our life vision and confidence in the ultimate outcome.

Melodrama may be an optimistic model *for* the world, but it is not a very reliable model *of* the world, at least not from a Christian perspective. In contrast to scripture, the melodramatic vision is based on a faith in the inherent goodness of human nature. Since all people are basically good and have a natural compassion for one another, pursuing self-interest is equivalent to serving the common welfare. As one writer explained, "If each individual, compelled by the circumstances that govern the pursuit of his own interests, acts for the good of all, then each is, for all intents and purposes, virtuous and well-intentioned, and one who strays is not inherently vicious but rather momentarily wayward, and his innate goodness will inevitably re-assert itself."[5] This vision provides an optimistic view of progress and social change based on a belief in human perfectibility. It also makes it seem that social problems are the fault of individuals, and not the result of life circumstances or a corrupt society; personal, not institutional, reform is all that is needed for progress to a better world.

In the melodramatic world, virtue is defined in domestic terms—marital fidelity, parental love, dutiful children—in a way that tends to make domestic life sacred and the public realm secular. The world of politics, work, and business is a kind of warfare in which success determines fairness and virtue. "Evil" is depicted as anything diverging from this notion of virtue. Villains neglect their duties, defile a woman's chastity, corrupt the innocent, threaten or abuse women or children.

We can see how these ideas can be turned into a formula that shapes a narrative in warrior epics like *Gladiator* and the Mel Gibson vehicle *The Patriot* (both 2000), which was described as "*Braveheart* to the tune of 'Yankee Doodle.'"[6] In these films, a reluctant hero is drawn into battle only when the villain threatens or harms his family. Political issues serve merely as a backdrop to the personal conflict. In contrast, *Snow Falling on Cedars* (1999), a story about interracial love and murder set in the aftermath of Pearl Harbor, maintains a deep personal drama, effectively integrating psychic, social, and historical forces, while also showing their interplay and effect on personal perceptions and decision making.

It is easy to see why a melodramatic representation of the world might be appealing to many people, including churchgoers. "In melodrama, self-empowerment against strong odds seems easily available through simple faith," scholars noted.[7] The emphasis is on the "good" individual whose heart is in the right place, and that is all that is needed for right living and a healthy society, not just laws and social policies, for example.

How does the melodramatic world compare with a Christian vision? First, carving the world up into black and white, good and evil, is a very simplistic view of life and the human condition that gives us stock characters, straightforward situations, and clean resolutions. Instead of the moral ambiguity and complex characterization we encounter in scripture, melodramatic characters are either completely good or completely corrupt. A character with mixed motivations engaged in complicated relational and ethical situations is more consistent with real life—affirming a biblical view—than black-and-white caricatures. This sentimental view also oversimplifies sin and locates redemption in individuals who need only "some magical outside assistance," as one writer put it.[8] The tendency to restrict virtue to the domestic realm limits the idea of Christian calling to personal, family, and church life.

Second, the assertion of a harmony of interests as a social basis cannot overcome the reality of human conflict in the affairs of life that result from sin. Woven into this view is a belief that humanity has to find its way back to some point of origin when human nature was pure and innocent—a humanistic ideal that Christians believe can only be achieved at Christ's return. The classic melodramatic pattern begins with a normal or ideal situation (domestic bliss or harmonious community) that is threatened by an external evil and ends with the defeat of the villain, restoration of the moral order, and salvation of the virtuous characters. Virtue always triumphs over evil.

Finally, melodrama gives an exaggerated place to emotion, especially fear and sympathy, making human feelings—and not scriptural principles, for example—universal and the ultimate judge of any situation. Sentimentality manipulates your emotions by telling you how you should feel; our feelings are kindled, but there is nothing of depth or importance for us to consider. We are invited to give the work emotional meaning, but there is little to imagine and even less to really think about besides how it makes us feel. "Sentimentality is destructive because it is unreal," one writer warned. "It severs emotions from their holistic context. And the more it is indulged, the more it has the power to exploit and twist genuine feeling."[9]

By draping a (dubiously) Christian perspective over the sentimental world of American melodrama, Christians can accept uncritically the ideals, beliefs, and values of the American mainstream culture. That so many Christians are such strong advocates of sentimentalism perhaps suggests a greater degree of cultural assimilation than we would care to admit.

The Classical Hollywood Film

Despite the shortcomings of melodrama, many Christians, as we have seen, are attracted to it. They are not alone. Melodrama in fact marks the structure and tone of the classical Hollywood film. Mainstream Hollywood films largely draw on the conventions of melodrama, stylistically embodying an optimism about human progress and perfectibility. Let's consider it in some depth.

The classical Hollywood film is driven by a cause-and-effect narrative centered on the actions of the main characters. Narrative causality refers to the way that one event causes another to happen in a story, each scene flowing into the next; very little happens without reason. This is not surprising when you realize that Americans tend to think that most events have some "knowable, physical cause." The inexplicable may be vaguely attributed to "God's will," but as one writer observed, "most Americans have difficulty even comprehending the notion, so prevalent in many other parts of the world, that 'fate' determines what happens in people's lives."[10]

When a Hollywood film begins, we are magically dropped in the middle of a story that is already in progress and receive a set of initial impressions about character traits and motivations that will hardly (if at all) change throughout the film. The characters' actions move the story along, while also revealing clearly defined traits, motivations, and goals. Hollywood heroes are idealized and identified with certain traits, the most important being self-reliance and goal achievement. Action and problems introduced in the beginning are fully resolved by the end—the detective solves the crime, the cowboy hero saves the community—allowing the viewer to leave the theater satisfied that all is right in the world again.

For example, when we first meet Indiana Jones (Harrison Ford) in *Raiders of the Lost Ark* (1981), we know from the opening action sequence that he is resourceful, confident, and determined, with a comic side and personal integrity. As one writer observed, Jones is a "larger than life character who does everything for the right reasons and somehow manages to survive every incredible situation he encounters."[11] These traits remain throughout his globe-trotting quest to find the Ark of the Covenant before the Nazis do and to stop Hitler's ambition for world domination. One event causes the next. U.S. intelligence agents assign Jones to retrieve the Ark. Jones travels to Nepal to get a hieroglyphic medallion that can direct him

Indiana Jones represents the American rugged individualist in his globe-trotting quest to find the lost Ark.

to the Ark. There in the Himalayas he finds his ex-flame Marion Ravenwood (Karen Allen), who owns the medallion. Nazi agents demand that Marion give them the medallion and threaten her with a red-hot poker. Indie comes to the rescue. He and Marion fly to Egypt, the last known resting place of the Ark. After a hair-raising chase through the streets of Cairo, Marion is kidnapped by the Nazis and held hostage in the desert. In pursuit of the Ark (and Marion now), Jones uses the medallion to locate an excavated tomb, finds the Ark, loses the Ark, gets the Ark again only to lose it again, and so on, with one event bringing about the next until the enemy is destroyed and Jones returns the Ark to the United States for safekeeping in an enormous government warehouse.

Let's turn our attention now to some of the key features of the cultural landscape of the classical Hollywood film.

The Wizard of Oz Syndrome

Hollywood films represent a world in which humans are at the center. I call it the Wizard of Oz Syndrome. Although they don't know it,

Dorothy and her friends have *within themselves* everything they need to secure their fate; their journey on the Yellow Brick Road brings them to that realization. Ultimately, they have no real need of the Wizard, a God figure whose pyrotechnical visage is unmasked, revealing only a bumbling old man.

Religion scholar Christian Scharen treated this myth as a kind of theology—"religion as something we humans do." He described it as a "highly optimistic accounting of human potential" and "an overly positive evaluation of human moral capacity, in that we are able to capture God's favor by our actions." Ultimately, such a view leaves us "with a God who can be manipulated by a human project of self-mastery." In a similar vein, commenting on American religions, political science professor Alan Wolfe said, "Rather than being about a god who commands you, it's about finding a religion that empowers you."[12]

Instead of portraying the frailty of human experience and the need for a source of redemption outside of ourselves, the classical Hollywood mythology invests humans with everything they need to secure their own destiny and salvation. It is a faith in the power and capacity of an individual to pull himself or herself up by the bootstraps, so to speak. We can see this in screenwriter Susannah Grant's description of the appeal of Erin Brockovich: "She's a normal but very decent person at her core. She doesn't do anything that any one of us couldn't do if we decided to do the right thing. And what's exciting about that for people is that it's not alienating. It gives you a sense of limitless possibility and your own power by virtue (of) watching hers."[13]

Writer, director, and star Zach Braff even described the screenplay of *Garden State* (2004) as "a Wizard of Oz journey through suburbia."[14] Main protagonist Andrew's journey culminates in him finding the strength within himself to put aside his mind-numbing medication and confront the world as it is. Of course Andrew's girlfriend Sam (Natalie Portman) serves as a guide on his path to self-realization, but the choice Andrew makes is ultimately his own.

This journey to self-realization is the backbone of many Hollywood stories. Characters often achieve heroic status by "making something of themselves." Heroism is a matter of self-fulfillment. The key to success is believing in yourself. American heroes are rugged individuals who live by a code of self-reliance. That they transcend their humble beginnings by working hard and exercising some exceptional gift in order to accomplish great things affirms the belief in America as the land of opportunity.

Co-producer Douglas Wick said that what he found fascinating about *Gladiator* (2000) was "the idea of taking a hero and then pulling away his social context, so all that's left is his inner life, and then finding out what he's made of, what resources he then has."[15] That Wick could be talking about any number of films, like *Cast Away* (2000), *Erin Brockovich* (2000), *The Patriot*, or *Master and Commander* (2003), shows the dominance of this theme in Hollywood productions and its popular appeal with audiences.

Some movies try to temper this underlying belief in basic human goodness. Films like *Kinsey*, *The Aviator* (both 2004), and *Catch Me If You Can* (2002) show a key event in the childhood of the main character: Alfred Kinsey's overbearing religious father, Howard Hughes's mother bathing him and instructing him to spell QUARANTINE, the family trauma of adolescent Frank Abagnale. Like the search for the meaning of "rosebud" in *Citizen Kane*, the suggestion is that these characters have each been corrupted by an early event. From my perspective at least, this is a feeble attempt to give a character more depth and complexity and also explain how basically good people are so terribly flawed.

Despite the popularity of the Hollywood style, life is not linear. We wander, stall, fall backwards, do things over, move ahead, circle around, start over, learn and relearn. And whatever hope we have in the human potential for goodness has to be tempered by our capability for evil and destruction. A *Books & Culture* review of the biopic *Ray* (2005) was a good illustration of what I am getting at here. It is worth quoting at length.

> Surely the life of Ray Charles is parabolic of the proclivity of Americans to believe that, if we only pull ourselves up by our bootstraps, we can triumph over any obstacle. We have a deeper faith in ourselves and our ability to solve problems than perhaps any people ever known, and it has never been stronger than it is today. As Christians we can applaud the "works" side of this success story; effort is required of us if we expect to accomplish anything in life. And to this extent we can confidently use *Ray* as a guide for facing adversity. But the philosophy of the film is basically humanistic, encouraged by each mini-drama in the life of Ray Charles, where he is never shown praying, and where even the Christianity of his wife is most evident in a conversation just after she has slept with him as a girl. This is a cancerous view of life, strong and destructive in our country today, and working actively against the gospel that declares us all incapable of solving our problems apart from the grace of God.[16]

In contrast to the Hollywood paradigm, scripture emphasizes the sovereignty of God, the human sinfulness and inadequacy that demands dependence on God's grace alone, and the necessity of centering all of life on the goal of glorifying God. The history of redemption recorded in scripture contains a mixed bag of saints and sinners. The cast of characters in Hebrews 11, for example, exhibited a variety of gifts, but they were all weak, flawed, and sinful; some had serious character faults, others displayed a distinct lack of talent and ability. They were, in other words, ordinary people—unable to save themselves and desperately in need of redemption.

Though sinful, these men and women are commended for their faithful living. The heroic status of this "cloud of witnesses" (Heb. 12:1) is credited to the power of God; they accomplished whatever they did because of God's grace and handiwork and certainly could not boast of their own works. For these reasons, "God is not ashamed to be called their God" (Heb. 11:16), and scripture presents them as models for people of faith who desire to serve God and love their neighbor as themselves.

Becoming God-Like Figures

One writer described "the magical world of movies" as a place "where ordinary men can become god-like figures who can control their own fates through their individual efforts and still have some real effect at making the world a better place in which to live."[17] Consistent with the melodramatic vision, Hollywood films present personalized and dramatized stories in which individual desires, ambitions, and goals rule. A central tension in this world is between the ideal of a pure individual with self-determining powers and communal needs and institutional limitations.

In short, Hollywood films deal with social issues by reducing them to personal matters. Social, political, and economic problems are presented as personal and individual—a sign of *individual* weakness and not a flaw of the social or political system—and therefore to be resolved at the personal level. For example, America's reluctance to become entangled in World War II is personalized in Rick's (Humphrey Bogart) struggle over Ilsa (Ingrid Bergman) in the timeless *Casablanca* (1942). Rick's love for Ilsa shakes him out of his isolationism and motivates him to help her and Victor Lazlo (Paul Henreid) escape the Germans. By oversimplifying complex issues, filmmakers can offer superficial resolutions—the gunfight, love conquering all—based on a widely accepted cultural belief in the inherent goodness of the individual, who is presented as a redeemer or Christ figure. This myth of individualism is so powerful in American culture that audiences find it plausible that an idealistic small-town Boy Rangers troop leader could single-handedly (well, with the help of an assistant/love interest) expose and defeat the corrupt political machinations of long-term, experienced senators in Frank Capra's classic *Mr. Smith Goes to Washington* (1939). Variations on *Mr. Smith Goes to Washington* are a mainstay of the American cinema: *Clear and Present Danger* (1994), *The Pelican Brief*

(1993), *The Firm* (1993), *Mission Impossible* (1996), and many other movies that feature heroic individuals who weed out the corruption in American institutions, whether government, the judicial and legal systems, or intelligence organizations. (One of the only exceptions is the lone district attorney who is unsuccessful in revealing the truth in *JFK* [1991].)

The happy ending when love conquers all accomplishes the same in romantic comedies, suggesting that we can find in personal relationships the peace and harmony that escape us in the conflicts and contradictions of the social world. In *You've Got Mail* (1998) the ruthless competition between companies in the corporate world is ameliorated easily enough by love and romance. Joe Fox (Tom Hanks) and Kathleen (Meg Ryan) transcend their "business" differences and find "personal" happiness and satisfaction in love and life. Even though he intentionally—and without caring—put her family-owned bookstore out of business! But the Shop Around the Corner bookstore is not just a business for Kathleen—it is her mother's legacy, and she feels deeply responsible for it. Leaving the store for the last time, she discloses her feelings in a voiceover: "I'm heartbroken. I feel as if a part of me has died, and my mother has died all over again. And no one can ever make it right." No one except Joe Fox, of course. In accord with the conventions of the romantic comedy, the same mega-bookstore owner who ruins Kathleen's life also restores it—love is a wonderful thing. Other than to simply accept it as an economic reality, the film never deals with large corporations destroying small businesses, even though this is a major theme in the film.

Resolving tensions and contradictions between the individual and the community is a perennial theme in American culture and fertile ground for artistic exploration. Some of the best drama on *ER*, for example, results from characters having to make medical, ethical, and social decisions based on personal morals and standards that might conflict with institutional policies and practices or the dictates of law.

But the cultural landscape of the Hollywood film clearly exaggerates individualism, favoring individual over corporate or institutional solutions to problems and conflicts. The emphasis on the individual corresponds to a lack of trust in institutions and also downplays the role of external forces in shaping human beings and impacting the course of events and even history.

Boyz N the Hood is a good illustration of how the choices people make occur "within the interaction of social, psychic, political, and economic forces of everyday experience." This film about coming of age in South Central Los Angeles "shows how communities affect their own lives, and how their lives are shaped by personal and impersonal

Boyz N the Hood shows how both personal and impersonal forces shape people's lives.

forces," one writer explained. Filmmaker John Singleton understood that "character is not only structured by the choices we make, but by the range of choices we have to choose from—choices for which individuals alone are not responsible."[18] This kind of portrayal of life and society can get people to think about faith not just for personal life and relationships but also for creating just social arrangements and institutions that serve the well-being of our neighbors. The authors of *Divided by Faith*, for example, showed how the cultural assumptions of individualism have impeded white evangelical efforts to combat racism; their individualistic perspective curtails their ability to understand the nature of the problems, and they miss "the racialized patterns that transcend and encompass individuals, and are therefore often institutional and systemic."[19] And so Christians of whatever persuasion could benefit from artistic representations that challenge them to think seriously about faith and cultural orientation both for personal and public life.

Radical Individualism

The focus on the individual can make storytelling more dramatic, especially in a culture that prizes individualism; it can also distort the reality it depicts. Focusing on an individual often downplays, if not denies, the part of collective action in our social environment and as an agent of change in history. *Amistad* (1997) and *Mississippi Burning* (1988), two historically based movies, were both criticized for giving too much of the credit for the abolitionist and civil rights movements respectively to individual heroes rather than the groups of people who made up the movements. By extolling the individual over community and institutional life, the struggle and sacrifice of many ordinary people can be lost in the stories of popular culture.

There are both positive and negative aspects of individualism. We all need a measure of freedom, independence, and self-governance. Individualism can be a positive force in that it fosters creativity and initiative; the defense of personal liberty ensures respect for equal rights for all people. But when focus on the self is taken to an extreme it can be a negative force, what research psychologist David Myers called "radical individualism." Radical individualism finds expression in popular sentiments like "Do your own thing," "If it feels good, do it," and "To love others, first love yourself."[20] In his appraisal of nineteenth-century American culture, the Frenchman Alexis de Tocqueville observed that Americans "form the habit of thinking of themselves in isolation and imagine that their whole destiny is in their hands." In exaggeration such attitudes can lead a person "to think of all things in terms of himself and to prefer himself to all."[21]

Today's radical individualism, Myers explained, draws on these kinds of egotistic attitudes; self-interest and self-indulgence outweighs social responsibility and moral obligation. But living for yourself is a diminished life, and God does not call us to be self-reliant individualists, isolated or alone, but to be members of a community. Scripture presents us as individuals gifted by God in order to contribute to the "common good" (1 Cor. 12:7), and it directs us to seek the kingdom of God and his righteousness above all else (Matt. 6:33–34). We are to live in relationship to others, accountable to God and responsible to one another (Phil. 2:3–4). Popular artworks extolling these values resonate with a Christian cultural landscape and can help us all to see more clearly as individuals, groups, and communities trying to find our way in contemporary society.

Outside Magical Assistance

In a hilarious episode of *The Simpsons*, Homer decides he is not going to church anymore. God comes down from heaven to have a conversation with him. Homer explains to God: "I'm not a bad guy. I work hard and I love my kids. So why should I spend half my Sunday hearing about how I'm going to hell?" "Hmm, you've got a point there," God replies. "You know, sometimes even I'd rather be watching football. Does St. Louis still have a team?" Homer reminds God, "They moved to Phoenix." Later Homer concludes, "So I figure I should try to live right and worship you in my own way." And God concurs.

This episode captured the attitudes (and Sunday practices, perhaps) of many Americans. According to surveys, most Americans see religion as something individual, primarily a private matter having to do with family and local congregation. But "living right" and worshiping God "in my own way" gives priority to American values associated with individualism and not to the authority of scripture or a church tradition. Humans can serve God as they please; the individual is his or her own final authority for right living and appropriate worship.

These attitudes can affect the way people understand God and the Christian message. According to a survey by the Barna Research Group, 89 percent of adults agreed, "there is a god who watches over you and answers your prayers." But as I showed earlier, the typical American

In a conversation with God (who has five fingers) Homer articulates American values and attitudes about religion.

thinks of God in generic terms. While a majority (68 percent), for example, believed the Christian faith had "all the answers to leading a successful life," 58 percent also thought that no single religion had "all the answers to life's questions and challenges." These attitudes led pollster George Barna to conclude that because "people turn to religion to provide them with insights and abilities to meet tangible goals, faith is used by many people as a means to a worldly, rather than eternal, end."[22] Religious convictions take a back seat to the myths and values of American individualism: self-interest and materialism.

The same Barna study also showed that 80 percent of Americans incorrectly believed that the Bible says that "God helps those who help themselves," a maxim attributed to Benjamin Franklin.[23] Not only are these words not found in the Bible, but the idea itself is inconsistent with scripture: "For it is by grace you have been saved, through faith—and this not from yourselves, it is the gift of God—not by works, so that no one can boast" (Eph. 2:8–9). And yet, 84 percent of evangelicals, 83 percent of Catholics, and 87 percent of mainline Protestants all agreed to some extent that "God helps those who help themselves" is true.[24] "The American penchant for self-reliance, achievement, and autonomy has invaded the realm of the afterlife," Barna observed. "People are more likely to count on their own abilities and character as a means to pleasing God or otherwise earning eternal peace than they are to accept a gift—even a spiritual gift—as taught by the Christian Church regarding the sacrificial death and subsequent atonement through Jesus Christ."[25]

In contrast to scripture, the belief that "God helps those who help themselves" implies that we are capable of securing our own salvation with a little help from God. The assumption is that God is not the source of redemption, but "some magical outside assistance," an aid for self-reliant individuals on their journey to personal salvation.

The movie *The Legend of Bagger Vance* (2000) is a vivid illustration. The main character, Rannulph Junuh (Matt Damon), has everything going for him. He's an exceptionally talented golfer, wealthy, and engaged to be married to a beautiful woman. But Junuh's life takes an unexpected turn when he goes off to fight in World War I; the horror and brutality of war devastates him. Unable to return to a hero's welcome, Junuh disappears, giving up everything—including golf and his fiancée.

Seemingly from out of nowhere, Bagger Vance (Will Smith) enters Junuh's life. Bagger's mission, as Junuh's caddie, is to help him "find his swing again." The game of golf becomes a metaphor for life. Director Robert Redford said, "It's a classic hero's journey, and Bagger Vance is a very heroic character, a spiritual character. He takes Junuh from the dark to the light. It's not about being black; it's about a journey of the soul. Junuh falls into darkness, and finds the light with a spiritual guide."[26] Near the end of the film, Junuh gets his life back together again, and as they approach the 18th green of the big golf tournament, Bagger Vance is going to leave. Junuh says to his angelic caddie, "I need you." And Bagger replies, "No. No you don't. Not anymore." Junuh just needed a little "magical outside assistance" on that fairway of life—another Yellow Brick Road to self-realization.

Bruce Almighty (2003) employs the same narrative strategy, but gives a somewhat different slant. The screenwriters blend a Christian theme with this story convention, leaving the film open to multiple interpretations. God (Morgan Freeman) tells Bruce (Jim Carrey) that the human problem is that they "keep looking up." He says, "People want me to do everything for them. What they don't realize is they have the power." Despite Bruce's plea for him to stay, God leaves telling Bruce he can handle things on his own now (a departing line close to that of Bagger Vance). But then it is only when Bruce surrenders to God's will that he finally finds real love and satisfaction in life. Director Tom Shadyac explained that the emphasis on *"keep* looking up means that we depend on God to do everything for us."[27] The director's intent was to motivate people to right action.

Movies like *It's a Wonderful Life* (1946), *The Preacher's Wife* (1996), *Michael* (1996), *The Family Man* (2000), *What Women Want* (2000), *Groundhog Day* (1993), and *City of Angels* (1998) also include characters that benefit from some magical outside assistance. A synthesis of American individualism and Christianity, this outlook diminishes the totalizing effect of sin while increasing the responsibility of the individual. It can also downplay, if not perhaps even eliminate to one degree or another, the need for Christ as Savior and Lord.

American sentimentality is often fused with Christian values. We can see evidence of this in *Forrest Gump* (1994), a movie applauded by many as a shining example of family (and so "Christian") values. Actor Tom Hanks, who played the slow-talking Forrest Gump, found this most ironic. He said, "A mother sleeps with the principal to get her son into school, and Forrest has a kid out of wedlock—now that's family values!"[28]

Gump is a simpleton "who can only operate at the speed of his own common sense," as Hanks puts it.[29] He does not depend on his intellect or even a moral system as a guide through life, but relies instead on an inherent goodness and an intuitive sense of right and wrong. "Forrest Gump has no opinion about anything," director Robert Zemeckis said.[30] And by avoiding making any moral decisions, Gump ends up both a Vietnam war hero and antiwar hero (and played to both conservative and liberal audiences).

The floating feather in *Forrest Gump* symbolizes the main character's life, blown by the winds of fate and destiny. Gump doesn't make life decisions so much as he just always seems to be in the right place at the right time, and God is there to provide some magical assistance to those who help themselves, whether the good-hearted Forrest or the angry and cynical Lieutenant Dan (Gary Sinise). The two dangerously spend the night in their boat at sea during a terrible storm, with Lieutenant Dan angrily arguing with God. They return to shore the next morning to find that all the other boats that were docked had been destroyed, leaving Forrest and Dan to monopolize the shrimp business. (Apparently, God had it in for the other shrimp boaters.)

In one sense, *Forrest Gump* is about combating loneliness. But the movie is grounded in traditional American mythology: in the land of opportunity anyone who works hard and obeys the social rules will be "healthy, wealthy, and wise." As one critic noted, *"Forrest Gump* celebrates innocence and slow-wittedness—not just as a handicap to be surmounted, but the key to worldly success."[31] Christians can enjoy this "life-affirming story," but we should also understand that it promotes the proverbs of Benjamin Franklin in *Poor Richard's Almanac* far more than the teachings of Jesus in Matthew, Mark, Luke, and John.

For the Love of Money

The attitudes, desires, and values of materialism are a powerful force in North American life. Over 40 percent of Americans attend church weekly, but 70 percent visit a mall.[32] And reality TV shows draw high ratings by offering contestants a shortcut to the American Dream: become rich overnight, find the love of your life, run a corporation, land a recording contract, and so forth.

A primary value in the consumer culture is immediate gratification; a basic belief is that acquiring things will make you a better person. It is as if the possession of material things will bring you love, happiness, satisfaction, and meaningful relationships *now*. The Barenaked Ladies satirize these attitudes in "Shopping": "Everything will always be alright / When we go shopping."

An underlying assumption in mainstream Hollywood films is that the goal in life is to become rich. This is so obvious, perhaps, that it is hardly worth stating. Nevertheless, a prosperous lifestyle is a central feature in the American popular arts. *The O.C.*, a television show popular among high school and college students, is set in an affluent community in Orange County, California. *"The OC* looks like

The world of *The O. C.* is characterized by a luxurious consumer lifestyle.

some landlocked Midwesterner's dream vision of Southern California," one reviewer noted. "Everybody's wealthy, driving SUVs, riding horses or going surfing."[33] The show focuses on Ryan Atwood, a high school kid from the other side of the tracks, who is taken in by the well-to-do Cohen family. In this upscale environment Ryan is able to shake free from his limiting past while enjoying the benefits of a world composed of stunningly beautiful young women, nightly parties, and a luxurious consumer lifestyle. A critic dubbed *The O.C.* "a dreamland untethered to reality" that presented the ultimate vision of consumer society.[34]

In a consumer society, acquiring wealth is the measure of accomplishment, not only a way to demonstrate social status but also an outward indication of an internal goodness. Wealth is even associated with spiritual well-being, a sign of God's blessing, and an affirmation that God does help those who help themselves. This can appear as a clear theme, as in *Forrest Gump*, where the side-effect of following the Golden Rule is to become "a gazillionaire." More often, however, affluence is an assumption in the story, as in movies like *Pretty Woman* (1990) ("No matter what they say, it's all about money") or *Jerry Maguire* (1996) ("Show me the money"), in which living happily ever after includes a high level of material success. And so even if a character desires love, truth, or freedom, the pursuit of these values usually occurs in tandem with expectations of wealth and satisfaction. The American myth *is* a rags-to-riches story after all.

"Living in a material world," as Madonna's song puts it, affects personal and communal identity. We don't just buy and sell goods; we pur-

In *Pretty Woman* (1990), the camera objectifies and sexualizes Vivian during the "shopping spree" montage sequence by focusing attention on her body parts.

chase dreams, experiences, and pleasures. In this sense, consumerism is a kind of salvation; purchasing a product is advertised as the solution to every problem. Material things are often invested with supernatural powers—a consumer purchase can transform an individual. And so it only takes one afternoon of conspicuous consumption (during which time she spends "obscene amounts" of Edward's money in a shopping spree) to transform Vivian from a hooker into a woman of privilege, in *Pretty Woman* (1990). We watch the transformation take place while Vivian goes in and out of a dressing room trying on clothing in an expensive boutique on Rodeo Drive. The Roy Orbison theme song plays on the soundtrack in a montage sequence that encourages a voyeuristic kind of looking. Modeling, as Vivian is in this scene, invites being looked at. The camera also objectifies and sexualizes her by featuring shots that focus our attention on her body parts: a bare back and breasts as a satin camisole slides down covering them, a long leg as she pulls up a sheer stocking. Sexual allure and beauty are Vivian's "assets" and means to realizing her "fairy tale," that is, getting her Prince Charming.

There are films like *Fight Club* (1999) that criticize the consumer society by suggesting that it emasculates men, robbing their lives of meaning and making them just another buttoned-down cog in the machine. Likewise, materialism is at the root of the disintegration of Lester and Carolyn's marriage in *American Beauty* (1999). When Lester tries to put a spark back into their romance, Carolyn interrupts his advance, concerned that Lester might spill beer on their expensive couch. Lester tells her, "This isn't life. It's just stuff. And it's become more important to you than living. Well, honey, that's just nuts." "The Burnhams' problem is that nearly all of their thinking and thirsting derive from contemporary media-driven American notions of success and contentment," film scholar Roy Anker explained. "Unbeknownst to them, they are thorough-going materialists philosophically, and devout consumers ethically, meaning that they expect to find contentment by acquiring all the rudiments of conventional American beauty."[35]

In the final sequence of *The Aviator* (2004), as Howard Hughes (Leonardo DiCaprio) loses control of himself, he repeats, "The way of the future, the way of the future, the way of the future." A voiceover reminds us that Hughes achieved his childhood dream to "fly the fastest planes ever built, make the biggest movies ever, and be the richest man in the world." But none of this prevents him from sliding into madness. As one critic observed, Scorsese "may as well have ended his film with a black tableau in white print: 'And what shall it profit a man, if he gain the whole world, and lose his own soul?' (Matt. 16:26)." He pointed out that this film "comes across as a severe critique of American celebrity worship, sexual obsession, and rampant materialism."[36]

And rock group U2 blasted in song "the decadence and danger of a consumer culture where buying and seeking pleasure are elevated to the level of life or death," Scharen pointed out. "The song 'Last Night on Earth' tells the story of a woman lost in the fast life, burning the candle at both ends, and embracing its inevitable self-destruction."[37]

> I went looking for spirit, but found alcohol / I went looking for soul, and I bought some style / I wanted to meet God, but you sold me religion.

Here is a song that depicts a woman disillusioned by the self-destructive pursuits of pleasure and purchasing power and the vacuity of style over substance.

Above a certain level of comfort material things cannot meet our emotional and social needs. And scripture is clear that we should not let materialism substitute for trust in God: "You cannot serve both God and Money" (Matt. 6:24). People who try to serve two masters, for example, experience tensions and contradictions and find themselves facing tough decisions. In his letter to Timothy, the Apostle Paul showed how a faith orientation shapes attitudes and behavior related to the pursuit of wealth and the possession of material things. Those who put their trust in these are on a path of destruction that can even lead to loss of faith.

> People who want to get rich fall into temptation and a trap and into many foolish and harmful desires that plunge men into ruin and destruction.

For the love of money is a root of all kinds of evil. Some people, eager for money, have wandered from the faith and pierced themselves with many griefs. (1 Tim. 6:9–10)

The Bible also presents us with a more complex understanding of poverty than the tenets of self-reliant individualism might allow. Laziness may be a reason for being poor (Prov. 10:4), but scripture also attributes social causes: "A poor man's field may produce abundant food, but injustice sweeps it away" (Prov. 13:23). And the writer of Proverbs is clear that those who oppress the poor show contempt for God (Prov. 14:31). Working within this framework, Simona Goi argued, "if some people fall in poverty because they are irresponsible, lazy, untrustworthy, self-indulgent, promiscuous, and given to theft and deception, it is also the case that people can become or stay wealthy because they are greedy, selfish, arrogant, deceitful, uncompassionate, and blind to the suffering of others." She continued, noting that these personal attributes do not tell the whole story. "Beyond individual sins, the fall has distorted domestic and international structures . . . so that they reward behaviors incompatible with the ideals of the Gospel."[38] As this writer proposed, Christian faithfulness involves not just changing "individual hearts" but also the cultural patterns and social arrangements that are manifestations of people's deep-seated beliefs about life and society.

"There is nothing wrong, and much that is right, about consuming to live," Rodney Clapp noted, while pointing out that at issue for those concerned "is that the affluent, technologically advanced West seems more and more focused not on consuming to live but on living to consume."[39] As living sacrifices, our wealth and possessions belong to God, and we are accountable for our use of the good gifts given to us (1 Tim. 6:17–19). People of faith have to guard against the secular desire to make consumption into an idol—a guide to life, personal health, emotional well-being, and the pursuit of happiness. In humility and thankfulness, we should perform acts of kindness for the poor while also confronting the unjust laws and social patterns that cause poverty. Popular artworks that deal with these issues show that they are not trivial but significant and deserving of our attention, both personally and collectively.

Summary

- American melodrama depicts the battle between good and evil in sharp and contrasting terms; evildoers are destroyed and the virtuous are rewarded.

- The classical Hollywood film focuses on the actions of a main character in pursuit of a goal, one event causing the next and leading to a complete and satisfying resolution.
- Hollywood heroes are idealized and identified with certain traits, the most important being self-reliance and goal-achievement.
- What the author calls the Wizard of Oz Syndrome is a very human-centered approach to life, with characters on a journey to self-realization.
- Hollywood films exaggerate individualism and deal with social issues by reducing them to personal matters.
- The belief that God is not the source of redemption, but "some magical outside assistance," is a cultural synthesis of American individualism and Christianity.
- The attitudes, desires, and values of materialism are a powerful force in North American life, and an underlying assumption in mainstream Hollywood films is that the goal in life is to become rich.
- Scripture warns against trusting in materialism as a means of salvation, while also presenting a more complex understanding of poverty than the tenets of self-reliant individualism allow.

Discussion Questions

1. How should Christians respond to melodrama? Explain why the melodramatic vision runs against the grain of the main tenets of the Christian faith.
2. What are the basic characteristics of the classical Hollywood film? How might these features work against portrayals of a Christian cultural landscape?
3. To what extent do you think people believe they should be healthy, wealthy, and successful because they deserve it for being "good"?
4. The author maintains that "the cultural landscape of the Hollywood film clearly exaggerates individualism, favoring individual over corporate or institutional solutions to problems and conflicts." How might such portrayals distort our understanding of similar events in the real world?
5. Generate a list of movies and consider ways they affirm or oppose the themes highlighted in this chapter—the classical Hollywood formula, melodrama, self-reliant individualism, religion, and materialism.

6. How does the general treatment of materialism in the Hollywood landscape compare with a Christian understanding of wealth and poverty?
7. As Christians, what should we make of the assumptions about materialism that are so prevalent in Hollywood films?

10

THE MESSAGE IN THE BOTTLE

LOVE, SEX, AND GENDER STEREOTYPES

This job of yours—it's murder on relationships.

    Paris Carver to James Bond in *Tomorrow Never Dies*

Nobody has sex like people have sex in the movies.

    Julianne Moore, Actor

Heroes are those men and women (or fictional characters) who somehow embody a culture's most important ideals and values. Most American heroes, for example, are ordinary people with common origins—not aristocrats or royalty—who achieve greatness by using their exceptional talents. Abraham Lincoln rose from a log cabin to the White House, and Martin Luther King Jr. became a leader of the civil rights movement. Peter Parker went from bookworm to Spider-Man superhero, and the dual identity of Superman echoed the alien immigrant experience in America.[1] Heroes represent qualities—abilities, attitudes, and motivations—a society finds admirable. Their success is meant to inspire the rest of us by implying that we are all capable of achieving something of the same.

As we saw in chapter 9, in North American culture, success is often equated with the acquisition of material things. And in a materialistic culture, "insatiability" is a primary trait of the consumer. "The consumer is taught that persons consist basically of unmet needs that can be requited by commodified goods and experiences," Rodney Clapp explained. "Accordingly, the consumer should think first and foremost of himself or herself and meeting his or her felt needs. The consumer is taught to value above all else freedom, defined as a vast array of choices."[2] Clapp's observations serve as a summary of the themes in the previous chapter by showing the act of consumption as a kind of religious ritual based on values associated with self-reliant individualism.

Every culture harbors some notion of the ideal life and the ideal person. This chapter looks at gender stereotypes, sex, and romance. As we have seen, the tendency of melodrama is to oversimplify. One result is the creation of stock characters based on gender. While social conditions have changed, the cultural attitudes exhibited in gender depictions remain rooted in the sentimentalism we associate with nineteenth-century Victorian culture. The Hollywood cultural landscape represents a polarized view of men and women that is riddled with contradictions.

Gender Stereotypes

Film scholar Robin Wood described the ideal male in Hollywood films as a virile, strong, unrestrained, and unattached man of action and adventure. His shadow, or opposite, is the "settled husband/father, dependable but dull."[3] These are images that associate masculinity with muscles, emotional restraint, dominance, aggression, and the capacity for violence. Adventurers like Indiana Jones are simply not the marrying type. If they do marry they don't make good husbands, like John McClane in the *Die Hard* films (1988, 1990, 1995), or their work activities threaten the family as in *Patriot Games* (1992).

There is no better illustration than the Ian Fleming creation James Bond. British Agent 007 is not just the ultimate spy, but also a handsome, womanizing, and unattached gentleman with a license to kill. Bond's globe-trotting missions always end with some evil genius foiled and beautiful women swooning, "Oh, James." In every new Bond film (over twenty and still counting), a woman might get "too close for comfort," as Bond admits to Paris (Teri Hatcher) in *Tomorrow Never Dies* (1997). But as Paris tells him, "This job of yours—it's murder on relationships." Independence marks the ideal man.

The parody *Austin Powers: International Man of Mystery* (1997) exaggerates these traits to make fun of them. Secret agent Austin Powers

(Mike Myers) is cryogenically frozen during the 1960s. His partner, Mrs. Kensington (Mimi Rogers), describes him as "The ultimate gentleman spy. Women want him, and men want to be him." That's the image we have of James Bond. But Powers—with crooked teeth, thick horn-rimmed glasses, and furry body hair—is sexually crude and lacks the sophistication of "Bond. James Bond." When he is revived in the 1990s to combat his nemesis, Dr. Evil, Powers finds that he has to conform to new sexual norms. At first, Powers maintains, "As long as people are still engaging in sex with many anonymous partners, while at the same time experimenting with mind-altering drugs in a consequence-free environment, I'll be sound as a pound." In contrast to the licentious Bond, however, Powers learns the 1990s' need for "freedom and responsibility. It's a groovy time," and becomes a "one woman man" by marrying his current partner Vanessa (Elizabeth Hurley), who will not tolerate him going around "shagging everyone."

In this and many Hollywood films, the role of the woman is to be the domesticator of these rugged individualists. Marriage represents the end of freedom for the male adventurer whose tendencies are to be unrestrained in love and life.

The ideal woman is to some extent the opposite of her male counterpart; a "wife and mother, mainstay of hearth and home" who stands in contrast to her shadow, the woman who is "erotic . . . fascinating but dangerous."[4] Women are represented in ways that define them by their sexuality and their appearance. They are to be "overtly sexy and attractive but essentially passive and virginal."[5]

Even though ideals and attitudes have changed, whatever new conceptions of women have emerged still find representation largely within traditional gender categories. Women "have long been divided into virgins and whores," Jean Kilbourne explained, but the cultural expectation now is that they are "supposed to embody both within themselves. This is symbolic of the central contradiction of the culture—we must work hard and produce and achieve success and yet, at the same time, we are encouraged to live impulsively, spend a lot of money, and be constantly and immediately gratified," she wrote. "This tension is reflected in our attitudes toward many things, including sex and eating. Girls are promised fulfillment both through being thin and through eating rich foods, just as they are promised fulfillment through being innocent and virginal and through wild and impulsive sex."[6] These conflicting images are captured in the deceitful belief that lurking beneath every proper woman is a nymphomaniac just waiting to attack any man—a dominant image in music videos.[7]

In many portrayals, women exist largely to take part in the man's fantasies and adventures. The man is active, the woman spirited but ultimately submissive, her identity largely dependent upon a man. However talented and beautiful, women need a man for complete happiness and certainty. We can see these images of men and women in a wide range of movies, including classics like *Casablanca* (1942) and *Rear Window* (1954), action films like *Raiders of the Lost Ark* (1981) and *True Lies* (1994), a family film like *City Slickers* (1991), and even animated features like *The Little Mermaid* (1989). The Christmas classic *It's a Wonderful Life* (1946) contrasts worldly success, individualism, and adventure with an ordinary life, community, and domesticity in the character of George Bailey.

There are other films, however, that rework these cultural patterns to question the viability of established gender ideals and roles. Stanley Kubrick explored the psychological dimension of these gender conceptions in his erotic and dream-like *Eyes Wide Shut* (1999). At a glamorous Christmas party, Bill Harford (Tom Cruise), a doctor, and his wife Alice (Nicole Kidman) both resist temptations to infidelity. The next night a discussion about marital faithfulness turns into an argument. Bill can't imagine his wife being unfaithful. But Alice confesses to lusting over a naval officer she once saw in a hotel lobby and how powerful the urge was to throw her entire life away for one night with him. Though only a sexual fantasy for Alice, "the revelation shatters the stability of Bill's world," film critic James Berardinelli noted. In a moment of realization his whole gendered world is turned upside down. His wife (and mother of their daughter) acting like the erotic woman shatters his self-perception as the virile adventurer who can keep her desires completely satisfied. His obsession leads him into a series of encounters in a sexual underworld "where he finds not only perversion and pleasure, but death and danger," as this critic put it. Berardinelli explained, "The way he reacts in each of these circumstances, and the manner in which he interacts sexually with his wife, displays a growing awareness concerning the ease of having *meaningless* sex with someone who is regarded as an object, and the difficulty of having *meaningless* sex with someone who is seen as a person."[8] A movie about eroticism in marriage, at one level, the film draws its dramatic import from the tensions in popular gender stereotypes.

In *American Beauty* (1999) the gender roles have been reversed. Carolyn (Annette Bening) is essentially the head of the family, focused on her career, a "natural" with a gun, and the primary economic provider (even before her husband Lester [Kevin Spacey] quits his job). In contrast, Lester is submissive and practically ignored by his wife and daughter. When Lester becomes infatuated with his daughter Jane's sexually alluring friend, Angela, he starts jogging and lifting weights to restore his muscles and also his masculinity (suggesting the action-

American Beauty questions the validity of accepted gender ideals and roles.

adventure hero). Though the film implies that this dysfunctional family is the result of the reversal of traditional roles, it ultimately also criticizes traditional gender roles. Lester realizes the shallowness of his actions at the end of the film and discovers that "macho conquest counts for nothing in the world as it really is," as one scholar put it.[9] Instead he comes to embrace his role as a father and realizes the value of his family.

In the martial arts film *Crouching Tiger, Hidden Dragon* (2000), the relationship between Li Mu Bai (Chow Yun-Fat) and Yu Shu Lien (Michelle Yeoh) is based on mutual trust and respect between relative equals. Both are courageous warriors of great strength and resourcefulness. Although they have been in love for many years, their personal gratification must wait until Li Mu avenges his master's death. This relationship stands in sharp contrast to those found in many Hollywood films that are based on rigid gender stereotypes, self-pleasure, and immediate gratification.

An Openhearted Love Fable

The blockbuster hit film *Pretty Woman* (1990) illustrates how these cultural ideals, beliefs, and assumptions about gender can inform characterizations, drive the story, and determine acceptable resolutions. Within two months of its release in 1990, *Pretty Woman* surpassed $100 million at the box office to become a certified blockbuster hit. The film went on to earn over $463 million worldwide. The video release spent 169 weeks on the top sell-through list in *Video Business*, putting it in league with *Pinocchio* and *The Wizard of Oz*.[10] *Pretty Woman* placed fourteenth on *Entertainment Weekly*'s list of the one hundred most popular movies of all time in 1994: "Never underestimate the power of a Cinderella story when it's being driven by Julia Roberts," the magazine concluded.[11]

The popularity of *Pretty Woman* makes it a useful illustration; it adheres to the classical Hollywood cultural pattern following the traditional marriage plot, while also representing contemporary ideas and attitudes about gender, sex, and marriage. In the traditional marriage or romance story, the woman's value is determined largely, though not exclusively, by her "virtue," that is, her chastity or virginity. As consumerism was increasingly associated with feminine culture in the twentieth century, there was a shift in a woman's value from chastity to sexual expertise and appearance, the latter dependent upon consumer skills (wardrobe, cosmetics, and so forth). In *Pretty Woman*, Vivian (Julia Roberts) has to "couple consumer knowledge and sexual knowledge in order to be valuable," one scholar explained.[12]

In an opening sequence, shots of Edward driving into Hollywood are intercut with shots of a woman (Vivian) waking up and getting dressed. That we are introduced to Vivian through shots of her arms, legs, and lips establishes her immediately as a sexual object and suggests a corresponding attitude toward her as a woman. The crosscutting makes an association between the two, setting up their fateful meeting on Hollywood Boulevard.

Edward gets lost en route to his Beverly Hills hotel; for a price Vivian will direct him there, and eventually she gets into the driver's seat to show Edward "what this car can really do." That the woman is doing the driving is a visual image suggesting that the traditional roles for men and women are reversed. The problem, according to the narrative, is

That the woman is doing the driving is a visual image suggesting the main characters' problems in *Pretty Woman* (1990) result from an inappropriate reversal of the traditional and proper roles for men and women.

that Edward and Vivian, who are basically good, have been led astray by harsh circumstances in their lives. As a result, they've become disoriented and acquired roles inappropriate for their gender. The resolution advanced, then, is for Edward and Vivian to help each other recognize their waywardness and accept their proper and established roles; they must fall in love and find fulfillment by entering into a state of marriage and becoming a legitimate family. Only in this way can they become whole people, complementing each another and restoring balance to the world of family and corporate capitalism.

A Hooker with a Heart of Gold . . .

Vivian is the classic prostitute with a heart of gold—basically good and forced less by choice than circumstances into her immoral profession. Vivian violates the ideal female role in two ways. She is, first of all, the erotic woman. And before she can regain her respect by marrying Edward, Vivian has to show real prospect as a marriage partner; her veiled potential as the traditional wife and mother has to be disclosed. Also, Vivian has assumed the traditional male role as the breadwinner in her household. She is an independent, self-reliant business entrepreneur who earns a living by exchanging pseudo-affection and sexual favors for money. She tells her roommate, "We say who, we say when, we say how much."

The film makes it easy for us to overlook the fact that Vivian is a Hollywood hooker. Aware of the conventions of the genre, right from the beginning we're waiting for this princess in disguise to be revealed for who she really is. As the story unfolds we come to see her as a small-town girl who is both a stunning beauty and tomboy familiar with the finer points of expensive cars. She's also softhearted and practices safe sex and dental hygiene. Consequently we're disturbed when the hotel manager and store clerks treat her with disrespect.

According to the gender logic of the narrative, Vivian's main problem is that she's an inexperienced shopper; she has to learn to enjoy being an avid consumer—the woman's role. When Edward awakens her saying, "Wake up. Time to shop," Vivian is reluctant. "More shopping?" she asks, dismayed. According to the narrative, for Vivian to be a suitable wife she has to stop earning a living and depend on a man to be the economic provider.

An afternoon spending "obscene amounts" of Edward's money in a shopping spree, a lesson from the hotel manager (Hector Elizondo) on

Pretty Woman preserves the traditional Cinderella story while also making personal pleasure the highest goal in life.

which fork to use at a formal dinner, and overnight Vivian is displaying upper-class social norms and behaviors. We are so charmed and captivated by Vivian that we let pass the probability that she will now become a snobbish socialite who will demand the flattery of store clerks on Rodeo Drive. She does return to the store to deride the saleswomen who earlier refused to help her. "Big mistake," she tells them holding up her packages.

In *Pretty Woman*, the ability to purchase and look good in fashionable clothing replaces Cinderella's glass slipper, as one scholar observed.[13] Through clothing (i.e., costuming) we become aware that Vivian is really a princess in disguise. Her physical beauty and sexual expertise, rather than her virginity, are her primary "assets," what makes Vivian valuable to Edward. And yet *Pretty Woman* preserves the traditional Cinderella theme that a woman's ambitions can only be realized through marriage to the right man. A direct and profane intertextual reference to Cinderella metaphorically links Vivian (as prostitute) and the classic mythical rags-to-riches figure. In *Pretty Woman* a poor girl marries a rich man who "saves" her from a life of poverty and unhappiness. In this contemporary retelling, however, the princess "saves him right back."

. . . Meets a Corporate Raider

At first Edward seems an unlikely fairy-tale prince. He is a ruthless, driven, controlling, and filthy rich business executive.[14] Edward fails repeatedly at relationships because he treats women like hookers, wanting them to be at his beck and call; Vivian finally fits the bill. The problem is that Edward consumes what others have constructed; he buys companies and sells them off in pieces to earn a profit. "You don't make anything and you don't build anything?" Vivian observes. "Sort of like stealing cars and selling them for parts?" To be the patriarchal head of a family, however, Edward needs a traditional occupation as a producer. Stacking glasses (symbolically) on his desk, he realizes this, and instead of taking over the Morse company, Edward creates a partnership; they go into the ship-building business together. The elderly Morse puts his hand on Edward's shoulder and the father figure says, "I'm proud of you."

The film does not critique Edward's avaricious business practices that include using political connections to leverage business affairs to his own advantage. In that sense the film allows, if not justifies, his corporate raiding, while indicating that the cause of his marauding career is the psychological trauma he experienced at an early age; his father abandoned the family and left them in a financial strait. In an act of retribution, Edward makes his father's company one of many victims in his spree of hostile takeovers, which begins to look like an emotional compensation for an absentee father. Something of Edward's sensitive side is disclosed by his piano playing, but ultimately what the rich bachelor really needs is a woman to humanize his business habits and domesticate him.

An Innocent Movie?

Film critic Roger Ebert described *Pretty Woman* as "an innocent movie" and "the sweetest and most openhearted love fable."[15] No doubt these features contribute to the film's continued popularity on video and DVD. In a sense, *Pretty Woman* is conservative in that it affirms very traditional roles for men and women. But the view of sex, gender, and marriage represented here calls for Christian appraisal.

The opening line of this storybook romance is, "No matter what they say, it's all about money." And everything in the story turns on money. In its display of excess and materialism, sex and the objectification of women, *Pretty Woman* flaunts the ideals, attitudes, and values of consumerism as a way of life. The film even depicts marriage in economic terms as a business arrangement primarily. When Edward (presumably) marries Vivian—his beck-and-call girl—only the status of their relationship changes. However much Christians affirm marriage, we do not have to accept assumptions about gender roles that commodify relationships and sex as a kind of economic exchange.

The dark side of prostitution is implied by the death of Skinny Marie, but in the world of the film (and parameter of the genre) streetwalking, though not an admirable profession, is cast as relatively safe and harmless. There are drug dealers in the streets, and Edward's lawyer Philip Stuckey (Jason Alexander) tries to rape Vivian, but the sexual encounters between Edward and Vivian are depicted as blissful, and being a prostitute has surprisingly little effect on Vivian.

In contrast, *Leaving Las Vegas* (1995) shows prostitution as a dehumanizing affair—cold, cruel, humiliating, and deadly dangerous. In this film human love and compassion, and even professional sex, are not sufficient for personal redemption. In contrast to the fantasy of *Pretty Woman*, Sera (Elizabeth Shue) and Ben (Nicolas Cage) cannot save each other. There is no fairy-tale ending for this man who has failed at relationships or the prostitute who longs for a better life.

Ultimately, *Pretty Woman* denies the importance of faith in anything beyond oneself. The film glorifies the pursuit of personal pleasure through leisure and consumption as the highest goal in life and promotes the value of immediate gratification. Like other mainstream Hollywood films treated in this book, *Pretty Woman* affirms the American myth.

The central characters have only to overcome the limitations of their past in a personal struggle to reach a gracious future that awaits them with open arms.

Gender Misconceptions

The gender stereotypes we find in popular culture are pervasive and alluring. Considering the dominance of this image system it is not surprising to find that they influence Christian perspectives. John Eldredge, for example, drew on this Hollywood cultural system to construct his notion of a "masculine design" in *Wild at Heart*.[16] His descriptions of men and women matched Robin Wood's treatment of Hollywood's gendered ideals. As Eldredge put it, men have three universal desires: "a battle to fight, an adventure to live, and a beauty to rescue." Women, in contrast, yearn only to be fought for, to share an adventure, and unveil their beauty.

Eldredge's concept of masculinity bore the image of the American cinema—James Bond, Indiana Jones, and especially *Braveheart* (1995). And Eldredge wanted to be like William Wallace, not Mother Teresa. It followed that he accepted the notion of a violent masculinity as normative and not socially constructed: "Aggression is part of the masculine *design*, we are hardwired for it," he asserted.

Wild at Heart perpetuated Hollywood stereotypes, casting men as warriors wielding swords not plowshares, and not ambassadors for Christ carrying on a ministry of reconciliation (2 Cor. 5:17–20). Women were to play the seductress, the damsel in distress, an ideal image that "hardly diverges from that of the makers of the Barbie Doll or the franchisers of Hooter's restaurants," as critics noted. "Rather than offering a subversive and invigorating message for a woman, Eldredge has endorsed the exploitative and oppressive conception that objectifies female sexuality and communicates that a woman has value only in her relationship to a man—insinuating that men and women cannot be completely whole unless engaged in some sort of romantic relationship."[17]

Eldredge transposed the frontier myth and its stock characters into a theory of gender that reads like an appropriation of movie genre conventions. The extent to which he found "an authentic masculinity" in the world of western novels and movies is disconcerting. It should convince us that the potential for cultural accommodation is real and Christians need to develop a critical awareness of the popular cultural landscape.

The polarized and contradictory view of men and women, as if they represent different values and even separate spheres in life, might dominate the Hollywood cultural landscape, but it contrasts with the biblical presentation. God charges the man and woman to work together in the cultivation of the creation and the advance of the kingdom. The woman described in Proverbs 31 is capable, caring, and morally upright, with business acumen. She is deserving of love, honor, and respect; her beauty and value lie in her integrity, character, strength, and faithfulness. In contrast to the male code of self-reliance, the Psalmist wrote, "The LORD is my strength and my shield; my heart trusts in him, and I am helped" (Ps. 28:7). The writer of Ecclesiastes made it clear that "Wisdom is better than weapons of war" (Eccles. 9:18). God uses the foolish, the weak, the lowly and despised to accomplish his purposes (1 Cor. 1:27–31). And Christians—male and female alike—are expected to exhibit the fruit of the Spirit: "love, joy, peace, patience, kindness, goodness, faithfulness, gentleness and self-control" (Gal. 5:22–23).

Scripture informs us that people gifted by God have a wide range and diversity of talents to be used in service of our neighbor (1 Cor. 12:14–26). But the popular-culture landscape is dominated by gender ideals rooted in extreme notions of masculinity and femininity that are misconceptions of God's image bearers. Christians should develop a critical posture toward these gender stereotypes, for they can dehumanize us, distorting our identities, relationships, and roles for service in God's kingdom.

You're My Density?

In *Back to the Future* (1985), Marty McFly (Michael J. Fox) has traveled back in time and is trying to orchestrate his future parents' date at the Enchantment Under the Sea dance. Trying to get George (his future father) to ask out his future mother, Marty says, "It's destiny, George. You and Lorraine are meant for each other." George fears rejection and doesn't know what to say. "Just tell her destiny has brought you to her and you think she's the most beautiful girl you've ever seen," Marty tells him. George, an avid science fiction reader, scribbles the line on a notepad, but he fumbles the delivery to Lorraine and it comes out as, "I'm your density—I mean destiny."

A powerful belief in the Hollywood landscape is that our ultimate destiny is to find that one person somewhere out there in the universe who will make life meaningful and complete. Such a romantic love is passionate and irresistible and can conquer anything, including barriers of social class, age, race and ethnicity, and personality conflicts. Indeed, popular artworks often treat love as an emotion that is its own authority, a kind of law of nature. It follows that finding a suitable partner is mostly a matter of listening to the calling of your heart. In many movies, people having little in common, and sometimes even a relationship characterized mostly by conflict, enter into long-term commitments based on an impulsive and what would normally appear to be an irrational decision.

The Notebook (2004), based on the Nicholas Sparks novel, forcefully illustrates the love-as-destiny myth with young love overcoming class differences, personality conflicts, and physical separation. Allie Hamilton (Rachel McAdams) and Noah Calhoun (Ryan Gosling) meet and fall passionately in love while Allie's family is vacationing at their summer home in North Carolina. Allie's wealthy parents disapprove of the working-class Noah; they cut short their vacation and take Allie home to Charleston, thinking this will end the relationship. After years of separation, Allie becomes engaged to a handsome and wealthy man; Noah continues to hope that by fulfilling his promise to restore his family's mansion, Allie will somehow come back to him. And through a variety of circumstances, eventually she does. Despite an often tempestuous relationship, they reunite and marry. In an emotionally effective plot device, the story is told in flashbacks; the now aged Noah reading their love story to an Allie suffering from Alzheimer's, reinforcing the basic tenet of the love-conquers-all myth: romantic love is destiny, more powerful than any force on earth. As one critic observed, *The Notebook* "insists on true, mystical, eternal love, till death do us part, and won't have it any other way."[18]

The love-as-destiny myth also drives the narrative of *Wedding Crashers* (2005). In this romantic comedy, divorce mediators John Beckwith (Owen Wilson) and Jeremy Grey (Vince Vaughn) have fine-tuned their methods for seducing women at weddings when romance is in the air and female attendees "throw their inhibitions to the wind." John is smitten at first sight by Claire Cleary (Rachel McAdams). She asks him, "What's true love?" "True love," he tells her, "is your soul's recognition of its counterpoint in another." Claire says, "It's a little cheesy but I like it." "I read it on a bumper sticker," John replies. Clichéd it is, but after a series of comic mishaps John and Jeremy predictably find their soul mates and marry the two daughters of Treasury Secretary William Cleary.

Even the smart and sassy *Sex and the City*, an exposé on the love lives of four single, thirtysomething, professional women in the Big Apple, insists on a basic optimism about heterosexual romance but without providing a basis for that optimism. Various episodes waver between cynicism and "the wishful thinking of hopeless romantics," as one writer observed. "The temptation is to resort to sentimentalism out of guilt for our cynicism. This is a shallow solution."[19] Even so, the individual search for love-as-destiny is a myth that is perpetuated in songs, music videos, movies, and television programs. It is a significant aspect of the

Characters on *Sex and the City* have no basis for their optimism about romance.

cultural landscape represented in stories dealing with romance, sex, and gender.

As Long As They Don't See "The Act"

The act that Shakespeare called "making the beast with two backs" represents, in both art and life, a ubiquitous human desire, "a drive so strong that it has ignited both great battles and intimate passions—sex."[20] Attitudes about depictions of sex (and violence) vary in different cultures. In Britain, depictions of drug use, violence, and profanity are more objectionable to most than sex, horror, blasphemy, and nudity. In Southeast Asia, graphic violence on the screen is accepted, but sex is forbidden. Japan is famous for its pornographic cartoons and gory, violent movies; pornography can be bought at convenience stores, and there is nudity on late-night television, but kissing in public is absolutely taboo.[21] In the United States, people complain about the levels of sex and violence in the media, although most Americans seem more concerned with sex than violence. Several people I know who worked at video stores told stories about parents asking about the sexual content of "the latest teen slasher flick." This store manager's account was typical: "When I tell them that there is little or no sex, but a multitude of killings and gratuitous gore, their response is always, 'Okay, as long as they don't see "the act."'"[22]

The range of American attitudes reveals a deep ambivalence. On the one hand, sex is "the ultimate expression of the American dream of freedom, liberation, and mobility." But sex can also be frightening and is seen as the source of many troubles; abuse, assault, sexually transmitted diseases, and especially AIDS make casual sex a "dangerous pastime."[23] Hollywood's treatment of love and sex is a good illustration of how the popular arts reflect a society they help to create. Almost half the people in one survey believed sex was permissible when people were "in love" and did not need to be reserved for marriage; over a quarter thought sex had nothing to do with love.[24] Surveys also showed that 70 percent of evangelical Christians engaged in premarital sex.[25] Not surprisingly, the long-awaited final kiss that once culminated many a movie romance has been replaced with sexual intimacy. Sex is used as an all too easy way to signify, and even substitute for, a deep and meaningful relationship. More often than not, characters don't need to get to know one another and develop trust; they only need to sleep together.

Sexual situations, however, can also be used effectively to disclose character traits, attitudes, and desires to the audience. Female characters, often defined by their sexuality, unfortunately, sometimes use their beauty and sexual allure to charm (*Grease* [1978]), disarm (*Charlie's Angels* [2000], *Urban Cowboy* [1980]), or manipulate men (*The Thomas Crown Affair* [1999]). The most extreme example is the femme fatale, a woman who is sexually alluring, but also treacherous (*Basic Instinct* [1992], *The Last Seduction* [1994]).

In the gangster film *Bonnie and Clyde* (1967) there is a suggestion that Clyde's wild criminal behavior can be explained at least in part as an attempt to compensate for his sexual impotence. The association of millionaire Noah Cross's (John Huston) business practices and his incestuous desires in the movie *Chinatown* gives the film a deeper moral dimension, suggesting corruption and violation at multiple levels. Bedroom play in *The Family Man* (2000) reveals the passionate love between Kate (Téa Leoni) and Jack (Nicolas Cage), who are receiving a little magical outside assistance.

Many movies depict sex in ways that affirm the gender patterns I described earlier. Masculinity is associated with sexual prowess, and losing your virginity is the theme of many teen films, from *Porky's* (1982) to *American Pie* (1999). In contrast, a woman is faced with the Madonna/whore complex. She is supposed to remain a lily-white virgin by resisting the advances of all those virile adventurers or be labeled a whore.

Of course, this is a real-life formula for disaster with women searching for love and companionship and men just wanting to score.

The plot of *American Pie* is structured in terms of these gender patterns. Four boys set losing their virginity before high-school graduation as their senior-year goal: "We will make a stand. We will succeed. We will get laid!" In one scene, Vicky (Tara Reid) asks her boyfriend, Kevin (Thomas Ian Nicholas), if he wants to "do it." Both surprised and excited, he answers with an enthusiastic, "Yeah!" "I love you," she says, with an expectant, "It's your turn." Disappointment covers both their faces as he replies, "That's not what I was thinking." Frustrated, she says, "Sex. It's always about sex." "Hey, it's not always about sex," he says in his defense. "I just thought it was about sex this time." For this young woman "doing it" was an affirmation of love and commitment; for the young man it was only recreational—even worse in this instance, a goal. Like most teenpics, however, *American Pie* concludes with the main characters at least discovering that the sure way to a sexual encounter is through a profession of love (however fleeting the sentiment).

Larger Realities

As expected perhaps, producers and merchandisers try to transform consumption into an erotic spectacle. Many scholars have pointed out that the images of sexuality in the media are designed to sell products by associating these images with erotic adventures. Sex sells, so the adage goes, and as I noted earlier, the consumer culture exerts an undeniable impact on the content of the popular arts and culture. Gratuitous sex and violence are often used to entice audiences, but they can also be used to make up for creativity in mainstream entertainment.

Sex is all too often shown as an "exciting amusement for people of all ages."[26] Caught up in swirling moments of romantic bliss, characters engage in all kinds of sexual encounters. But as actress Julianne Moore said, "Nobody has sex like people have sex in the movies—on tables, on the floor, flailing around, clothes ripping, hitting each other. It's ridiculous!"[27] Sex can also be treated "as potentially redemptive, offering individuals and society a seemingly endless source of pleasure and transcendence."[28]

Media depictions of "impulsive sexuality" can make the world seem more sexual. "As people heavily exposed to televised crime see the world as more dangerous, so people heavily exposed to pornography or sexually oriented rock videos see the world as more sexual,"[29] David Myers explained. He summarized the social science research: "Repeatedly viewing violence desensitizes people to violence and shapes their perceived reality. Erotic images likewise tend to distort people's perceptions of sexual reality, decrease the attractiveness of their own partners, prime men to perceive women in sexual terms, make sexual coercion seem more trivial, and provide mental scripts for how to act in sexual situations."[30]

However alluring these images and portrayals may be, we should be aware that far too many depictions of sex in the popular arts simply ignore larger realities of life. In many movies, music videos, and television shows, decisions about sexual intimacy are often based on the value of self-gratification and are devoid of emotional, ethical, and religious considerations.

Though few, there are counterexamples. In *The Horse Whisperer* (1998), Annie (Kristin Scott Thompson) is unhappy in her marriage and falls in love with Tom (Robert Redford), whose wife left him. They each see the other as the ideal partner. Their attraction builds in the story, taking them to the edge of an affair. In a poignant scene Tom says, "Annie, this is where I belong, this is who I am. Is this what you want?" When Annie affirms that she does, Tom asks if she can tell that to her family, to her husband and daughter. "If you had a chance to go home and change things, would you?" he asks her. She responds, "You can't ask me that. It's not that simple." But Tom replies, "It is." In the end, their larger commitments in life—personal identity, integrity, family, and work—overpower their sensual desires.

Likewise, episodes in the television program *Law & Order: SVU* deal with the terrible brutality of abuse and assault, showing that deep hurt can result from sex, and this can negatively affect people's self-image and emotional well-being. The bedroom is often the place in which the precarious fine line between love and hate is crossed in sin-troubled human relationships.

Yet, the media has often failed to show this side of sex, instead glamorizing and trivializing it in shows like *Sex and the City*. According to a writer in *The New Republic*, "none of these women is hurt by sex," in fact they "are constantly humiliated, insulted, and embarrassed without the slightest effect on their egos or their self-esteem."[31] Given the conventions of the genre, regular viewers (I would assume) recognize these characters as urban female composites and expect them to encounter all kinds of relationships and situations related to the show's central topic. Nevertheless, there are in reality consequences for sexual behavior that are connected with deep emotional dynamics.

In real life, sex can be "about power, the power to define other human beings and their worth," as one writer noted.[32] Media representations can do the same, whether *Sex and the City*, a film like *Closer* (2004) that explored sexual desire, betrayal, and intimacy, or MTV videos.

Evoking Meaning

Is there a proper place for the erotic in popular art? Like everything else in life, there is an ethical dimension to the creation of art; artists have to exercise moral restraints in their representations of life. They (and also critics) have to make judgments about what should appear offstage and, just as important, when and how sexual activities should be portrayed onstage.

What makes portrayals of sex moral or immoral as subject matter is the manner of treatment. "Even at its most explicit, film can never put the viewer directly into the most intimate sexual situations, and that's probably a good thing," a film director explained. "What film can do is evoke the meaning people attach to sexual relationships."[33] Erotic depictions do not have to be voyeuristic—a temptation always to be resisted—but can be put in a proper context, so as to engage the audience at the level of meaning and not simply adolescent curiosity.

Musicians have explored a range of topics centered on love and sex. In "A Man and a Woman," a song about his marriage, U2's Bono sings, "I could never take a chance of losing love to find romance." With vivid adult imagery, Springsteen looks at the loneliness and alienation of a meaningless sexual encounter with a prostitute who resembles a former lover in "Reno."

In John Sayles's film *Lone Star* (1996), Sam (Chris Cooper) returns to his hometown in hope of renewing a relationship with Pilar (Elizabeth Peña), his high-school sweetheart. Their romance was broken up by their parents, presumably because they objected to an Anglo-Mexican marriage. One night in the restaurant after closing, Pilar plays "Since I Left You, Baby" on the jukebox (her mother, who owns the place, hasn't changed the songs since she was ten). She and Sam playfully circle each other and begin to dance in a highly erotic moment that rekindles their romance. There is a tenderness in the scene's hint of both nostalgia and hope. Film critic Janet Maslin pointed out that Sayles "films a startlingly tender bedroom scene between these two without nudity or graphic sex and without failing to communicate that they are deeply in love."[34] This scene reaches another level of meaning as part of the film's project to revise the western frontier myth by showing different racial groups coexisting—even falling in love—and not just warring with each other.

A popular artwork represents just a slice of life; it can't cover all aspects of a topic and every possible perspective on an issue. In most cases, we would not want to judge an artwork based on portrayals of immoral moments; rather, we should think critically about the overall perspective given to the issue. Instead of simply condemning erotic elements, our critique should be directed toward the artist's treatment and an understanding and evaluation of their inclusion in the whole artwork. What meanings, values, and perspectives does the entire film, for instance, bring to its depiction of sexual acts?

How might we reflect on the relationship between Rose and Jack in *Titanic*, for example? The now rather famous sex scene sums up many of the film's themes: forbidden love, class differences, and individual freedom. Jack's sketching of Rose in the first-class stateroom is a kind of foreplay; their sexual liaison that takes place in the next scene happens on the lower deck in the backseat of a car. When Rose initiates the encounter, Jack is pretending to be her chauffeur; this role playing conforms to the fantasy of the working-class boy fulfilling the sexual desires of the uptown girl. However clichéd and unbelievable, Jack and Rose have passionate, sweating, and panting sex that steams up the car windows in what *Variety* called "an effectively intense and sensual sequence."[35] Jack takes Rose "to the stars," both arousing and fulfilling her passions, a feat her fiancé, Cal, is apparently unable to accomplish. (Remember: Rose says Jack saved her in *every* way.)

Rose and Jack consummate their love in an illicit sexual encounter that is for Rose a declaration of independence. By leaving the nude drawing for her fiancé to find, Rose makes her disdain for him clear. She expects it will end their engagement (and her mother's control over her). Rose's mother and fiancé have been shown as selfish and oppressive; viewers want Rose to be free of them. Our intense dislike of them makes the lovemaking between Jack and Rose more acceptable to the audience, as does our knowledge of the impending catastrophe.

An Inseparable Part of Being Human

A widely reported study by the Kaiser Family Foundation in 2005 revealed a trend in television programming toward more sexual subject matter. Seventy percent of the TV shows surveyed included some sexual content, ranging from discussions about sex to scenes involving kissing or intercourse.[36] This figure was up from 56 percent in 1998 and 64 percent in 2002. And in another survey 51 percent of the teenagers reported getting their information about sex from movies and TV shows like FOX's teen drama *The O.C.* that "embraced current teenage sexual mores."[37]

While Christians do well to recoil from destructive patterns that result from our culture's obsession with sex, we should not abandon it as a topic for artistic treatment or criticism. Sexuality is an inseparable part of being human; that we have bodies and sexual urges is one aspect of being fearfully and wonderfully made in the image of God. Scripture treats the full range of human sexuality, everything from marital faithfulness to adultery, rape, and incest. In presenting these topics, it gives us a perspective on sex.

When from the roof of his palace David sees the beautiful Bathsheba bathing, he finds her irresistible (2 Sam. 11:2), but there are consequences for sexual behavior that are connected with deep emotional dynamics. David is overwhelmed with guilt because of his adultery with Bathsheba (Ps. 51); the affair weakens his authority as ruler and father. Calvin Seerveld described the Song of Songs as "a bundle of straightforward, erotic love lyrics of amazing vitality and passion," while showing how these chapters actually criticize Solomon.[38] The Song of Songs depicts him as a man of flesh and blood, whose sinful desire to add the Shulammite maiden to his harem is finally frustrated by her faithfulness to her betrothed. Solomon comes across as ostentatious, lustful, and even foolish, trying to seduce this woman.

While rejecting lust and promiscuity, scripture affirms and encourages sex as a celebration of human love and marriage, a good gift from God that can be playful and exciting, wonderful and mysterious, an ecstatic enjoyment of human love. Sex allows humans to reach a level of intimacy that can be mysterious and even in some sense spiritual; scripture likens the covenantal relationship between God and the church to a marriage (Isa. 62:5; Rev. 21:2).

Perhaps in reaction against our culture's preoccupation with sex, some Christians draw on the Victorian sentiment of romantic love: the belief in a love that is pure but passionless, beautiful and eternal, but close to sexless. Though I have not read them, I understand this is a view presented in Christian romance novels, in which not even married couples engage in sex. According to one report, in these Christianized love stories, "no bodices get ripped, no loins throb, no breasts heave, and the cover is more likely to feature a wedding dress than a shirtless Fabio. And while a kiss is still a kiss, it no longer sends the hero on an inexorable journey to the 'pulsing flower of her womanhood.'"[39] Secular romance novels might diminish sexuality by detaching it from deep and committed relationships and turning it into fleeting encounters with strangers, but Christian stories of love and relationships that deny the force of sexual passion and desire, and even avoid consideration of sex, can also distort and cheapen human life.

There are Christians who want to treat sexual sin as the worst kind, even though a life of purity in thought and deed is virtually impossible. According to one survey, over half of the men said they had erotic thoughts every day or several times a day.[40] Jesus equated the fantasy with the act: "anyone who looks at a woman lustfully has already committed adultery with her in his heart" (Matt. 5:28).

Even so, some Christians tend to think of themselves as nice, decent people, loving and kind, moral and righteous. But morality too easily becomes moralism, a list of dos and don'ts mostly related to sexual behavior. People can think of themselves as righteous and set apart from sinners if they avoid making outward or visible mistakes in this area of life, even if their faith is compromised by a trust in more tangible things—money, career, social status, and their ill-perceived moral uprightness. Reducing sin to sexual immorality can also lead people to believe that they are free from the demands of faithfulness to God in most other areas of life.

"Sex and art go together. They have been friends for generations," James Wall pointed out. "Sex and exploitation have also spent time together. Our task is to encourage the first relationship and discourage the second."[41] In sum, the popular arts treat sex in a variety of ways. We have to learn to distinguish between portrayals that denigrate humanity and those that affirm it, criticizing the former without also condemning the latter.

Summary

- Hollywood's cultural landscape presents a polarized view of men and women.
- The ideal man is a virile, strong, unrestrained, and unattached man of adventure.
- The ideal woman is a wife, mother, and a mainstay of hearth and home.
- Christians should be critical of these misconceptions of God's male and female image bearers, for they distort our identities, relationships, and roles for service in God's kingdom.
- Christian treatments of sex will situate the variety of sexual experiences in the proper context of human love and marriage, while rejecting the practices of lust and promiscuity.
- Though the popular arts often present alluring images and portrayals of sex, these depictions of sex often ignore the larger realities of life.

Discussion Questions

1. Describe gender stereotypes prevalent in films, TV programs, and music videos, and evaluate them from your Christian perspective.

2. "While Christians do well to recoil from our culture's obsession with sex," the author contends, "we should not abandon it as a topic for artistic treatment or criticism." Is there a proper place for the erotic in popular art? If so, how should it appear in a Christian cultural landscape?
3. Spend some time talking about a Christian perspective on sex.
4. Can you think of popular artworks that treat sex appropriately?

A HISTORY OF VIOLENCE

CHARTING THE TERRAIN

Violence is the ultimate conflict and conflict is the ultimate drama.

Clint Eastwood, Actor and Director

Sex and violence are all-encompassing fantasies that permeate every possible market. Screenwriting needs them more than the other forms of media—because the numbers have to be bigger.

Paul Schrader, Filmmaker

In the wake of *The Passion*'s box-office success in 2004, Hollywood marketing firms began surveying the religious community hoping to be able to discover something of their tastes and preferences. Now, if faith-based movie websites were any indication, many people identifying themselves as Christian exhibited a penchant for sentimental, melodramatic fare that was clean and wholesome. Paradoxically, these same moviegoers turned out in huge numbers for Gibson's movie, which critics deemed one of the most violent pictures they'd ever seen.

A 2005 MarketCast study showed that at least some Christians were far less troubled with violence than sex, nudity, and profanity in the media. "What you find is that people with conservative religious doctrine are the most likely to see movies rated R for violence," a MarketCast executive said.

"If you compared it to liberals, it's a third more."[1] Indeed, a CBN writer acknowledged, "*The Passion* has shown that Christian audiences may not mind sitting through a violent, bloody movie if there is a spiritual message of inspiration."[2] Apparently, even though they were uneasy with the levels of onscreen violence, some Christian critics still found favor with Gibson's films, from *Braveheart* (1999) and *The Patriot* (2000) to *The Passion*. One minister said, "I've described the *Passion* to some as *Braveheart* goes to church."[3] Religion columnist Terry Mattingly pointed out that *Braveheart* "was bloody violent and its wedding was followed by a nude wedding night," while also noting, "Many conservative believers cheered and began to have second thoughts about their R-rating phobias."[4]

According to one study, these conservative Christians used "factual basis and patriotic lessons" to justify the violence.[5] This kind of critical response is evidence of attitudes associated with the approaches we considered in chapter 7; *The Passion* provided a clear illustration as the measure of acceptable content (here violence), for these critics depended on the movie's support of a specific "Christian" moral or social vision, and not dramatic justification for example. "This isn't just violence for violence's sake," the head of an evangelical youth ministry said, "This is what really happened, what it would have been like to have been there in person to see Jesus crucified."[6]

But many film critics cringed at the level of violence in the movie. In what was a positive review, Roger Ebert called *The Passion* "the most violent film I have ever seen." He warned his readers, "You must be prepared for whippings, flayings, beatings, the crunch of bones, the agony of screams, the cruelty of the sadistic centurions, the rivulets of blood that crisscross every inch of Jesus' body."[7] Even so, evangelical leaders—many who had denounced R-rated movies for undermining "traditional values"—persuaded parents and youth ministers to take young people to see it. For some it might have been their first time seeing an R-rated film.

Violence is a staple in American entertainment, appearing in songs and music videos, action films, and even animated cartoons. The American Academy of Pediatrics estimated that by the age of eighteen the average American child will have seen about 200,000 acts of violence on television alone.[8] Young children (under the age of 8) do not easily distinguish between real life and fantasy, and social science research has shown that viewing violence in the media can desensitize them to cruelty and shape perceptions of reality by making the world seem "more menacing."[9] Research has also shown that media depictions make violence seem more common than it is, minimize the consequences of violent acts, and imply that violence is a common way of solving disputes.[10]

And so there is good reason for us to be attuned to treatment of violence in popular culture. "Humankind has had more bloodthirsty eras but none as filled with *images* of violence as the present," George Gerbner observed. "We are awash in a tide of violent representations the world has never seen . . . drenching every home with graphic scenes of expertly choreographed brutality."[11] In this chapter we will chart the violent terrain of the popular-culture landscape.

Regeneration through Violence

Violence has a central place in American mythology as a means of justice and retribution. It is also a means of salvation for a community of "good" people threatened by an external evil. Robert Jewett and John Shelton Lawrence showed that popular American narratives, like those in traditional western movies and comic books, adhere to a distinctively American "monomyth":

> A community in a harmonious paradise is threatened by evil: normal institutions fail to contend with this threat: a selfless superhero emerges to renounce temptations and carry out the redemptive task: aided by fate, his decisive victory restores the community to its paradisal condition: the superhero then recedes into obscurity.[12]

Jewett and Lawrence described this myth as an American appropriation of Judeo-Christian redemption dramas. "The supersaviors in pop culture function as replacements for the Christ figure, whose credibility was eroded by scientific rationalism," they explained. "Figures such as Neo in *The Matrix* seem explicitly designed to offer contemporary moviegoers this new Christ—one who has dropped the ineffectual baggage of the Sermon on the Mount. Instead, he and his shooting partner Trinity carry a duffel bag full of pistols, guns, and explosives needed to destroy the command center of political evil."[13]

In what one scholar called the "epic moment" in the frontier clash between savagery and civilization, an act of violence by the rugged, individual hero saves the imperiled community in *Shane* (1953) and countless westerns. This frontier myth celebrated "regeneration through violence," the restoration of the community's fortunes and values secured by means of the destruction of an evil threat.[14] The classic western myth implies that one man drawing quicker than another can ultimately resolve all problems. This frontier formula sets up violence as the necessary and sufficient resolution to all the problems the story has raised, and audiences have grown accustomed to finding dramatic satisfaction in a violent resolution.

The popularity of westerns began to erode in the 1970s, but George Lucas's *Star Wars* series (starting in 1977) codified the western myth in space; action-adventure films like the *Die Hard* series (1988, 1990, 1995) transport the same formula into contemporary settings. The mythic space of the action-adventure film is the global village of today's transnational economy. This contemporary setting is an imagined landscape like that of the Great Plains that evokes the fictions of the western: a foreign "wilderness" inhabited by cutthroat corporate executives, corrupt political dictators, drug czars, mercenaries, and especially heartless terrorists, whose barbaric cruelty and acts of wanton violence and destruction make them the new savages. In the wild west, outlaws held up stagecoaches, trains, and frontier banks; in present-day action-adventure films, international outlaws hijack planes and raid corporate vaults and Federal Reserve buildings. The arch villain in the *Mission Impossible* sequel, *MI–2* (2000), goes even further by demanding corporate stock options—the gift that keeps on giving.

These films are so formulaic they can be described as *Die Hard* on a boat (*Under Siege* [1992]), a train (*Under Siege 2: Dark Territory* [1995]), a bus (*Speed* [1994]), a plane (*Executive Decision* [1996]), and in a tunnel (*Daylight* [1996]). In these action films, the source of the evil "Other" is personified, usually racially distinguished or connected in some way with "foreigners," thereby locating evil outside the community (i.e., America), which is good and worth saving (as in the traditional western). In the struggle to secure law and order and protect civilization, individual instincts about right and wrong are valued over the legal establishment, which is portrayed as corrupt or ineffectual. Violent solutions are preferred to legal processes, and in the action-adventure genre, the more powerful the weapon and spectacular the villain's destruction, the better.

A music video by a popular evangelical musician showed how Christians can uncritically appropriate this mythology.[15] The artist stars in the video as the western redeemer-hero. He sings, "I'm authorized and deputized to blow you [Satan] clean away." Western theme songs are woven into the soundtrack as he destroys a number of demons with a pearl-handled spiritual six-shooter. Finally, he kills Satan and, like all cowboys, rides out of town on a horse, having completed his violent mission for God. Such a synthesis of Christian themes and American mythology signals cultural accommodation, and Christians should be leery of identifying violence with the gospel message in this way. Even more, as followers of the Prince of Peace, we should challenge the central place violence has in American mythology as a means to regenerate a community and its values.

Religion, however, is often used "either as a force for justifying and legitimating violence or as a device for enhancing the entertainment value of violence," according to one study.[16] Films such as *Saving Private Ryan* (1998) and *Tombstone* (1993) featured religion in some way as "supportive of redemptive and righteous violence."[17] The warriors in *Braveheart* are blessed by the priest before going off into battle to fight the English. In contrast, other films used religion to support immoral violence and explain the violent actions of fanatics in films like *Se7en* (1995), *A Time to Kill* (1996), and *Contact* (1997). According to this study, in only three of the top 180 films from 1990 to 1998 was "religious faith portrayed as even remotely leading to the rejection of violence."[18]

In similar fashion, Peter Chattaway argued that in the films *Kill Bill* (2003), *The Punisher* (2004), and *Man on Fire* (2004) all the characters' "violent vendettas are portrayed as at least somewhat justified, and there even seems to be a hint of divine sanction hanging over their efforts." In *Kill Bill*, after surviving an attack, The Bride says, "When fortune smiles on something as violent and ugly as revenge, it seems proof like no other that not only does God exist—you're doing his will." Similarly in *Man on Fire*, when Creasy decides to seek revenge against the kidnappers his "vendetta is given a religious tinge, through the film's repeated references to the Scriptures and St. Jude, the patron saint of lost causes whose pendant Pita gives to Creasy," Chattaway explained.[19]

We All Got It Comin' Kid

Of course, there are films that represent a challenge to traditional portrayals of violence. By giving us a more complex characterization, Clint Eastwood's *Unforgiven* (1992) departs from the stark contrast between good and evil in traditional westerns. The plot takes on a downward spiraling effect, driven by a series of incidents in which characters refuse to forgive. In *Unforgiven*, "there are no white hats to root for and even the villains are ambivalent figures," one film critic observed. "The darkness at the core of this film is Eastwood's sorrowful view of human nature, Protestant in its sense of original sin."[20] "Deserve's got nothin' to do with it," Eastwood's character William Munny says, turning the concept of total depravity into a frontier slogan. "We all got it comin' kid." In one scene Sheriff Little Bill (Gene Hackman) mercilessly beats a hired assassin in the street. By showing the townspeople responding in horror and disgust to this violence, the film suggests that those of us in the audience should do likewise. The antiviolent message of *Unforgiven*, however, is largely undermined by taking the traditional shoot-out to extraordinary lengths, with Will Munny (Clint Eastwood) killing a record number of men.[21] Still, to some extent, *Unforgiven* demonstrates how a different cultural perspective can be employed in a traditional genre in ways that challenge the dominant value system.

In the Bedroom (2001) shows the grief and agonizing struggles of parents who have lost their son. Eventually, they seek revenge, as if a violent act of retribution will take away their unbearable pain and resolve their personal and emotional conflicts. But the film's ending suggests that while the small New England town has returned to some kind of state of normalcy, things will never be the same for these people; violence is not the regenerative force they imagined it would be.

The New Zealand film *Once Were Warriors* (1994) is a penetrating look at the effects of alcohol and violence among Maori people living in a working-class urban environment. The violence that a warrior is capable of brings only physical and emotional pain in a domestic setting, violating people and destroying their relationships and lives.

A History of Violence (2005) evoked the western and worked with the conventions of traditional Hollywood genre films; it pits the goodness of small-town life against the corruption of the big city, a local hero and family man against mobsters. The story is informed by a belief in the American Dream and the possibility of wiping the slate clean and starting all over again. For all its action, the film centers thematically on character and not story, dealing with the human predilection for violence and its consequences for individuals and a community. The film's title is nuanced, suggesting something about the main character, but also about the nature and meaning of violence on which the filmmaker wants audience members to reflect. Director David Cronenberg accomplishes this, as critics noted, by taking care "to show the immediate consequences of violence—such as what a shotgun can do to someone's face—without rubbing our noses in it."[22]

Ultimately, the film settles nothing, provides no answers, but instead poses questions for viewers to contemplate. When is violence justified? Under what conditions can we allow killing? Why do we associate violence with masculinity? What are the effects of acts of violence? And these issues are wed to our emotional reactions and thoughtful responses. Why is violence popular? Why do we laugh or cheer at certain scenes of violence, for example?

Violent Masculinity

Jackson Katz argued persuasively that there is a trend in American culture to intensify an equation of masculinity with the capacity for violence. He called this a *tough guise*: "the front that so many boys and men put up based on an extreme notion of masculinity that emphasizes toughness and physical strength, and gaining the respect and admiration of others through violence or the implicit threat of it."[23] Young men learn this masculine ideal and the ways to act it out through media representations that associate manhood with being violent. Masculinity is measured only by strength or weakness.

Another writer, William Pollack, described this phenomenon as a "mask of masculinity, a mask that most boys and men wear to hide their true inner feelings, and to present to the world an image of male toughness, stoicism, and strength, when in fact they feel desperately alone and afraid." He argued that boys are socialized according to a "Boy Code," a set of unwritten rules, behaviors, and expectations that put boys into a "gender straitjacket" that is a distorted and unrealistic image of masculinity. "When a boy tries to see his own genuine attributes, his true self, in the mirror, he can't; he only sees how he falls short of this impossible and obsolete ideal," he explained. "Is it any wonder, then, that he may later become frustrated, depressed or angry, suffer low self-esteem, fail to succeed in intimate relationships, or even turn violent?"[24]

Fight Club (1999), which featured "some of the most brutal, unremitting, nonstop violence ever filmed," as one reviewer put it, illustrates the

Fight Club (1999) suggests that the consumer society emasculates men, robbing their lives of meaning and making them just another buttoned-down cog in the corporate machine.

concept of violent masculinity.[25] Emasculated by the consumer culture and unable to sleep at night, the Narrator (Edward Norton) finds solace (though under false pretense) in a support group for men with testicular cancer. (The castration metaphor is obvious.) There he meets Bob, a former body builder, who has developed feminine features resulting from his cancer treatment. Trying to comfort the sobbing Narrator, Bob rasps in a high-pitched voice, "We're still men," with the Narrator affirming, "Yes, we're men. Men is what we are."

Everything changes when the Narrator meets Tyler Durden (Brad Pitt). Tyler wants a nostalgic return to a world where men were hunters: "In the world I see—you are stalking elk through the damp canyon forests around the ruins of Rockefeller Center. . . . You'll climb the wrist-thick kudzu vines that wrap around the Sears tower. And when you look down, you'll see tiny figures pounding corn, laying strips of venison on the empty car pool lanes of some abandoned superhighway." A fistfight outside a local bar gives them both such cathartic release that they eventually organize a secret Fight Club with ritualized beatings that help young men restore their sense of masculinity. Though the film eventually casts a negative spin on this violent ritual, it is, as one reviewer noted, "dazzling entertainment that wants us to luxuriate in violence as we condemn it."[26] The Narrator, who described himself as a "thirty-year-old boy" at the beginning of the film, experiences a personal transformation, becoming tough, confident, and independent. But cultivating a "tough guise" detaches him from his true emotions; eventually he recognizes the inhumanity of this conception of manhood. Ultimately, however, it is hard not to see the film at least metaphorically as an argument for a violent masculinity. Ebert called it "a celebration of violence in which the heroes write themselves a license to drink, smoke, screw and beat one another up."[27]

Katz and Pollack both showed that this form of violent masculinity is a social construction—cultural ideals, beliefs, attitudes, and assumptions that take shape as a pose, a falsehood that in reality hides our humanity, "reducing us all as human beings, and eventually making us strangers to ourselves and to one another—or, at least, not as strongly connected to one another as we long to be."[28]

To the extent that a violent masculinity has become a cultural norm, Katz argued that violence has been gendered "masculine," expected of men, but considered unusual for women. An article in *Newsweek* examined a growing increase in girl-on-girl violence, attributing it also to being culturally conditioned. "Historically, boys received messages from the culture that connect masculinity with physical aggression, while girls received opposite messages, encouraging passivity and restraint," the writer noted.[29] That seemed to be changing with the emergence of such "sheroes" as Sydney Bristow in *Alias* and Uma Thurman in *Kill Bill*, giving girls "tacit permission to alter their behavior."[30] Though rates of male violence remain higher, the rise of female violence lends support to the view that violence is not inherently male, but a social construction.

Lives Are Shattered

Of course, the biblical account of the history of redemption is laced with every imaginable act of human depravity—ugly sexual acts, but also deceit, murder, slavery, oppression, theft, swindling, violence, and so on—confirming the sinfulness of humanity and the wretchedness of a fallen world.[31] Isaiah gave the Israelites a graphic prophetic portrait of the impending invasion by the Assyrians: "Whoever is captured will be thrust through; all who are caught will fall by the sword. Their infants will be dashed to pieces before their eyes; their houses will be looted and their wives ravished" (Isa. 13:15–16). Can you imagine that scene in a movie? Or what about Samson slaying a thousand men with the jawbone of an ass (Judg. 15)? (Something similar occurs in scenes in *Braveheart*.) The sinking ship in *Titanic* perhaps gives us a sense of the view from Noah's ark as the flood waters rose (Gen. 7). The assassination of Eglon in Judges 3, with its combination of intrigue, gruesome detail, and humor, reads like a scene from a James Bond movie.

Even though the Bible explores the whole range of human depravity, the stories are always told with a certain perspective. The Bible does not overlook or excuse the evil it depicts; it shows evil and depravity as real but also at odds with the best of human experience. There are emotional and social consequences for our actions, and people are morally responsible for evil acts they perform.

Dead Man Walking (1995) probes life's worst tragedies and deepest sufferings, human grief, the struggle to forgive, and the need for spiritual redemption. The film contains horrific scenes of violence and rape that, while difficult to watch, reveal the depth of evil that has taken place and that these characters are struggling with. Most films and television programs make violence seem more common than it is and create the impression that it is the best way of solving disputes. Instead, this film treats violence as an invasion in the course of everyday life and investigates the consequences. People are robbed of their dreams, lives are shattered, and families are torn apart in grief. Even people of faith struggle to find meaning and overcome their loss, to act justly and show mercy, and to understand forgiveness. Yet the film depicts Matthew Poncelet (Sean Penn) as a human being capable of not only murder but of faith

Dead Man Walking (1995) probes life's worst tragedies and deepest sufferings, human grief, the struggle to forgive, and the need for spiritual redemption.

and repentance. Based on this portrait of humanity, the film tells a story and makes a case against capital punishment.

Dead Man Walking showed that all people, because we are all created in God's image, have inherent dignity and worth, even as we are all sinners. In contrast, the contract assassin Vincent (Tom Cruise) in *Collateral* (2004) callously murders without reason because he believes "millions of galaxies of hundreds of millions of stars and a speck on one in a blink, that's us. Lost in space. The universe don't care (about you)." That we have an inherent worth because we are created in God's image is a powerful assumption that should serve as a key criterion for Christian evaluation of portrayals of violence.

Even if we are overrun with popular artworks that indulge evil, we should resist the temptation to try to balance them out with portraits of life on the bright side—a penchant that can also lend support to artworks that bear little resemblance to reality. Being "born again" does not make people immune to the struggle with sin and free from the discomfort that accompanies the ambiguity and complexity of life. God does not spare the redeemed from the harsh realities of life. Accidents do happen, and they can shake our world; disease and death are as real for Christians as for anyone else. Popular artworks that explore human situations with honesty and sensitivity can help us come to terms with emotional trials that might occur in real life.

As I noted earlier, individual responses to popular artworks are influenced by a host of factors, including age, gender, and viewing skills, among others. Judgments about the appropriateness of depictions of violence are grounded in life perspectives. Even one of the staunchest supporters of family values in the media could still applaud what he considered to be "good, old-fashioned American violence."[32] That it often just depends on who's doing the killing and who's getting killed indicates an ideological bias.

Blessed Are the Peacemakers?

Ridley Scott's *Kingdom of Heaven* (2005), based on historical events between the Second and Third Crusades, seemed sure to generate controversy given its release amidst the events of 9/11 and the war in Iraq. The film centered thematically on "right action" and the idea of different religious groups living together peacefully. "The way I see it is that we're living in this world, which we share, and there has always been jostling for power and war over . . . money, power, land, religion, oil, water—and yet we share this place," Scott explained. "We should be able to live in harmony. Surely that's what any God—whoever your God may be—would tell you. That it's about humanity. If it isn't about that, then I'm not sure what it's about."[33] The director wanted "to demonstrate that Christians, Muslims and Jews could live together in harmony—if only fanaticism were kept at bay."[34]

Curiously, a British writer thought the film's balanced treatment of religious groups would prove a detriment in trying to capture the Christian market. "Evangelical Christians went to see *The Passion of the Christ* because it buttressed their own faith position," he noted. "They may not welcome being told that Jesus, Mohammed and Jehovah are all much of a muchness."[35] Most critics, including evangelical ones, found *Kingdom* a fair treatment of all religious groups. *Kingdom* "says very little about the religions on either side of the battle," a CBN writer thought, adding, "The movie does however contain a moral lesson that people of different nations and religions should strive for peace. That is as close as this movie comes to inspiration."[36]

That Scott and screenwriter William Monahan took some historical liberties for dramatic reasons was no surprise. But the inclusion of a love story between Balian and Sybilla, though not unexpected in a Hollywood spectacle, was puzzling to some mostly because it was left undeveloped. A writer on the CBN website asked, "But why create a fictional romance in a historical epic and then do very little to make viewers care anything about that story?"[37] The reason may have been that the producers hoped to duplicate the box-office success of *The Passion* by tapping into the same audience. At least one writer thought this accounted for the restrained handling of the love story "without the usually de rigueur dollop of on-screen eroticism." What Gibson realized, and Ridley Scott was apparently trying to exploit, was that Christian audiences "have no problem with blood and guts—it's just sex they're saving till they're married."[38]

While reviewers generally found the film to be "an ostensibly fair-minded, even-handed account" of the historical events, they found fault with the measure of violence in the movie, which was "filled with scene after scene of choreographed mayhem," as a *New York Times* reviewer put it. This critic charged that Scott even used violence to drive the narrative: "After starting with a bang, Mr. Scott tries to keep us in his storytelling grip with many more visceral, frenetically violent scenes."[39]

In contrast, the film's violence was of far less concern among Christian critics. "The movie has no objectionable nudity, blasphemy, profanity, or nuance," one reviewer noted, adding that aside from some historical inaccuracies "there is little in it to offend and less to recommend it."[40] Another pointed out that Scott lived up to his "reputation for bloody war movies," but concluded only that "The violence, while painting a realistic portrait of what battle would have looked like at the time, may be disturbing for younger viewers. This movie earns its R rating."[41] Again, as noted earlier, the depiction of violence was justified by claims of historical authenticity (and these reviewers apparently knew these methods of violence were historically accurate). One evangelical movie website even provided a detailed account of the violent acts in the film.

> Balian runs a man through with a sword and then pushes him into his blacksmith's fire. Men are shot down with arrows, and we see and hear the missiles impacting in their chests and heads. The camera lingers on a dying man with a spear through his throat. Swords cleave heads and slash open guts, with blood spraying across victim and attacker alike. A knight rams a dagger into the neck of a Muslim courier, and blood sprays across the room. Balian stomps on the neck of fallen foe, and we hear the neck bones snap. He then stabs another foe through the slit of his facemask.[42]

But no critical discussion followed; the reviewer's conclusion, though vague, seemed simply dismissive of all the violence in the film. "People of faith may object to individual moments, statements or characters, but *Kingdom of Heaven* is neither spiritually extreme nor malicious," he wrote. "As for violence—that's another matter altogether."[43] Why were other individual moments, statements, or characters identified as concerning people of faith, but not the brutal and graphic depiction of violence?

A critic for the Crosswalk website went so far as to make a positive association between violence and Christianity. "If Scott wants our admiration—as well as filmmaking that accurately reflects history—perhaps he should portray Christians as both warriors and righteous," she charged. "Has he heard of the Just War Theory?" This reviewer noted that the film contained "Extreme wartime violence throughout film, particularly stabbings, throat-slitting and beheadings," but offered no critical commentary whatsoever on this aspect of the film. Ironically, in a review that was itself laden with ideological assumptions, she criticized *Kingdom of Heaven* as harboring the director's personal and political agenda. To Godfrey's (Liam Neeson) declaration of fighting for "a better world—a land of conscience, where Muslims and Christians get along," she responded sarcastically, "What a lovely thought. Let's all join hands and sing a few rounds of 'We Are the World.'"[44] So much for the beatitude, "Blessed are the peacemakers, for they will be called sons of God" (Matt. 5:9).

Against the Grain of Faith

The causes of real-life violence are "complex and interrelated," a report by the National Association for the Education of Young Children concluded. "Among the significant contributors are poverty, racism, unemployment, illegal drugs, inadequate or abusive parenting practices, and real-life adult models of violent problem-solving behavior."[45] Media violence is only one factor, and as you can see from this list, not the most significant one.

According to the National Television Violence Study (NTVS), the three main effects of viewing televised violence are "learning aggressive attitudes and behaviors, desensitization to violence, and increased fear of becoming victimized by violence."[46] Depictions of violence do not necessarily lead to aggressive attitudes and behaviors. Many factors ranging from "biological and psychological factors to social and cultural ones" play a role. "Peer influences, family role models, social and economic status, educational level, and the availability of weapons can each significantly alter the likelihood of a particular reaction to viewing violence on television." And it is not just depictions of violence that should concern us, but the manner of treatment, the perspective the artist brings to acts of violence. "If the consequences of violence are demonstrated, if violence is shown to be regretted or punished, if its perpetrators are not glamorized, if the act of violence is not seen as justifiable, if in general violence is shown in a negative light, then the portrayal of violence may not create undesirable consequences," the NTVS study pointed out. "But if violence is glamorized, sanitized or made to seem routine, then the message is that it is an acceptable, and perhaps even desirable, course of action." Again we see the importance of being able to view media representations with a critical eye.

Just as important as the concern about the relation of media and real-life attitudes and behaviors is the extent to which media depictions shape people's perceptions of reality. In testimony before a congressional subcommittee in 1981, George Gerbner, who did pioneering work on the effects of television violence, said:

> The most general and prevalent association with television viewing is a heightened sense of living in a "mean world" of violence and danger. Fearful people are more dependent, more easily manipulated and controlled, more susceptible to deceptively simple, strong, tough measures and hard-line postures. . . . They may accept and even welcome repression if it promises to relieve their insecurities. That is the deeper problem of violence-laden television.[47]

The discourse over media violence shows the complexity of our engagement with the popular arts and also the relationship between art and life perspectives; popular art figures importantly in the ongoing process of cultural orientation.

Sociologist Robert Bellah made use of Robert Jewett's analysis of superheroes to help explain the "peculiarly American approach to empire" and propensity to divide the world into good and evil. Writing on the brink of the war in Iraq, he pointed out that Protestantism was a source of this dualistic tendency that was "now secularized and pervasive in our popular culture, disseminated by movies, television and video games," he explained. "At a deeper level, our infatuation with technology plays into this idea: technology, particularly military technology, will give us the equivalent of the supernatural invincibility of superheroes."[48] Bellah drew eerie parallels between popular culture and American attitudes and social policy showing the extent to which our understandings of national meaning and purpose can be informed by the narratives of popular culture.

The illustrations in this chapter show that criticism can be driven by ideological concerns. I hope they will also convince readers of the importance of developing rigorous tools for analysis of popular art and culture in order to reduce the risk of cultural accommodation. Hollywood films may affirm a national mythology that gives the appearance of consensus, and their melodramatic appeal makes them charming and seemingly harmless. Christians, however, should adopt a critical posture toward sentimentalized cultural values that run against the grain of faith. We need to be more aware of self-interest and self-reliance, a lust for power, violent resolutions to problems, materialism, stereotypes based on race, sexual orientation, gender, or disability, and even a humanistic outlook. American values? Perhaps, but definitely not Christian values.

Summary

- Violence is central to American mythology as a means of justice, retribution, and as salvation from evil; however, while the Bible depicts evil and violence as real, it also shows it at odds with the best of human experience.
- There is a trend in American culture to intensify an equation of masculinity with the capacity for violence, and Christians should work at being critical of this social construction.
- Christians need to develop tools for analysis of popular art and culture in order to reduce the risk of cultural accommodation.

Discussion Questions

1. What place does violence hold in American mythology and the Hollywood landscape? How should we think about this as Christians?
2. How is violence in the Bible different from the violence we see in Hollywood films?
3. Can you think of popular artworks that treat violence appropriately?
4. Is violence artistically necessary? Can art do without it?

CONCLUSION

If movies try to appeal to everybody, they can't improve. The best movies are really specific and authentic.

Amy Pascal, Chair, Columbia Pictures

People come to a movie to be entertained first. We have to master the art of filmmaking and create a powerful story before we think about how we're going to put some kind of Christian message in the film.

Ralph Winter, Film Producer

In 1999 *Entertainment Weekly* dubbed Christian popular culture "entertainment's newest boom industry."[1] But despite all the hoopla, industry insiders were still trying to galvanize the "Christian" audience into a consistent and driving force in music, television, and film. *The Prince of Egypt* (1998) was heavily marketed (and merchandised) in the evangelical community and received good reviews, but it did mediocre box office and was outperformed by animated competitors *A Bug's Life* and *Mulan*. Contemporary Christian music sales appeared to have reached a plateau by 2002. In 2005, PAX-TV still languished in the Nielsen ratings.[2]

Other specific efforts in the wake of *The Passion* (2004) were hardly successful. NBC touted *Revelations* (2005) as "a breakthrough faith-based thriller, a latter-day *Da Vinci Code* and a spiritual *X-Files*."[3] Looking for a ratings boost, the network ran the six-hour miniseries into May sweeps, "hoping for a heavenly result." After a positive start (and negative reviews), however, ratings fell steadily.[4] Warner Bros. film *Constantine* (2005), however, seemed like a sure bet. "Imagine the spiritual warfare of *This Present Darkness* done in the gritty style of *Fight Club*" is how one evangelical magazine described the *Matrix*-like movie starring Keanu

Reeves. This example of "Hollywood's fascination with the spiritual and the supernatural," however, managed only mediocre reviews and mild box office.[5] SONY was just as successful with the low-budget *The Exorcism of Emily Rose* (2005), a film that actually exceeded box-office expectations by drawing fans of horror films and churchgoers.

Of course, productions are always a gamble; the trick is to reduce the risk. Based on the successful video and DVD sales of the first two *Left Behind* films, SONY joined with Cloud Ten Pictures to produce a third installment. Hoping to imitate the success of the *Lord of the Rings* film trilogy, Disney (once boycotted by the Southern Baptists and other conservative groups) made *The Chronicles of Narnia: The Lion, the Witch and the Wardrobe* (2005). Although the distributor found it tricky "aggressively courting Christian fans who can relate to the story's biblical allegory while trying not to disaffect secular fans," *Narnia* garnered solid reviews and was a resounding box-office success, outpacing its Christmas-season rival, *King Kong*.[6]

When *The Da Vinci Code* opened in theaters in May 2006, critics panned the film. "*Da Vinci* is a dud—a dreary, droning, dull-witted adaptation of Dan Brown's religioso detective story that sold 50 million copies worldwide," a *Rolling Stone* critic wrote. "Here's the sure way to quiet the protesters: Have them see the movie. They will fall into a stupor in minutes. I know it bored me breathless." A "busy, trivial, inoffensive film," was how a *New York Times* critic described it. And my local religion editor wrote, "You can stop worrying that a controversial piece of fiction will make people lose their faith. . . . In fact, if your faith is shaken by this movie or the book on which it's based, you seriously need to go back to Sunday school. It's about as theologically threatening as an Indiana Jones movie, though not nearly as exciting."[7]

There was little doubt however, that much of the "manufactured hysteria over *The Da Vinci Code*" was meant to draw the churchgoing crowd into theaters. SONY was chasing after the "Passion dollar," which according to one report had become a trade term "meaning attracting those religious moviegoers who ensured the success of recent Christian-themed films such as *The Chronicles of Narnia* and *The Passion of the Christ*." A *New York Times* critic wrote facetiously that film studios couldn't open a film anymore "without provoking some kind of culture war skirmish, at least in the conflict-hungry media. Recent history—*The Passion of the Christ*, *The Chronicles of Narnia*—suggests that such controversy, especially if religion is involved, can be very good business." The hyped-up debate over the novel's theological and historical assertions and speculation about its influence was all "part of Columbia Pictures' ingenious marketing strategy," he wrote. "Thus we have had a flood of think pieces on everything from Jesus and Mary Magdalene's prenuptial agreement to the secret recipes of Opus Dei, and vexed, urgent questions have been raised: Is Christianity a conspiracy? Is *The Da Vinci Code* a dangerous, anti-Christian hoax? What's up with Tom Hanks's hair?"[8]

A cottage industry sprang up with books, DVDs, and study guides countering the religious and historical tenets put forth in *The Da Vinci Code*, along with video games, cookbooks, and tourist guides to help travelers follow in the footsteps of characters Robert Langdon and Sophie Neveu as they trekked about the crucial sites in France, England, and Scotland. AAA travel agents reported a 25 percent increase in bookings to Europe for the summer of 2006. Given the tremendous pre-release awareness the film finished first on its opening weekend and exceeded analysts' expectations (despite the negative reviews). Sony reported an estimated box office of $77 million in the U.S. and $224 million worldwide, the company's "biggest worldwide opening ever." The film outpaced the *Harry Potter* and *Lord of the Rings* films in global box-office debut and finished second to *Star Wars, Episode III: Revenge of the Sith* (2005) that did $253 million worldwide.[9] But like most summer releases, *The Da Vinci Code* quickly faded in the face of competition from a slew of action-packed blockbusters, as did the controversy surrounding it.

Hoping for a Heavenly Result

Producers found it difficult to define and predict the tastes of the "Christian" audience. But one thing was certain: the portion of that market composed of fundamentalists and evangelicals no longer thought that only films based on Bible stories or rated G were appropriate for consumption. "The truth is, followers of Christ are everywhere and every-day folks," said Jonathan Bock, Grace Hill Media consultant. "It would naturally follow that a large percentage of Christians are watching—and enjoying—*Desperate Housewives*, *The Amazing Race*, *American Idol* and even Red Sox–Yankee games."[10]

Surveys indicated that most Americans who identified themselves as religious watched pretty much what everyone did. Researchers at MarketCast, a leading Hollywood marketing firm, discovered "when it comes to popular movies and popular shows, tastes don't differ at all" between religious and nonreligious, the company president said. "But when it comes to movies, people distinguish between moral issues and entertainment issues. And most people, even the very religious, are very happy with their movies."[11]

Not surprisingly, film producers assumed most of the Christian audience would simply turn out for standard Hollywood fare. And if churchgoers were already happily attending movies, all they needed to do was clean them up a bit to draw in more conservative viewers.

The *New York Times* reported that film studios were hiring religious marketing consultants "to scan their family-friendly scripts for objectionable content and to devise marketing plans to reach the Christian audience." Producers, it seemed, were mostly interested in simply tailoring mainstream productions by "sanding the edges off dialogue that might offend churchgoers."[12] Director Taylor Hackford said he deleted obscenities and any profane use of the word "God" from the Ray Charles biopic, *Ray* (2004), to appease a Christian financier.[13]

Perhaps *Time* film critic Richard Corliss got it right: "Hollywood doesn't necessarily want to make Christian movies. It wants to make movies Christians think are Christian."[14] News reports confirmed that producers were not as interested in exploring "religion" as they were in commercial exploitation. "I think religion is becoming prevalent as a part of commerce. To the extent that you can sell religion, it's just like sex," one producer said of the increase in spiritual programming.[15] All the attention the entertainment industry was giving to the religious market prompted at least one reporter to ask, "But are churches being turned into commercial venues and congregations transformed into box office targets?"[16] Such an important question was easily overlooked, or perhaps deemed unimportant in the rush to take advantage of the entertainment industry's post-*Passion* venture with the churchgoing market. The strategy used to market *The Da Vinci Code*, however, generated some sparks in the religious community that could advance the discourse about the nature of cultural engagement and a fitting place for the church in the highly commercialized world of Hollywood.[17]

Offering Something Distinctive

The film, television, and music industries are all hit-driven businesses: a small number of huge commercial successes offset losses incurred by the greater number of productions. In this environment there is little room for failure. That's why there is so much imitation; to reduce investment risk, executives like to copy success. "Everybody wants something new, but they want something new that worked last week or last year," a studio executive said.[18] An unyielding cycle emerges. Producers claim they're only giving the audience what it wants. Critics lament that in deference to its bottom line, Hollywood makes too many products that are mediocre at best, lacking creativity and depth in story, theme, and characterization.

Family-friendly films in particular—the kind many Christians advocate—tend to depict a world where all issues are plain and simple.

Evildoers are destroyed, the virtuous rewarded. The "good" characters have within themselves everything they need to secure their destiny and only have to come to that self-realization. As we have seen, that is the theme of countless films from *Rocky* (1976) to *Cinderella Man* (2005), *The Wizard of Oz* (1939) to *The Incredibles* (2004). Sometimes characters get a little magical assistance from a divine source as in *The Legend of Bagger Vance* or *The Family Man* (both 2000).

This is not to say that television networks should abandon family programs or that Hollywood studios should not make G- and PG-rated films. Nor does it excuse the gratuitous inclusion of profanity, sex, and violence in programming aimed at young viewers. But given the circumstances described above, Christians are perhaps in a position now to offer something distinctive. Were more Christians to think about popular art in terms of faith perspective, they would actually have an opportunity to not only buy tickets but also to begin to shape the entertainment industry.

Let me offer just one example of what I'm getting at here. To reiterate a point made earlier, the Judeo-Christian tradition maintains that all people have dignity and worth because they are created in the image of God, but people also have a tendency to do evil. Redemption comes from experiences that make people aware of their own brokenness and insufficiency. As I showed in a previous chapter, films like *Magnolia* (1999) or *The Apostle* (1997) resonate with this kind of perspective. The characters have a moral ambiguity that fits with real life and makes for good drama—and interesting movies. Both films are not appropriate for young children.

As we've seen, the best popular artworks transform the real world into an imaginary one with ideals, values, attitudes, and assumptions woven into characterizations and storylines. Communicating cultural ideals and values, offering social and cultural criticism, providing social unity, and contributing to the collective memory are all good purposes for the popular arts. When faith communities think of Hollywood not as an evangelistic tool or simple entertainment provider but as an important participant in our cultural discourse, they will become more than a market share and be in a position to shape the popular arts and culture.

Films like *Saving Private Ryan* (1998) celebrate and honor the sacrifices of our armed forces. *Million Dollar Baby* (2004) sparked debate about euthanasia. *Crash* (2005) deals with racism. *Good Night, and Good Luck* (2005) probes the role of news media in keeping those with political power accountable to the people. *Syriana* (2005) looks deeply into the relationship between geopolitics and oil. *A History of Violence* (2005) explores the potential presence of violence in all of us. *Munich* (2005) discloses the tragic downward spiraling effects of the perpetuation of bloodshed. People of faith can engage these films by reflecting on the perspective they represent as they address issues of concern to us all.

A society benefits from a media that offers a range of perspectives, including faith-informed ones. The postmodern culture has, in principle at least, created a climate more open to this possibility. "Can you imagine someone asking Woody Allen to make his films less Jewish? Or Oliver Stone, less socio-political? Or Spike Lee, less African-American?" filmmaker Rik Swartzwelder asked. "It doesn't even matter if you like or agree with any of those filmmakers or their films. What is undeniable is that their singular perspectives helped each of them to stand out."[19]

All people of faith can contribute to the collection of meanings that make up our culture, not only by telling stories or writing songs but also by offering critical evaluations that exhibit faith-informed perspectives. This attitude, however, should not be confused with the kind of cultural arrogance exhibited by some who self-righteously judge their own values as superior to any others and for that reason would like to dominate the media of popular culture. Hopefully, faith-based contributions would result in an entertainment media that is more creative and honest, just and pluralistic. Making room for multiple voices to be heard in the cultural marketplace can foster an environment where people respect and listen to one another.

Most people go to a movie without even reading a review, so there is no necessary correlation between the quality of a film and the number of people who see it. Christians can help make a difference by making informed decisions about the popular art they consume, casting their consumer votes for good, interesting, and entertaining works that are excellent and praiseworthy.

Interpretive Communities

There are many other issues that deserve our attention but are beyond the scope of this work: contemporary debates regarding the entanglement of free speech, censorship, and media access; tensions between the industry's drive to maximize audience and profits and concerns about artistic quality and social responsibility; the status of popular art as art and fears that its influence has exceeded reasonable limits.

One way we can make progress in working through these matters is by establishing what scholars call an *interpretive community*. An interpretive community is made up of a group of people capable of discernment and active interpretation—friends, teachers, pastors, church members, reviewers who write for publications or websites, and others who share a common vision for engaging popular art. Such a community could be helpful in fostering a vision that might serve as a context for our engagement with popular art. Cultivating a common understanding can help producers, critics, and patrons work through issues based on some agreed-upon ideals, beliefs, values, and assumptions about faith, perspective, popular art, and culture.

Artists have to be supported by investors, production companies, critics, and audiences. It would also help to have producers and investors partner on projects that will "entertain" with artistic integrity and Christian perspectives. We need works of romance, adventure, and imagination that make us cry, laugh out loud, and wonder deeply about what life is like in God's world. We need more critics to help moviegoers evaluate films, as well as support for media literacy programs in schools and churches. Scholarly and popular treatments of critical issues would give us a better understanding of the contemporary situation. In other words, rather than pointing to isolated achievements, however valuable they are, like some Christians have done with *Chariots of Fire* (1981) or *The Passion*, for example, a communal effort promises to be more lasting and far reaching.

I hope, then, to see you at the movies, a concert, or in front of the television—not as passive consumers but as increasingly discriminating viewers and listeners. Remember, a lot of the delight and meaning of popular art comes from your engagement as a Christian. So have fun and be mindful of the contours of cultural landscapes. Keep the "eyes of your heart" wide open as you venture into the imaginative worlds that popular artists create. Talk about them with others to sort things out, giving artistic visions serious consideration—perhaps in ways that suggest trying a perspective on for size—based on a faith-informed outlook. For if we admire those artworks that bring together artistic merit and a Christian faith orientation, why not also applaud those fine works of art that honestly explore the human experience even while representing a different view of life?

The popular arts matter. Movies, concerts, music videos, and television programs are ways that people talk about themselves and others, consider the ups and downs of everyday life, and explore important matters that concern us all. Christians can serve their neighbors with popular art and criticism that helps us all understand and feel deeply the brokenness of our world and recognize the destructiveness of sin and the joy of forgiveness and redemption.

APPENDIX

A MATRIX FOR ANALYSIS

Asking questions is part of what it means to be human. Asking questions in the light of the grace of God in Jesus Christ is part of what it means to be Christian.

Daniel Migliore, *Faith Seeking Understanding*

A matrix is "something within which something else originates or develops." The idea behind this matrix for analysis is to generate criticism of popular art by suggesting questions for inquiry. The list contains questions I've invented or gleaned from a variety of sources, most of which appear in the relevant readings. Not all of these questions will apply to every artwork. Every work makes certain assumptions and addresses issues in particular ways, each requiring a different angle of inquiry and investigation before making an evaluation. Deciding which ones to pursue is part of the critic's task. Selecting and addressing some of the most important concerns as they relate to an individual work will help you identify the subject and lead you into a discussion of content and evaluation.

There are many illustrations throughout this work that suggest ways to make judgments about popular artworks. They show that it is possible to appreciate certain aspects of a work, while also being critical of others. You don't have to be a scholar to do this kind of criticism. Sometimes it's just a matter of getting a sense of the right questions to ask.

A Matrix for Analysis of Popular Artworks

Cultural Product

- Was this artwork a box-office or commercial success? To what elements can you attribute its success or failure (for example, star power, artistic quality, marketing)?
- Who is the intended audience? Is this artwork aimed at a particular group (for example, age, race, class, gender, religion)?
- What might people from these different groups take notice of in this artwork? How might they interpret it? How would this compare with your understanding?

Main Features of the Cultural Landscape

- What ideals, values, beliefs, attitudes, and assumptions are displayed? Which ones are glamorized or denigrated?
- What kinds of representations exist in this popular artwork?
- Who or what is being glorified?
- What does it glamorize or sensationalize? Make fun of? Put down?
- What is of value in life? Worth experiencing? Sacrificing or even dying for?
- What are the keys to success and happiness?
- Who are the heroes or villains? What makes him or her a hero or a villain?
- To what extent is the artistic portrayal faithful to the contours of a Christian cultural landscape?

Key Aesthetic Features

- How does the artwork deliver its message? Consider dialogue, narrative features, casting, acting, lighting, cinematography, musical or visual style, and so forth.
- What key symbols, metaphors, or images are used? What do they suggest about the meaning communicated in this artwork?
- Does the inclusion of a particular event or information contribute to plot or character development? If so, how? If not, why?
- Identify emotions that the artwork elicited—anger, delight, sadness, and so forth. How did the artwork bring out these feelings? Evaluate these means.

The Matter of Perspective

- From whose perspective is the story told?
- What key issues, concerns, problems, or questions are addressed? How does the song or story address these issues? How are they resolved?
- What constitutes good and bad conduct? According to the artwork? According to viewers?
- Are people punished or rewarded for wrongdoings?
- Can you discern a political perspective or agenda?
- How does your own perspective affect your understanding and appreciation of this artwork?

The World behind the Work of Art

- What beliefs, goals, convictions, and concerns can you find?
- To what extent is the vision represented in this artwork consistent with a Christian perspective?

God

- Does God exist in the world of the artwork? Or are the events and affairs of life directed by human effort alone? How do you know?
- How is God represented? Physically? Does God have a nonverbal or nonnarrative presence?
- What role does God play, if any?

Creation

- What beliefs and assumptions does the artwork represent about the world we live in?
- What is appealing or ugly? Enticing or repulsive? On what does the artwork lavish its most loving stare (for example, nature, sex, violence, people)?
- What is the nature of reality? How does it compare with the Christian view of the creation as good but stained by sin?
- Is this a moral universe? How are right and wrong determined?
- Is the universe ultimately material or spiritual? Is it indifferent, mean, or friendly? How does the artwork indicate this?

Humans

- How are humans portrayed? Are they inherently good or evil? Are characters one-dimensional, that is, all good or all evil?
- How does this view compare with a Christian understanding of human beings as created in God's image but fallen in sin?
- What motivates characters? Are they motivated by what they believe? What do they believe? What is the force of their convictions? How believable are these depictions?
- Which motivations are good and which are bad? How does the artwork suggest approval or disapproval?
- Are individuals portrayed as anything other than self-centered? Are they motivated by a higher goal, belief, or concern?
- What are the characters' needs (material, social, spiritual) and how are they met?
- How are men and women portrayed? What ideals, beliefs, values, and assumptions define masculinity and femininity? Are men and women seen as equal partners in life?
- How are characters identified? Race or ethnicity, class, vocations, or sexual orientation? How are they portrayed along these lines?
- Are people, regardless of race or ethnicity, class, or gender, seen as sharing equally?
- Are minority groups seen as stereotypes or figures of fun?
- Which characters do we establish an allegiance with? How does the filmmaker create this allegiance? What makes the character attractive or unattractive?
- How could characters have been presented differently? What other courses of action could have been pursued in the narrative? What other possible outcomes are there?

Nature of Evil

- What beliefs and assumptions are embedded in this representation of evil?
- What is the source and nature of evil? Is evil personal, social, or cultural? How does the artwork explain the existence of evil?
- What would you identify as "sin" in the story? Does the narrative designate it as such, and, how? If not, how does the narrative treat it?

Nature of Redemption

- What beliefs and assumptions does the artwork represent about hope and redemption?
- What are the means and nature of redemption?
- What are the possibilities for redemption in the world of the artwork?
- What elements or possibilities for grace exist in the story?
- Docs genuine forgiveness or reconciliation take place between people? Between God and humanity?

Authority

- What authority, if any, exists other than the self?
- To what extent do social institutions—family, school, church, business, government—wield authority?
- Does the artwork affirm a belief in absolute individual freedom? How does it depict social institutions?
- Do you get a sense that there are creational laws, or is the source of law from within the individual?

Sexuality

- Does the inclusion of an erotic scene deepen our understanding of the characters and their situation?
- How does this scene contribute to the meaning of sexuality?
- What do these two people really feel and think about one another?
- Do they love in the romantic sense? Is each escaping from the idea of a more personal relationship? Is this a purely sexual arrangement?
- Are sexual relationships portrayed in a way that you find acceptable? Why or why not?
- How do the beliefs and attitudes in this portrayal compare with a Christian understanding?

Violence

- Is violence the only possible or acceptable solution to problems? How does the narrative establish this situation?

- Is violence glorified? How are acts of violence justified in the narrative?

Map of Reality

- Does the artwork invite us to transfer its meaning to the real world?
- In what ways does the artwork resonate with your life experience and perspective as a Christian?
- How would you evaluate the map of reality this artwork represents?

Relevant Readings

Anker, Roy M. *Catching Light: Looking for God in the Movies.* Grand Rapids: Eerdmans, 2004.

Roy Anker examines a variety of films using literary and theological frameworks, taking into account not just themes and lines of dialogue, but all the tools of the cinema as a storytelling medium. Anker organizes the films into four categories: tales of darkness, stories of Christian grace, contemporary fairy tales, and movies with characters in secular settings who are "found" in their lostness.

Blake, Richard A. *Afterimage: The Indelible Catholic Imagination of Six American Filmmakers.* Chicago: Loyola Press, 2000.

Blake provides a study of how Catholic backgrounds have influenced the works of Martin Scorsese, Alfred Hitchcock, Frank Capra, John Ford, Francis Ford Coppola, and Brian De Palma.

Brand, Hilary, and Adrienne Chaplin. *Art and Soul: Signposts for Christians in the Arts.* Carlisle, Cumbria, UK: Solway, 1999.

A helpful guide for Christians engaging in the arts. The authors encourage Christian artists to cultivate a Christian worldview through which they can approach art.

Clapp, Rodney. *Border Crossings: Christian Trespasses on Popular Culture and Public Affairs.* Grand Rapids: Brazos Press, 2000.

A collection of essays by Clapp regarding Christian engagement with various aspects of American culture including holidays, family values, television, jazz, and Winnie-the-Pooh.

Dark, David. *Everyday Apocalypse: The Sacred Revealed in Radiohead, The Simpsons, and Other Pop Culture Icons.* Grand Rapids: Brazos Press, 2002.

David Dark argues for a new understanding of the word *apocalypse* as meaning revelatory and examines apocalyptic tendencies in certain forms of popular art including *The Simpsons*, Beck, and *The Matrix*.

Detweiler, Craig, and Barry Taylor. *A Matrix of Meanings.* Grand Rapids: Baker Academic, 2003.

In a book aimed at garnering greater appreciation for popular culture, Detweiler and Taylor propose allowing pop culture to influence theology and biblical interpretation. Advertising, celebrities, music, movies, television, fashion, sports, and art are all mined for their potential contributions to faith.

Forbes, Bruce David, and Jeffrey H. Mahan, eds. *Religion and Popular Culture in America.* Berkeley: University of California Press, 2000.

A collection of essays organized around four relationships between religion and popular culture: religious content and themes in popular culture, popular culture's influence on traditional religions, popular culture's creation of its own myths, and religion and popular culture in dialogue with each other.

Godawa, Brian. *Hollywood Worldviews: Watching Films with Wisdom & Discernment.* Downers Grove, IL: InterVarsity Press, 2002.

Godowa, believing all films contain redemption stories, aims to educate his readers in discerning these stories along with the worldviews and values communicated in films. Through advocating discernment he hopes to move Christians away from the traditional roles of cultural desertion or cultural immersion.

Greeley, Andrew. *God in Popular Culture.* Chicago: Thomas More Press, 1988.

Greeley proposes that God can be encountered in popular culture and develops his theory by examining what he calls the "religious imagination" and specific manifestations of popular culture.

Hughes, Richard T. *Myths America Lives By.* Urbana: University of Illinois Press, 2003.

Hughes examines the American Creed and five other dominant American myths (the Chosen People, Nature's Nation, Christian Nation, Millennial Nation, and Innocent Nation) and their origin and impact on America.

Johnston, Robert K. *Reel Spirituality: Theology and Film in Dialogue.* Grand Rapids: Baker Academic, 2000.

Theology professor Robert Johnston, interested in the spiritual significance of film, develops an approach for theological dialogue with film that is intent on gaining theological insights while remaining respectful of film as an art form.

Joseph, Mark. *Faith, God, and Rock & Roll.* Grand Rapids: Baker, 2003.

In this follow-up to his book *The Rock & Roll Rebellion*, Mark Joseph considers Christian musicians who are engaged in mainstream music culture, and argues that Christians can better serve God by being a part of the dominant culture rather than limiting their voice to the Christian music subculture.

Joseph, Mark. *The Rock & Roll Rebellion.* Nashville: Broadman & Holman, 1999.

Mark Joseph provides a history of the emergence and development of the Contemporary Christian Music (CCM) genre and makes the case that Christians need to expand out of CCM into the larger mainstream music culture.

Lawrence, John Shelton, and Robert Jewett. *The Myth of the American Superhero.* Grand Rapids: Eerdmans, 2002.

Lawrence and Jewett explore the historical and spiritual facets of the American Superhero myth and its inherent threat to American democratic values.

Laytham, D. Brent, ed. *God Is Not: Religious, Nice, "One of Us," an American, a Capitalist.* Grand Rapids: Brazos Press, 2004.

Six essays that examine popular cultural-political distortions of God and state—*who God is not* in an attempt to better understand *who God is*.

Lynch, Gordon. *Understanding Theology and Popular Culture.* Malden, MA: Blackwell, 2005.

Lynch provides an introduction to popular culture and religion, an overview of methodological frameworks for a religious and theological study of popular culture, and a theological aesthetics of popular culture.

Marsh, Clive, and Gaye Ortiz, eds. *Explorations in Theology and Film: Movies and Meaning.* Malden, MA: Blackwell, 1997.

A collection of essays that attempt to draw upon and further the idea of theology and film in dialogue, with an emphasis on treating film as film.

Martin, Joel W., and Conrad E. Ostwalt Jr., eds. *Screening the Sacred: Religion, Myth, and Ideology in Popular American Film.* Boulder: Westview, 1995.

Martin and Ostwalt present three approaches toward religious film criticism: theological, mythological, and ideological, and structure a collection of essays around each type of criticism.

Miles, Margaret R. *Seeing and Believing: Religion and Values in the Movies.* Boston: Beacon Press, 1996.

Miles offers a scholarly examination of religion and values in film from a cultural studies perspective. In the book, religion is primarily understood in terms of the relationships and practices between people in faith communities and is examined in film only in that dimension.

Moore, T. M. *Redeeming Pop Culture: A Kingdom Approach*. Phillipsburg, NJ: P&R Publishing, 2003.

Moore advocates a "kingdom approach" toward popular culture, which is characterized by approaching culture prayerfully, intelligently, purposefully, critically, dialogically, and redemptively.

Romanowski, William D. *Pop Culture Wars: Religion & the Role of Entertainment in American Life*. Downers Grove, IL: InterVarsity Press, 1996.

Romanowski provides a historical survey of popular culture in North America, arguing that popular culture fulfills the same roles and functions as "high culture" in transmitting cultural values. As a result he encourages the Christian church to end its avoidance of the popular arts and to instead critically and creatively engage popular culture.

Scharen, Christian. *One Step Closer: Why U2 Matters to Those Seeking God*. Grand Rapids: Brazos Press, 2006.

In an honest and accessible analysis, the author draws on biblical texts and theological tradition to interpret the band's music and activism. U2 exhibits a "theology of the cross," a vision of the world that does not ignore "the present realities of doubt, despair, suffering, and injustice."

Schultze, Quentin J., Roy M. Anker, James D. Bratt, William D. Romanowski, John William Worst, and Lambert Zuidervaart. *Dancing in the Dark: Youth, Popular Culture, and the Electronic Media*. Grand Rapids: Eerdmans, 1991.

The authors offer the idea that there is a dependent relationship between youth and the electronic media, and they recommend methods for the evaluation and redemption of popular art and entertainment.

Schultze, Quentin J., ed. *American Evangelicals and the Mass Media*. Grand Rapids: Academie Books, 1990.

One of the first books to examine American evangelicals' relationship with television, radio, magazines, books, music, and the press, the book is composed of original essays investigating both the historical and contemporary connection between evangelicals and the media.

Scott, Bernard Brandon. *Hollywood Dreams and Biblical Stories*. Minneapolis: Fortress, 1994.

Viewing popular films as communicators of common American myths, Scott attempts to create a critical conversation between the myths portrayed in Hollywood movies and specific biblical passages.

Seerveld, Calvin. *Bearing Fresh Olive Leaves: Alternative Steps in Understanding Art.* Carlisle, Cumbria, UK: Piquant, 2000.

In *Bearing Fresh Olive Leaves* Seerveld demonstrates the importance of art in God's world, explains the nature of redemptive art, and argues the need for Christian communities to support Christian artists.

Turner, Steve. *Imagine: A Vision for Christians in the Arts.* Downers Grove, IL: InterVarsity Press, 2001.

A book designed for Christians in the arts that provides thoughtful ideas about what Christian art and Christian engagement in the arts should look like.

Wall, James M. *Church and Cinema: A Way of Viewing Film.* Grand Rapids: Eerdmans, 1971.

In this pioneering book in religious film analysis James Wall establishes a methodology he terms "a continuum of perception" and proposes that Christians evaluate the particular vision of life a film presents rather than just the plot or characters.

Wuthnow, Robert. *All in Sync: How Music and Arts Are Revitalizing American Religion.* Berkeley: University of California Press, 2003.

Sociologist Robert Wuthnow argues that art and music contribute to the stability of American Christianity (in terms of church attendance) and play an important role in spiritual growth.

Zuidervaart, Lambert. *Artistic Truth: Aesthetics, Discourse, and Imaginative Disclosure.* Cambridge, UK: Cambridge University Press, 2004.

In this deeply philosophical work Zuidervaart introduces a new hermeneutic of artistic truth and examines the aesthetic, linguistic, and epistemological foundations of contemporary art.

Selected Web Resources

The Center for Parent/Youth Understanding (https://www.cpyu.org/store .aspx?id=76885) provides media reviews, resources, and analysis of youth culture for parents and teens.

Christianity Today Movies (http://www.christianitytoday.com/movies/) features reviews of current and DVD releases, a discussion forum, interviews, and commentaries.

CultureWatch (http://www.dickstaub.com/), the website of Dick Staub's Center for Faith and Culture, provides commentary on the "meaning, messages and belief system" in popular culture.

Hollywoodjesus.com (http://www.hollywoodjesus.com/index.htm) gives a spiritual take on movies, music, television, and books.

Internet Movie Database (http://www.imdb.com/) is an extensive collection of movie information (over 6.3 million individual film/TV credits and counting) with searchable features including details, credits, awards and nominations, links to reviews, summaries, trivia, and more.

Ransom Fellowship (http://www.ransomfellowship.org/) offers movie reviews and discussion guides.

Rotten Tomatoes (http://www.rottentomatoes.com/?bc=41) has over 127,000 titles and 644,000 review links in its ever-growing database and gives a rating summary of critical reviews (including films on opening weekend) and links to the reviews themselves.

NOTES

Introduction

1. Alex Kuczynski, "Groundhog Almighty," *New York Times*, December 7, 2003, http://www2.kenyon.edu/Depts/Religion/Fac/Adler/Misc/GroundhogDay.htm.

2. Quotations taken from Michael P. Foley, "Phil's Shadow," *Touchstone: A Journal of Mere Christianity,* online version, http://www.touchstonemag.com/docs/issues/17.3docs/17–03–012.html; Kuczynski, "Groundhog Almighty."

3. Lance Morrow, "The Ugly Side of 'American Beauty'," CNN.com, posted March 24, 2000, http://archives.cnn.com/2000/SHOWBIZ/Movies/03/24/morrow3_24.a.tm/index.html.

4. Timothy Gould, "Pursuing the Popular," *Journal of Aesthetics and Art Criticism* 57:2 (Spring 1999), 126.

5. Brian J. Walsh and J. Richard Middleton, *The Transforming Vision: Shaping a Christian Worldview* (Downers Grove, IL: InterVarsity Press, 1984), 35.

6. George M. Marsden, *The Outrageous Idea of Christian Scholarship* (New York: Oxford University Press, 1997), 10.

7. Margaret R. Miles, *Seeing and Believing: Religion and Values in Movies* (Boston: Beacon Press, 1996), 25.

8. H. R. Rookmaaker, *Art Needs No Justification* (Downers Grove, IL: InterVarsity Press, 1978), 38.

9. Calvin Seerveld, *Bearing Fresh Olive Leaves: Alternative Steps in Understanding Art* (Toronto: Tuppence Press, 2000), 11.

10. "New Study Examines the Impact of Gibson's "Passion' Movie," Barna Update, online version, July 10, 2004, http://www.barna.org/FlexPage.aspx?Page=BarnaUpdate&BarnaUpdateID=167; Brandon S. Centerwall, "Television and Violence: The Scale of the Problem and Where to Go from Here," *JAMA* 267, no. 22 (June 10, 1992), 3059–63.

11. Andrew M. Greeley, "The Catholic Imagination of Bruce Springsteen," *America*, February 6, 1988, 112.

12. William A. Dyrness, *Reformed Theology and Visual Culture: The Protestant Imagination from Calvin to Edwards* (Cambridge: Cambridge University Press, 2004), 4.

13. Jonathan Edwards, *The Works of Jonathan Edwards*, vol. 2, ed. Edward Hickman, 10th ed. (London: Henry G. Bohn, 1871), 263.

14. Miles, *Seeing and Believing*, 23.

15. John C. Lyden, *Film as Religion: Myths, Morals, and Rituals* (New York: New York University Press, 2003), 19–20.

16. A. O. Scott, "Being Super in Suburbia Is No Picnic," *New York Times*, November 5, 2004, E1, E13.

17. David Kelley, "Superhero Me!" The Objectivist Center, November 22, 2004, http://www.objectivistcenter.org/mediacenter/articles/dkelley_rff-the-incredibles.asp. See also Wendy McElroy, review of *The Incredibles*, The Future of Freedom Foundation, April 2005, http://www.fff.org/comment/com0504b.asp.

18. Jesse Kornbluth, "The Ultimate Power Player," *BUZZ*, June–July 1996, 76–79; "Praise Jesse," *BUZZ*, September 1996, 28.

Chapter 1 State of the Art: Worldly Amusements No More

1. Elizabeth Guider and Adam Dawtrey, "Slump or Bump?" *Variety*, August 15–21, 2005, 1, 49; Scott Bowles, "Hollywood Needs a Good Run," *USA Today*, January 23, 2006, 1–2D.

2. Jeff Leeds, "Marketing of 'Narnia' Presents Challenge," *New York Times*, October 12, 2005, E1.

3. Steven Levitan, "Hollywood's 'Elite': We're Not Villains," *USA Today*, December 13, 2004, 15A.

4. Ralph Winter and Mark Joseph, "Passion Changes Everything," *National Review Online*, February 25, 2004, http://www.nationalreview.com/comment/winter_joseph200402250840.asp.

5. Dann Halem, "Onward Christian Movies," *Premiere*, March 2004, 44. Estimates vary depending on how they are identified (self-identification or denominational affiliation), but the number of evangelicals in the U.S. is somewhere between 20 and 58 million people age 18 or older. See "The American Religious Landscape and Politics, 2004," *The Pew Forum on Religion & Public Life*, http://pewforum.org/publications/surveys/green.pdf.

6. Scott Bowles, "Hollywood Turns to Divine Inspiration," *USA Today*, April 14–16, 2006.

7. Quoted in Os Guinness, *Fit Bodies Fat Minds: Why Evangelicals Don't Think and What To Do about It* (Grand Rapids: Baker, 1994), 62.

8. H. J. Kuiper, "Moving Pictures," *Banner*, December 4, 1931, 1076.

9. James M. Wall, *Church and Cinema: A Way of Viewing Film* (Grand Rapids: Eerdmans, 1971), 31.

10. Tim Stafford, "Good Morning, Evangelicals!" *Christianity Today*, November 2005, 43.

11. Carl McClain, *Morals and the Movies* (Kansas City: Beacon Hill Press, 1970), 17.

12. See William D. Romanowski, *Pop Culture Wars: Religion & the Role of Entertainment in American Life* (Downers Grove, IL: InterVarsity Press, 1996).

13. Chris Salmon, review of Delirious? *Time Out*, May 19–26, 1999, 105.

14. Desson Howe, "'Left Behind': Heaven Help Us," *Washington Post*, online edition, February 2, 2001, http://www.washingtonpost.com/wp-srv/entertainment/movies/reviews/leftbehindhowe.htm.

15. Quoted in Daniel Fierman and Gillian Flynn, "The Greatest Story Ever Sold," *Entertainment Weekly*, December 3, 1999, 59.

16. Music Business Solutions, http://www.mbsolutions.com/biz/Info12.html.

17. Richard Mouw, *When the Kings Come Marching In: Isaiah and the New Jerusalem*, rev. ed. (Grand Rapids: Eerdmans, 2002), 65.

18. Quoted in Joan Brasher, "PAX TV to Launch Aug. 31," *CCM Update*, August 24, 1998, 2.

19. Dick Rolfe, "Give Families Choice of Editing Movies," *Grand Rapids Press*, June 14, 1993, A11.

20. Regie Hamm quoted in "For the Record," *CCM Update*, March 13, 2000, 8.

21. Doug LeBlanc, "Crossover Dreams," *Moody*, September–October 1997, 34.

22. John W. Styll, "Intro," *CCM Magazine*, June 1991, 4.

23. Chris Willman, "Faithful in Her Fashion," *Los Angeles Times*, April 16, 1991, F3.

24. Todd Hertz, "The Discontent between Business and Artistry," *Christianity Today*, online version, posted August 28, 2003, http://www.christianitytoday.com/ct/2003/134/43.0.html.

25. Chuck Eddy, review of *Heart in Motion*, *Entertainment Weekly*, April 5, 1991, 64; John Leland, "The Return of the Good Girls," *Newsweek*, May 20, 1991, 57.

26. Quoted in William D. Romanowski, "Where's the Gospel?" *Christianity Today*, December 8, 1997, 44–45.

27. Quoted in Walter Scott, "Personality Parade," *Parade* 24, November 1991, 2.

28. Quoted in "Gospel Gold: CeCe Winans Reflects on 16 Years of Gospel Recording," *Grand Rapids Press*, January 16, 2001, B8.

29. Quoted in Jeff Jensen and Gillian Flynn, "The Next Temptation," *Entertainment Weekly*, December 10, 1999, 46.

30. Quoted in Christine Wicker, "Even R-rated Films Suggest Redeeming Messages to Believers with Eyes to See," *Dallas Morning News*, June 6, 1998, 1G.

31. Dallas Jenkins, "Leaving Behind Family Entertainment," Christiancinema.com, July 30, 2003, http://www.christiancinema.com/catalog/newsdesk_info.php?newsdesk_id=42; Brian Orme, "Faith and Film: An Interview with Filmmaker Dallas Jenkins," *Relevant Magazine*, online version, July 22, 2005, http://www.relevantmagazine.com/print.php?sid=5201.

32. Paul C. Stevens, "The Christian in the MGM Lion's Den: A Content Analysis of Changing Evangelical Attitudes toward Motion Pictures in Christianity Today Film Reviews from 1956 to 1985" (PhD diss., Regent University, 1989), 49.

33. ChristianityTodayMovies.com, http://www.christianitytoday.com/movies/features/about us.html.

34. Eric Metaxas, "Shrek: Happily Ever Ogre," *Books & Culture*, July–August 2001, 5.

35. "Editor's Note: Shrekked," *Books & Culture*, September–October 2001, 3.

36. Samantha M. Shapiro, "All God's Children," *New York Times Magazine*, September 5, 2004, 46; Jeffery L. Sheler, "Nearer My God to Thee," *U.S. News & World Report*, May 3, 2004, 60, 66.

37. Terry Hemmings, then president of Reunion Records, quoted in James Long, "Terry Hemmings: Dropped in the Desert," *Contemporary Christian Music*, March 1997, 20.

38. Fierman and Flynn, "The Greatest Story Ever Sold," 59.

39. Ted Olsen, "Newsweek Discovers Christian Music about Six Years Late," *Christianity Today*, online version, posted September 9, 2001, http://www.christianitytoday.com/ct/2001/128/12.0.html.

40. Mark Joseph, *The Rock & Roll Rebellion: Why People of Faith Abandoned Rock Music—And Why They're Coming Back* (Nashville: Broadman & Holman, 1999), 246. See also Mark Joseph, *Faith, God, and Rock & Roll: How People of Faith Are Transforming American Popular Music* (Grand Rapids: Baker, 2003).

41. Mark A. Shibley, "Contemporary Evangelicals: Born-Again and World Affirming," *Annals of The American Academy of Political and Social Science* 558 (July 1998), 67.

42. See "Media and Technology," Barna Group, online version, http://www.barna.org/FlexPage.aspx?Page=Topic&TopicID=27; Lynn Robinson, "Christians and the Arts," *re:generation quarterly* 5, no. 4 (Winter 1999–2000), 12; Richard Corliss, "The Gospel According to Spider-Man," *Time*, August 9, 2004, 72.

43. Sharon Waxman, "The Passion of the Marketers," *New York Times*, July 18, 2005, C3.

44. Cited in Adam Nagourney and Janet Elder, "Americans Show Clear Concerns on Bush Agenda," *New York Times*, online version, November 23, 2004, http://www.nytimes .com/2004/11/23/national/23poll.html?ex=1133154000&en=a54f82b5208d650c&ei=5070 &oref=login&pagewanted=2&th&oref=login.

45. A survey conducted by John Evans's Texas-based Movie Morality Ministries cited in Joe Maxwell, "The New Hollywood Watchdogs," *Christianity Today*, April 27, 1992, 39–40.

46. "Media and Technology," Barna Group, online version, http://www.barna.org/Flex Page.aspx?Page=Topic&TopicID=27; "Harry Potter's Influence Goes Unchallenged in Most Homes and Churches," Barna Update, online version, May 1, 2006, http://www.barna .org/FlexPage.aspx?Page=BarnaUpdateNarrow&BarnaUpdateID=237.

47. David G. Myers, *The American Paradox: Spiritual Hunger in an Age of Plenty* (New Haven: Yale University Press, 2000), 206.

48. Michael S. Horton, "Precious Moments in American Religion," *Modern Reformation*, January–February 1997, 7.

49. Of course, not everyone in the business did this. Charlie Peacock is one notable exception, as his book makes clear. See *At the Crossroads: An Insider's Look at the Past, Present, and Future of Contemporary Christian Music* (Nashville: Broadman & Holman, 1999).

50. Warren I. Susman, *Culture as History: The Transformation of American Society in the Twentieth Century* (New York: Pantheon, 1984), 288.

Chapter 2 The Smoke Goes Upwards: Faith and Culture

1. See Charles Lyons, *The New Censors: Movies and the Culture Wars* (Philadelphia: Temple University Press, 1997), 165.

2. "Why Hollywood Doesn't Like You," *Christianity Today*, August 10, 1998, 64.

3. James Dobson and William Fore quoted in Lyons, *The New Censors*, 164–65.

4. Terry Eagleton, *The Idea of Culture* (Oxford: Blackwell, 2000), 2.

5. Clifford Geertz, *Interpretations of Culture* (New York: Basic Books, 1973), 89.

6. Ibid., 452.

7. Robert N. Bellah et al., *Habits of the Heart* (Berkeley: University of California Press, 1996), 27.

8. William Shakespeare, *As You Like It*, Act 2, Scene 7.

9. Gordon J. Spykman, *Reformational Theology: A New Paradigm for Doing Dogmatics* (Grand Rapids: Eerdmans, 1992), 219.

10. Calvin Seerveld, "What Makes a College Christian?" in *In the Fields of the Lord: A Seerveld Reader*, ed. Craig Bartholomew (Toronto: Tuppence Press, 2000), 122.

11. Paul Tillich, *Theology of Culture* (New York: Oxford University Press, 1959), 42.

12. Kenneth A. Myers, *All God's Children and Blue Suede Shoes: Christians and Popular Culture* (Westchester, IL: Crossway Books, 1989), 51.

13. Abraham Kuyper, "Sphere Sovereignty," in *Abraham Kuyper: A Centennial Reader*, ed. James D. Bratt (Grand Rapids: Eerdmans, 1998), 488.

14. Norman Stone quoted in *Telling Images: The Role of Christians in Arts and Media* (London: Arts Centre Group, 1996), 23.

15. Quoted in Scott Stossel, "The Man Who Counts the Killings," *Atlantic Monthly*, May 1997, 98.

Chapter 3 Terms of the Trade: Studying Popular Art and Culture

1. Julia Reed, "A Campus Culture Which Spurns the Misfits," *Sunday Telegraph*, April 25, 1999, 31.

2. Richard Barsam, *Looking at Movies: An Introduction to Film* (New York: W. W. Norton, 2004), 422; Warren I. Susman, *Culture as History: The Transformation of American Society in the Twentieth Century* (New York: Pantheon, 1984), 7; Lawrence Grossberg, Ellen Wartella, and D. Charles Whitney, *MediaMaking: Mass Media in a Popular Culture* (Thousand Oaks, CA: Sage Publications, 1998), 191–92.

3. James H. Olthuis, "On Worldviews," in *Stained Glass: Worldviews and Social Science*, ed. Paul A. Marshall, Sander Griffioen, and Richard Mouw (Lanham, MD: University Press of America, 1989), 29.

4. Albert M. Wolters, *Creation Regained: Biblical Basics for a Reformational Worldview* (Grand Rapids: Eerdmans, 1985), 3.

5. Olthuis, "On Worldviews," 31; Brian J. Walsh and J. Richard Middleton, *The Transforming Vision: Shaping a Christian Worldview* (Downers Grove, IL: InterVarsity Press, 1984), 38.

6. Lambert Zuidervaart, *Artistic Truth: Aesthetics, Discourse, and Imaginative Disclosure* (Cambridge: Cambridge University Press, 2004), 66.

7. Calvin Seerveld, "What Makes a College Christian?" in *In the Fields of the Lord: A Seerveld Reader*, ed. Craig Bartholomew (Toronto: Tuppence Press, 2000), 122.

8. George M. Marsden, *Fundamentalism and American Culture: The Shaping of Twentieth-Century Evangelicalism, 1870–1925* (New York: Oxford University Press, 1980), 230.

9. Joel W. Martin, "Introduction: Seeing the Sacred on the Screen," in *Screening the Sacred: Religion, Myth, and Ideology in Popular American Film*, ed. Joel W. Martin and Conrad E. Ostwalt Jr. (Boulder: Westview, 1995), 6. Myths, as many scholars have observed, tend toward total claims, and a key feature of postmodern thinking is a deep suspicion of myths or "metanarratives" as supposed universal visions that are blind to their own historical and socially constructed nature.

10. Susman, *Culture as History*, 10, 11.

11. Ibid., 8.

12. Jon Horowitz quoted in Mark I. Pinsky, *The Gospel According to the Simpsons: The Spiritual Life of the World's Most Animated Family* (Louisville: Westminster John Knox Press, 2001), 1.

13. Christian Scharen, *One Step Closer: Why U2 Matters to Those Seeking God* (Grand Rapids: Brazos Press, 2006), 39.

14. John Wiley Nelson, *Your God Is Alive and Well and Appearing in Popular Culture* (Philadelphia: Westminster Press, 1976), 16. See also Gregor T. Goethals, *The TV Ritual: Worship at the Video Altar* (Boston: Beacon Press, 1981), 7; Davin Seay with Mary Neely, *Stairway to Heaven: The Spiritual Roots of Rock 'n' Roll—From the King and Little Richard to Prince and Amy Grant* (New York: Ballantine, 1986), 7–8; John C. Lyden, *Film as Religion: Myths, Morals, and Rituals* (New York: New York University Press, 2003), 47.

15. Thomas Schatz, *Hollywood Genres: Formulas, Filmmaking, and the Studio System* (Philadelphia: Temple University Press, 1981), 46.

16. See Richard Slotkin, *Gunfighter Nation: The Myth of the Frontier in Twentieth-Century America* (New York: Maxwell Macmillan International, 1992), 628–43.

17. Robert Benne and Philip Hefner, *Defining America: A Christian Critique of the American Dream* (Philadelphia: Fortress Press, 1974), 8.

18. Since *Rocky* played in theaters the art museum's steps became a top tourist attraction with people running up them, re-creating that symbolic moment of ascent in the film.

19. Michael Ryan and Douglas Kellner, *Camera Politica: The Politics and Ideology of Contemporary Film* (Bloomington: Indiana University Press, 1988), 112.

20. Quoted in David Sterrit, "The Man behind *Rocky*," *Christian Science Monitor*, January 13, 1977, 12. For a full treatment see Daniel J. Leab, "The Blue Collar Ethnic in Bicentennial America: *Rocky*," in *American History/American Film: Interpreting the Hollywood Image*, ed. John E. O'Connor and Martin A. Jackson (New York: Ungar, 1979), 257–72; Ryan and Kellner, *Camera Politica*, 111.

21. See Joel W. Martin, "Redeeming America: *Rocky* as Ritual Racial Drama," in *Screening the Sacred: Religion, Myth, and Ideology in Popular American Film*, ed. Joel W. Martin and Conrad E. Ostwalt Jr. (Boulder: Westview, 1995), 125–33.

22. Bono quoted in Bill Flanagan, *U2 at the End of the World* (New York: Dell, 1996), 171.

Chapter 4 Close Encounters of the High, Low, and Divine Kind: Reimagining the Popular Arts

1. Stanley Cavell, *The World Viewed: Reflections on the Ontology of Film* (New York: Viking Press, 1971).

2. IG, *A Refutation of the Apology for Actors* (1615), 57–58, cited in Julia Briggs, *This Stage-Play World: Texts and Contexts, 1580–1625*, 2nd ed. (New York: Oxford University Press, 1983, 1997), 264.

3. Briggs, *This Stage-Play World*, 266, Heywood quotation, 269.

4. Harry S. Stout, *The Divine Dramatist: George Whitefield and the Rise of Modern Evangelicalism* (Grand Rapids: Eerdmans, 1991), xviii.

5. Warren I. Susman, *Culture as History: The Transformation of American Society in the Twentieth Century* (New York: Pantheon, 1984), 284.

6. Quoted in Tim Stafford, "Taking on TV's Bad Boys," *Christianity Today*, August 19, 1991, 16.

7. Quoted in Dan Wooding, "'The Prince of Egypt' is a Profound Biblical Epic," *Movieguide*, December A [*sic*], 1998, 4.

8. Christine L. Pryor, "Dreamworks Delivers Moses," *NRB*, December 1998, 24.

9. Morris H. Chapman, president of the executive committee of the Southern Baptist Convention, quoted in Laurie Goodstein, "Some Christians See 'Passion' as Evangelism Tool," *New York Times*, February 5, 2004, A18.

10. Quoted in "Gibson's Passion Gets an Evangelical Blessing," *Christian Century*, July 26, 2003, 14.

11. Jarvis Ward, Mission America Coalition, e-mail message to author, August 1, 2005.

12. Quoted in Melody Green and David Hazard, *No Compromise: The Life Story of Keith Green* (Chatsworth, CA: Sparrow Press, 1989), 162.

13. Quotations taken from Jay R. Howard and John M. Streck, *Apostles of Rock: The Splintered World of Contemporary Christian Music* (Lexington: University Press of Kentucky, 1999), 58–59 (emphasis mine).

14. Gary Richard Drum quoted in Howard and Streck, *Apostles of Rock*, 262.

15. Hilary Brand and Adrienne Chaplin. *Art and Soul: Signposts for Christians in the Arts* (Carlisle, Cumbria, UK: Paternoster Publishing, 1999), 89.

16. James Traub, "The Statesman: Why, and How, Bono Matters," *New York Times Magazine*, September 18, 2005, 83.

17. Steve Turner, *Hungry for Heaven: Rock and Roll and the Search for Redemption* (London: Virgin, 1988), 14.

18. Robert K. Johnston, *Reel Spirituality: Theology and Film in Dialogue* (Grand Rapids: Baker Academic, 2000), 57.

19. David John Graham, "The Uses of Film in Theology," in *Explorations in Theology and Film*, ed. Clive Marsh and Gaye Ortiz (Malden, MA: Blackwell, 1997), 36.

20. George Barna, *Index of Leading Spiritual Indicators* (Dallas: Word Publishing, 1996), 73.

21. Quentin J. Schultze, "Keeping the Faith: American Evangelicals and the Media," in *American Evangelicals and the Mass Media*, ed. Quentin J. Schultze (Grand Rapids: Academie Books, 1990), 33. George Barna concluded: "Credible research has yet to be conducted which shows that the media are an effective means of leading people into a true relationship with Jesus Christ, or even leading them into a local church where that relationship can be fostered." George Barna, *The Barna Report: What Americans Believe* (Ventura, CA: Regal Books, 1991), 31.

22. "New Study Examines the Impact of Gibson's 'Passion' Movie," Barna Update, online version, July 10, 2004, http://www.barna.org/FlexPage.aspx?Page=BarnaUpdate&BarnaUpdateID=167.

23. Theodore Baehr, *Hollywood's Reel of Fortune: A Winning Strategy to Redeem the Entertainment Industry* (Ft. Lauderdale: Coral Ridge Ministries, n.d.), 5.

24. David Novitz, "Ways of Artmaking: The High and the Popular in Art," *British Journal of Aesthetics* 29, no. 3 (Summer 1989), 214.

25. Erwin Panofsky, "Style and Medium in the Motion Pictures," in *Film Theory and Criticism: Introductory Readings*, ed. Gerald Mast, Marshall Cohen, and Leo Braudy, 4th ed. (New York: Oxford University Press, 1992), 244.

26. William D. Romanowski, *Pop Culture Wars: Religion & the Role of Entertainment in American Life* (Downers Grove, IL: InterVarsity Press, 1996), 85–86, 200–202.

27. Matthew Arnold, *Culture and Anarchy*, ed. J. Dover Wilson (Cambridge: Cambridge University Press, 1932; repr., 1988), 6, 204.

28. Allan Bloom, *The Closing of the American Mind* (New York: Simon & Schuster, 1987), 185, 322, 69.

29. Arnold, *Culture and Anarchy*, 130.

30. H. J. Kuiper, "Foolish Song," Editorial, *Banner*, May 5, 1944, 412.

31. David Noebel, *The Marxist Minstrels: A Handbook on Communist Subversion of Music* (Tulsa: American Christian College Press, 1974), 5, 218.

32. Michael S. Horton, "Precious Moments in American Religion," *Modern Reformation*, January–February 1997, 7.

33. Edward Baxter Perry quoted in Lawrence Levine, *Highbrow/Lowbrow: The Emergence of Cultural Hierarchy in America* (Cambridge, MA: Harvard University Press, 1988), 134–35.

34. Brand and Chaplin, *Art and Soul*, 19.

35. Howard and Streck, *Apostles of Rock*, 46–47.

Chapter 5 Mapping Reality: Popular Art and Culture

1. Paul Oskar Kristeller, "The Modern System of the Arts," in *Renaissance Thought II: Papers on Humanism and the Arts* (New York: Harper & Row/Harper Torchbooks, 1965), 174.

2. Nicholas Wolterstorff, *Art in Action: Toward a Christian Aesthetic* (Grand Rapids: Eerdmans, 1980), 5.

3. By Shand, "Why White People Watch Bad TV," *George*, August 1998, 38.

4. Noël Carroll, *A Philosophy of Mass Art* (New York: Oxford University Press, 1998), 196.

5. Ibid., 281.

6. Jack Nachbar and Kevin Lause, eds., *Popular Culture: An Introductory Text* (Bowling Green: BGSU Popular Press, 1992), 5.

7. "New Study Examines the Impact of Gibson's "Passion' Movie," Barna Update, online version, July 10, 2004, http://www.barna.org/FlexPage.aspx?Page=BarnaUpdate &BarnaUpdateID=167.

8. Stephen Whitty, "In Today's Films, Morality Is Missing in Action," *Grand Rapids Press*, December 23, 1998, D6.

9. John G. Cawelti, *Adventure, Mystery, and Romance: Formula Stories as Art and Popular Culture* (Chicago and London: University of Chicago Press), 27.

10. Kenneth Burke, "Literature as Equipment for Living," in *The Philosophy of Literary Form: Studies in Symbolic Form*, 3rd ed. (Berkeley: University of California Press, 1973), 293–304.

11. Todd Gitlin, "Pop Goes the Culture," *U.S. News & World Report*, June 1, 1998, 70.

12. Barbie Zelizer, "Reading the Past Against the Grain: The Shape of Memory Studies," *Critical Studies in Mass Communication* 12 (June 1995), 214.

13. Leland Ryken, *The Liberated Imagination* (Wheaton, IL: Harold Shaw Publishers, 1989), 35.

14. Zelizer, "Reading the Past Against the Grain," 214.

15. George Lucas quoted in John Culhane, "George Lucas: The Mastermind of the *Star Wars* Family," *Families*, March 1982, 49.

16. Marc Peyser and David J. Jefferson, "Sex and the Suburbs," *Newsweek*, November 29, 2004, 51.

17. Nicholas Wolterstorff, *Art in Action: Toward a Christian Aesthetic* (Grand Rapids: Eerdmans, 1980), 89.

18. Calvin Seerveld, *Rainbows for the Fallen World: Aesthetic Life and Artistic Task* (Toronto: Tuppence Press, 1980), 79–82.

19. "Gibson's Passion Gets an Evangelical Blessing," *Christian Century*, July 26, 2003.

20. Quoted in Mark Olsen, "A Passion to Convey a Director's Vision," *Los Angeles Times Calendar*, February 27, 2005, E19.

21. On this issue see David Hazony, "Breach of Faith," *Azure: Ideas for the Jewish Nation* 18 (Autumn 2004), 13–19.

22. Calvin Seerveld, *A Christian Critique of Art and Literature*, rev. ed. (Sioux Center, IA: Dordt College Press, 1995), 21.

23. Margaret R. Miles, *Seeing and Believing: Religion and Values in the Movies* (Boston: Beacon Press, 1996), 22.

Chapter 6 Measuring Christian Distinction: Moral, Ideological, and Theological Approaches

1. "Michael Moore Film Fest Draws Competition," *Baltimore Sun*, online version, http://www.baltimoresun.com/entertainment/movies/sns-ap-people-moore,1,1021520 .story?coll=bal-movies-utility.

2. Ron Strom, "Red-Staters Challenge Michael Moore Film Fest," http://worldnetdaily .com/news/article.asp?ARTICLE_ID=45133.

3. Quoted in Strom.

4. Quoted in Strom.

5. Quoted in "Michael Moore Film Fest Draws Competition."

6. Peter Travers, "Matrix No! Master Yes!" *Rolling Stone*, November 27, 2003, 102; Chris Utley, review of *Matrix Revolutions*, Hollywood Jesus, http://www.hollywoodjesus .com/matrix_revolutions.htm.

7. Michael Medved, "'Kill Bill' Mocks Innate Revulsion toward Cruelty," *USA Today*, October 22, 2003, 21A; Mark Caro, review of *Kill Bill, Vol. 1*, *Chicago Tribune*, online version, October 9, 2003, http://metromix.chicagotribune.com/movies/mmx-031009movies-review-mc-killbillvol1,0,6955179.story?coll=mmx-movies_top_heds.

8. Quoted in Cathleen Falsani, "Cardinal Takes a Crack at 'The Da Vinci Code,'" *Chicago Sun-Times*, online version, January 9, 2004, http://www.suntimes.com/special_sections/falsani/cst-nws-fals09.html.

9. Msgr. Francis Maniscalco quoted in Jeffrey L. Sheler, "Debating *Da Vinci*," *U.S. News & World Report*, May 22, 2006, 50.

10. John Coffey, "Engaging with Cinema," *Cambridge Papers* 8, no. 1 (March 1999), 3.

11. Roger Ebert, review of *Schindler's List*, rogerebert.com, http://rogerebert.suntimes.com/apps/pbcs.dll/article?AID=/19931215/REVIEWS/312150301/1023.

12. Les White, "My Father Is a Schindler Jew," *Jump Cut*, 1994, 4.

13. Drew Trotter, "The Movies and America," *Books & Culture*, May–June 2005, 46.

14. Roger Ebert, review of *Saving Private Ryan*, rogerebert.com, http://rogerebert.suntimes.com/apps/pbcs.dll/article?AID-/19980724/REVIEWS/807240304/1023.

15. Jon Pareles, "The Dixie Chicks: America Catches Up with Them," *New York Times*, online version, May 21, 2006, http://www.nytimes.com/2006/05/21/arts/music/21pare.html?_r=1&th&emc =th&oref=slogin.

16. Quoted in David Barsamian, "Bruce Cockburn: The Progressive Interview," *Progressive*, March 2005, 44.

17. Maria McFadden, "The Cider House Rules—Not!" *Human Life Review* (Spring–Summer, 2000), 124; "Hard Cider ('The Cider House Rules' as Meditation on Abortion)," *Commonweal*, March 24, 2000, 5; Steven Isaac, review of *The Cider House Rules*, Pluggedin Online, http://www.pluggedinonline.com/movies/mov ies/a0000542.cfm.

18. Paul W. McNellis, "Abortion as a Sacramental Moment? The Misguided Morality of 'The Cider House Rules,'" *America*, April 1, 2005, 16.

19. Amy Taubin, "Up in Arms on the Home Front," *Village Voice*, online version, December 8–14, 1999, http://www.villagevoice.com/film/9949,taubin,10750,20.html.

20. James Berardinelli, review of *The Cider House Rules*, ReelViews, http://www.realviews.net/movies/c/cider.html.

21. Danny Carrales quoted in Jeff Jensen and Gillian Flynn, "The Next Temptation," *Entertainment Weekly*, December 10, 1999, 44.

22. Kenneth Turan, review of *Brokeback Mountain*, *Los Angeles Times*, online version, December 9, 2005, http://www.calendarlive.com/movies/turan/cl-et-brokeback9dec09,0,186375.story; Stephen Holden, "Riding the High Country, Finding and Losing Love," *New York Times*, online version, December 9, 2005, http://movies2.nytimes.com/2005/12/09/movies/09brok.html?ex=1139806800&en=3feb72ced6aae239&ei=5070.

23. Lisa Ann Cockrel, review of *Brokeback Mountain*, ChristianityTodayMovies.com posted December 16, 2005, http://www.christianitytoday.com/movies/reviews/brokeback mountain.html.

24. Roger Ebert, review of *Brokeback Mountain*, rogerebert.com, December 16, 2005, http://rogerebert.suntimes.com/apps/pbcs.dll/article?AID=/20051215/REVIEWS/51019006/1023; Holden, "Riding the High Country"; Turan, review of *Brokeback Mountain*.

25. John Petrakis, "Heartbreak Mountain," review of *Brokeback Mountain*, *Christian Century*, January 24, 2006, 43.

26. Unsigned review of *Brokeback Mountain*, Catholic News Service, http://www.catholic news.com/data/movies/05mv682.htm.

27. Daniel Mendelsohn, "An Affair to Remember," *New York Review of Books* 53, no. 3 (February 23, 2006), 12–13.

28. Jeffrey Overstreet, review of *Brokeback Mountain*, Lookingcloser.org, http://look ingcloser.org/movie%20reviews/A-G/brokebackmountain.htm.

29. Steven D. Greydanus, review of *Brokeback Mountain*, Decent Films Guide, http://www.decentfilms.com/sections/reviews/2645.

30. Ibid.

31. Jeffrey Overstreet, review of *Kingdom of Heaven*, Lookingcloser.org, http://looking closer.org/movie%20reviews/H-P/kingdomofheaven.htm.

32. Jeffrey Overstreet, "What Others Are Saying," ChristianityTodayMovies.com, http://www.christianitytoday.com/movies/reviews/brokebackmountain.html#ff.

33. Cockrel, *Brokeback Mountain*.

34. David John Graham, "The Uses of Film in Theology," in *Explorations in Theology and Film*, ed. Clive Marsh and Gaye Ortiz (Malden, MA: Blackwell, 1997), 43.

35. Clive Marsh, "Film and Theologies of Culture," in *Explorations in Theology and Film*, 23.

36. Robert K. Johnston, *Reel Spirituality: Theology and Film in Dialogue* (Grand Rapids: Baker Academic, 2000), 16–17.

37. Craig Detweiler and Barry Taylor, *A Matrix of Meanings: Finding God in Pop Culture* (Grand Rapids: Baker Academic, 2003), 22.

38. Joel W. Martin and Conrad E. Ostwalt Jr., eds., *Screening the Sacred: Religion, Myth, and Ideology in Popular American Film* (Boulder: Westview, 1995), 15, 17.

39. Robert K. Johnston, *Useless Beauty: Ecclesiastes through the Lens of Contemporary Film* (Grand Rapids: Baker Academic, 2004).

40. Joel W. Martin, "Introduction: Seeing the Sacred on the Screen," in *Screening the Sacred*, 4. That these critics tended to privilege films that lent themselves to theological consideration indicates once again the presuppositional nature of the enterprise. Of course there is nothing unusual about this; every critic tends to look for what suits best the salient features of his or her approach (even as this might suggest its limitations).

41. Martin and Ostwalt, eds., *Screening the Sacred*, 13–14.

42. David Jasper, "On Systematizing the Unsystematic," in *Explorations in Theology and Film*, ed. Clive Marsh and Gaye Ortiz (Malden, MA: Blackwell, 1997), 237.

43. Martin and Ostwalt eds., *Screening the Sacred*, 6.

44. Roy M. Anker, *Catching Light: Looking for God in the Movies* (Grand Rapids: Eerdmans, 2004).

45. Conrad E. Ostwalt Jr., "Hollywood and Armageddon: Apocalyptic Themes in Recent Cinematic Presentation," in *Screening the Sacred*, 62.

46. Gordon Lynch, *Understanding Theology and Popular Culture* (Malden, MA: Blackwell, 2005).

47. Andrew M. Greeley, "The Catholic Imagination of Bruce Springsteen," *America*, February 6, 1988, 110–15; J. Richard Middleton and Brian J. Walsh, "Theology at the Rim of a Broken Wheel: Bruce Cockburn and Christian Faith in a Postmodern World," *Grail* 9.2 (June 1993), http://crc.sa.utoronto.ca/articles/BrokenWheel.html; Rodney Clapp, "God Is Not a Stranger on the Bus," in *God Is Not . . .*, ed. D. Brent Laytham, (Grand Rapids: Brazos Press, 2004), 23–38.

48. Larry E. Grimes, "Shall These Bones Live? The Problem of Bodies in Alfred Hitchcock's *Psycho* and Joel Coen's *Blood Simple*," in *Screening the Sacred*, 25.

49. Detweiler and Taylor, *A Matrix of Meaning*, 304.

50. Brian Godawa, *Hollywood Worldviews: Watching Films with Wisdom & Discernment* (Downers Grove, IL: InterVarsity Press, 2002), 15–17. Godawa defined redemption as "the recovery of something lost or the attainment of something needed" (15).

51. Paul W. McNellis, "Abortion as a Sacramental Moment? The Misguided Morality of 'The Cider House Rules,'" *America*, April 1, 2005, 16.

52. Cardinal Tarcisio Bertone quoted in Maureen Dowd, "The Vatican Code," *New York Times*, online version, March 27, 2005, http://www.nytimes.com/2005/03/27/opinion/27dowd.html.

53. And *JFK* reportedly had "an extraodinary effect on the public's consciousness" convincing people that there was a conspiracy to assassinate President Kennedy. See Marcus

Ruskin, "JFK and the Culture of Violence," *American Historical Review* 97, no. 2 (April 1992), 487. For survey results see Bill Carter, "Dan Rather Returns to the Assassination," *New York Times*, February 4, 1992, B1, B3; Ron Rosenbaum, "Taking a Darker View," *Time*, January 13, 1992, 54-56. Surveys since the publication of the Warren Commission Report show most Americans have always been skeptical of the lone gunman theory. See Art Simon, *Dangerous Knowledge: The JFK Assassination in Art and Film* (Philadelphia: Temple University Press, 1996), 16.

54. Noël Carroll, *A Philosophy of Mass Art* (New York: Oxford University Press, 1998), 309–10. Carroll argued that with respect to the process of engagement with narrative artworks in terms of moral values, the direction "is not *from the text to the world* by way of newly acquired and interesting moral propositions," but rather "*from the world to the text*" (340).

55. Murray Smith, "Engaging Characters," in *The Philosophy of Film*, ed. Thomas E. Wartenberg and Angela Curran (London: Blackwell, 2005), 162.

56. "Da Vinci Code Confirms Rather Than Changes People's Religious Views," Barna Update, May 15, 2006, http://www.barna.org/FlexPage.aspx?Page=BarnaUpdateNarrow Preview&BarnaUpdateID=238.

57. Bill Johnson quoted in John Dart, "Hollywood Softens," *Grand Rapids Press*, April 12, 1997, B2.

58. Bob Smithouser, Pluggedin Online, http://www.pluggedinonline.com/movies/mov ies/a0000621.cfm.

59. Alonso Duralde, "Alexan-dreck," *Advocate*, December 21, 2004, 54.

60. Ken James, Christian Spotlight at the Movies, http://christiananswers.net/spotlight/ movies/pre2000/i-americanbeauty.html.

Chapter 7 Popular Art as Art: Marking the Aesthetic

1. City of the Angels Film Festival website, http://www.cityofangelsfilmfest.org/home .htm.

2. Jeff Jensen and Gillian Flynn, "The Next Temptation," *Entertainment Weekly*, December 10, 1999, 44.

3. Richard A. Blake, *Afterimage: The Indelible Catholic Imagination of Six American Filmmakers* (Chicago: Loyola Press, 2000), xvi, 11–12, xiii.

4. Ibid., xiv, xviii.

5. Terry Eagleton, *The Idea of Culture* (Oxford: Blackwell, 2000), 30.

6. Calvin Seerveld, *Bearing Fresh Olive Leaves: Alternative Steps in Understanding Art* (Toronto: Tuppence Press, 2000), 8, 130.

7. See Lambert Zuidervaart, *Artistic Truth: Aesthetics, Discourse, and Imaginative Disclosure* (Cambridge: Cambridge University Press, 2004), 9. Zuidervaart described the aesthetic as "the intersubjective exploration, interpretation, and presentation of aesthetic signs."

8. Sut Jhally, *Dreamworlds: Desire/Sex/Power in Rock Video* (Amherst: University of Massachusetts, 1990), educational video.

9. Quotes taken from Jon Pareles, "Bruce Almighty," *New York Times*, April 24, 2005, sec. 2: 1, 24.

10. Michel Gondry quoted in Kevin Lally, "Brain Twister," *Film Journal International*, April 2004, 20.

11. Nicholas Wolterstorff, *Art in Action: Toward a Christian Aesthetic* (Grand Rapids: Eerdmans, 1980), 96–121.

12. C. S. Lewis, preface to *The Screwtape Letters* (New York: Macmillan, 1961), 10.

13. Quoted in Steve Erickson, "Interview with Manohla Dargis," Senses of Cinema, http://www.sensesofcinema.com/contents/02/23/dargis.html.

14. See Howard S. Becker, *Art Worlds* (Berkeley: University of California Press, 1982).

15. Margaret R. Miles, *Seeing and Believing: Religion and Values in the Movies* (Boston: Beacon Press, 1996), 8.

16. John D. Hagen Jr., "It's Time to Take Sides: Catholicism, Yes; Popular Culture, No," *Commonweal*, September 22, 1995, 19–21.

17. Richard Alleva, *Commonweal*, September 22, 1995, 21–23.

Chapter 8 Cultural Landscape: Toward a Christian Framework

1. Springsteen quoted in Kurt Loder, "Bruce!" *Rolling Stone*, February 28, 1985, 23.

2. Keith Dudzinski quoted in Merle Ginsberg, "The Fans," *Rolling Stone*, October 10, 1985, 31.

3. Springsteen quoted in Brian D. Johnson, "The Boss," *Maclean's*, September 2, 1985, 26.

4. Ginsberg, "The Fans," 31.

5. Dave Osborne quoted in ibid., 69.

6. Quoted in Jon Pareles, "Bruce Almighty," *New York Times*, April 24, 2005, sec. 2, 1, 24.

7. Ibid.

8. Andrew M. Greeley, "The Catholic Imagination of Bruce Springsteen," *America*, February 6, 1988, 112.

9. Ibid., 114. Recall Blake's idea of "afterimage" in chapter 7.

10. Quoted in Pareles, "Bruce Almighty."

11. Roger Ebert, review of *Magnolia*, rogerebert.com, January 7, 2000, http://rogerebert.suntimes.com/apps/pbcs.dll/article?AID=/20000107/REVIEWS/1070303/1023.

12. Quoted in Robert D. Ballard with Jean-Louis Michel, "How We Found *Titanic*," *National Geographic*, December 1985, 718.

13. Josh Burek, "The Gospel According to Neo," *Christian Science Monitor*, online version, May 9, 2003, http://www.csmonitor.com/2003/0509/p16s01-almo.htm.

14. Gregory Bassham, "The Religion of *The Matrix* and the Problems of Pluralism," in The Matrix *and Philosophy: Welcome to the Desert of the Real*," ed. William Irwin (Chicago: Open Court, 2002), 114. In the same volume, see also Deborah Knight and George McKnight, "Real Genre and Virtual Philosophy," 188–201.

15. Janet Maslin, "'The End of the Affair': When Passion Turns to Poison," *New York Times*, online version, December 3, 1999, http://www.nytimes.com/library/film/120399affair-film-review.html.

16. Paul Schrader, *Transcendental Style in Film: Ozu, Bresson, Dreyer* (Berkeley: University of California Press, 1972), 71.

17. Quoted in Douglas Rowe, "Whirling Dervish Director Scorsese Deals with Mortality in Flick," *Grand Rapids Press*, October 31, 1999, F8.

18. Thomas J. Burke Jr., "Understanding Man and Society," *Imprimis* 29, no. 1 (January 2000), 5.

19. Roger Ebert, review of *The Apostle*, rogerebert.com, January 30, 1998, http://rogerebert.suntimes.com/apps/pbcs.dll/article?AID=/19980130/REVIEWS/801300301/1023.

20. David Denby, "The Gospel Truth," *New York Magazine*, online version, January 12, 1998, http://www.newyorkmetro.com/nymetro/movies/reviews/1975/.

21. James Berardinelli, review of *Munich*, ReelViews, http://www.reelviews.net/movies/m/munich.html.

22. Dave Tomlinson, *The Post-Evangelical* (London: Triangle, 1995), 129.

23. David Schaap, "Strange Things Happen All the Time," *Perspectives: A Journal of Reformed Thought*, October 2000, 22.

24. Adrienne Munich and Maura Spiegel, "Heart of the Ocean: Diamonds and Democratic Desire in *Titanic*," in *Titanic: Anatomy of a Blockbuster*, ed. Kevin S. Sandler and Gaylyn Studlar (New Brunswick: Rutgers University Press, 1999), 166.

25. Paul Schrader, interview by Garry Wills at the Festival of Faith & Writing, Calvin College, Grand Rapids, MI, March 31, 2000.

26. Quoted in Benjamin Svetkey, "Bleak Chic," *Entertainment Weekly*, November 3, 1995, 36.

27. Hilary Brand and Adrienne Chaplin, *Art and Soul: Signposts for Christians in the Arts* (Carlisle, Cumbria, UK: Paternoster Publishing, 1999), 77.

28. Kathleen Norris, "Why the Psalms Scare Us," *Christianity Today*, July 15, 1996, 21.

Chapter 9 The American Melodramatic Way: Individualism, Religion, and Materialism

1. Todd McCarthy, review of *Titanic*, *Variety*, November 3, 1997, 4.

2. Stephen Holden, "Off to Save America with Cape and Mask," *New York Times*, on-line version, October 28, 2005, http://movies2.nytimes.com/2005/10/28/movies/28zorr.html?th&emc=th.

3. George Barna, *The Barna Report: What Americans Believe* (Ventura, CA: Regal Books, 1991), 89.

4. Carl F. H. Henry, *Christian Countermoves in a Decadent Culture* (Portland, OR: Multnomah, 1986), 32.

5. Jeffrey D. Mason, *Melodrama and the Myth of America* (Bloomington: Indiana University Press, 1993), 12.

6. George Will, "'The Patriot'—Story of America's Fight for Life," *Grand Rapids Press*, July 6, 2000, A14.

7. Michael Ryan and Douglas Kellner, *Camera Politica: The Politics and Ideology of Contemporary Film* (Bloomington: Indiana University Press, 1988), 112.

8. Alan Trachtenberg, *The Incorporation of America: Culture and Society in the Gilded Age* (New York: Hill and Wang, 1982), 81.

9. Roberta Bondi, "Sentimentally Yours," *Christianity Today*, August 10, 1998, 29.

10. Gary Althen, *American Ways: A Guide for Foreigners in the United States* (Yarmouth, ME: Intercultural Press, 1988), 34.

11. Patrick D. Anderson, "From John Wayne to E.T.: The Hero in Popular American Film," *American Baptist Quarterly* 2, no. 1 (1983): 16–31.

12. Christian Scharen, *One Step Closer: Why U2 Matters to Those Seeking God* (Grand Rapids: Brazos Press, 2006), 109–10. Wolfe quoted in Jerry Adler, "In Search of the Spiritual," *Newsweek*, August 29, 2005, 52.

13. Quoted in Steve Chagollan, "One for All," *Variety* (supplement), March 5–11, 2001, 4.

14. Quoted in Mark Olsen, "Just Follow the Yellow Brick Road," *Sight and Sound* 14, no. 12 (2004), 10.

15. Quoted in Chagollan, "One For All," 44.

16. Drew Trotter, "The Movies and America," *Books & Culture*, May–June 2005, 46.

17. Patrick D. Anderson, "From John Wayne to E.T.: The Hero in Popular American Film," *American Baptist Quarterly* 2, no. 1 (1983), 20.

18. Michael Eric Dyson, "Between Apocalypse and Redemption: John Singleton's *Boyz N the Hood*," in *Film Theory Goes to the Movies*, eds., Jim Collins, Hilary Radner, and Ava Preacher Collins (New York: Routledge, 1993), 215, 223.

19. Michael O. Emerson and Christian Smith, *Divided by Faith: Evangelical Religion and the Problem of Race in America* (New York: Oxford University Press, 2000), 90.

20. David G. Myers, *The American Paradox: Spiritual Hunger in an Age of Plenty* (New Haven: Yale University Press, 2000), 7.

21. Alexis de Tocqueville, *Democracy in America*, ed. J. P. Mayer (New York: Knopf, 1991), 506–8, quoted in ibid., 162.

22. George Barna, *Index of Leading Spiritual Indicators* (Dallas: Word Publishing, 1996), 14, 23.

23. Ibid., 80.

24. George Barna, *The Barna Report: What Americans Believe* (Ventura, CA: Regal Books, 1991), 80. In another survey, 57 percent thought that a combination of good works and faith in God secured one's salvation. Cited in David Van Biema, "Does Heaven Exist?" *Time*, March 24, 1997, 73.

25. Barna, *Index of Leading Spiritual Indicators*, 71–72.

26. Quoted in CultureWatch, http://www.dickstaub.com (Center for Faith and Culture), May 2001.

27. Tom Shadyac, hollywoodjesus.com, interview by a group of Christian film reviewers, http://www.hollywoodjesus.com/newsletter056.htm.

28. Tom Hanks quoted in Josh Young, "Ground Control to Major Tom," *George*, April 1998, 108–9.

29. Quoted in ibid., 108.

30. Quoted in Jerry Adler, "'Tis a Gift to Be Simple," *Newsweek*, August 1, 1994, 59.

31. Adler, "'Tis a Gift to Be Simple," 58.

32. Barna, *Index of Leading Spiritual Indicators* (Dallas: Word Publishing, 1996), 33; Frank Newport, "America Remains Predominantly Christian," Gallup News Service, online version, April 21, 2000 URLS; Public Broadcasting Service, *Affluenza* Teacher's Guide, online version, http://www.pbs.org/kcts/affluenza/treat/tguide/tguide1.html.

33. Phil Gallo, "California Dreaming," *Variety*, August 11–17, 2003, 27.

34. Ibid.

35. Roy M. Anker, *Catching Light: Looking for God in the Movies* (Grand Rapids: Eerdmans, 2004), 350.

36. Drew Trotter, "The Movies and America," *Books & Culture*, May–June 2005, 42.

37. Scharen, *One Step Closer*, 65.

38. Simona Goi, "Christian Politics: Between or Beyond Red and Blue?" *Perspectives: A Journal of Reformed Thought*, June–July 2005, 21.

39. Rodney Clapp, *Border Crossings: Christian Trespasses on Popular Culture and Public Affairs* (Grand Rapids: Brazos Press, 2000), 126.

Chapter 10 The Message in the Bottle: Love, Sex, and Gender Stereotypes

1. See Gary Engle, "What Makes Superman So Darned American?" in *Popular Culture: An Introductory Text*, ed., Jack Nachbar and Kevin Lause, (Bowling Green: BGSU Popular Press, 1992), 331–43.

2. Rodney Clapp, *Border Crossings: Christian Trespasses on Popular Culture and Public Affairs* (Grand Rapids: Brazos Press, 2000), 143, 145.

3. Robin Wood, "Ideology, Genre and Auteur," *Film Comment*, January–February 1977, 47.

4. Ibid.

5. Jean Kilbourne, *Deadly Persuasion: Why Women and Girls Must Fight the Addictive Power of Advertising* (New York: Free Press, 1999), 130.

6. Ibid., 145.

7. Sut Jhally, *Dreamworlds: Desire/Sex/Power in Rock Video*, educational video (Amherst: University of Massachusetts, 1990).

8. James Berardinelli, review of *Eyes Wide Shut*, ReelViews, http://www.reelviews.net/movies/e/eyes_wide.html.

9. Roy M. Anker, *Catching Light: Looking for God in the Movies* (Grand Rapids: Eerdmans, 2004), 348.

10. *Video Business*, November 8, 1999, 35.

11. "The Big Pictures: America's 100 All-Time Favorite Films," *Entertainment Weekly*, April 29, 1994, 28.

12. Hilary Radner, "Pretty Is as Pretty Does: Free Enterprise and the Marriage Plot," in *Film Theory Goes to the Movies*, ed. Jim Collins, Hilary Radner, and Ava Preacher Collins, (New York: Routledge, 1993), 60.

13. Ibid., 56–76. Aspects of the analysis here were informed by this essay, and also Madonne Miner, "No Matter What They Say, It's All about Money," *Journal of Popular Film & Television* 20, no. 1 (Spring 1992): 8–14; Thomas E. Wartenberg, "Pretty Woman: A Fairy Tale of Oedipalized Capitalism," in *Unlikely Couples: Movie Romance as Social Criticism* (Boulder: Westview, 1999), 67–88.

14. One scholar compared Edward's controlling temperament to that of Martin in *Sleeping with The Enemy*, a film that came out the year after *Pretty Woman* and starred Julia Roberts as a victim of domestic abuse. See Jane Caputi, "Sleeping with The Enemy as Pretty Woman Part II?" *Journal of Popular Film & Television* 19:1 (Spring 1991), 2–8.

15. Roger Ebert, review of *Pretty Woman*, rogerebert.com, http://rogerebert.suntimes.com/apps/pbcs.dll/article?AID=/19900323/REVIEWS/3230305/1023.

16. John Eldredge, *Wild at Heart: Discovering the Secret of Man's Soul* (Nashville: Thomas Nelson, 2001). Quotations are taken from 9, 10, 13, 16, 22.

17. Mark Mulder and James K. A. Smith, "Are Men Really Wild at Heart?" *Perspectives: A Journal of Reformed Thought*, October 2004, 21–22.

18. Stephen Holden, "When Love Is Madness and Life A Straightjacket," *New York Times*, June 25, 2005, E1.

19. Nathan L. K. Bierma, "Hopeless Romantics: Belief and *Sex and the City*," Sure of What We Hope For: Essays on Belief, http://www.nbierma.com/writing/belief/sexandcity.html.

20. *History of Sex: Ancient Civilizations*, (New York: A&E Television Networks, 1996), educational video.

21. William D. Romanowski, *Pop Culture Wars: Religion & the Role of Entertainment in American Life* (Downers Grove, IL: InterVarsity Press, 1996), 316.

22. Brian Logan, letter in *Premiere*, December 1999, 24.

23. Robert T. Michael et al., *Sex in America: A Definitive Survey* (Boston: Little, Brown, 1994), 8.

24. Ibid., 233.

25. Cited in Philip Yancey, *Designer Sex* (Downers Grove, IL: InterVarsity Press, 2003), 5.

26. Marc Silver, "Sex and Violence on TV," *U.S. News & World Report*, September 11, 1995, 64.

27. Quoted in Rob Tannenbaum, "Now, Moore Than Ever," *Premiere*, March 2000, 66.

28. Michael et al., *Sex in America*, 8.

29. David G. Myers, *The American Paradox: Spiritual Hunger in an Age of Plenty* (New Haven: Yale University Press, 2000), 205.

30. Ibid., 206.

31. Lee Siegel, review of *Sex and the City*, *New Republic*, November 18, 2002, 31.

32. William H. Willimon, "Recreational Sex," *Christian Century*, April 19, 2005, 20.

33. Kimberly Peirce (director of *Boys Don't Cry*) quoted in Glenn Kenny, "Breaking the Sex Barrier," *Premiere*, March 2000, 63.

34. Janet Maslin, "Lone Star," *New York Times*, online version, June 21, 1996, http://www.nytimes.com/library/filmarchive/lonestar.html.

35. Todd McCarthy, review of *Titanic*, *Variety*, November 3, 1997, 12.

36. Jennifer C. Kerr, "Study Says There Is More Sex on TV," Breitbart.com, http://www.breitbart.com/news/2005/11/09/D8DP1U5O4.html.

37. Seventy percent also said they get information about sex from their parents. Michelle Tauber, "Young Teens and Sex," *People*, January 31, 2005, 91.

38. Calvin Seerveld, *The Greatest Song: In Critique of Solomon* (Palos Heights, IL: Trinity Pennyasheet Press, 1963, 1967), 14.

39. David Briggs, "Christian Romance Novelists Leave Bodices, Faith Intact," *Grand Rapids Press*, October 13, 1997, A12.

40. Cited in Philip Elmer-Dewitt, "Sex," *Time*, October 17, 1994, 70.

41. James M. Wall, *Church and Cinema: A Way of Viewing Film* (Grand Rapids: Eerdmans, 1971), 83.

Chapter 11 A History of Violence: Charting the Terrain

1. Joseph Helfgot quoted in Sharon Waxman, "The Passion of the Marketers," *New York Times*, July 18, 2005, C3.

2. Elliott Ryan, review of *The Kingdom of Heaven*, CBN.com, http://www.cbn.com/entertainment/screen/elliott_KingdomofHeaven.asp.

3. Daniel Harrell, "Random Notes and Reflections on Mel Gibson's *The Passion of the Christ*," Park Street Pulpit, March 5, 2004, http://www.parkstreet.org/pulpit/dhpassion.shtml.

4. Terry Mattingly, "Movies after the Passion, Part I," Terry Mattingly On Religion, May 19, 2004, http://tmatt.gospel com.net/column/2004/05/19/.

5. Neal King, "Truth at Last: Evangelical Communities Embrace *The Passion of the Christ*," in *Re-Viewing The Passion: Mel Gibson's Film and Its Critics*, ed. S. Brent Plate (New York: Palgrave Macmillan, 2004), 155.

6. Ron Luce, president of Teen Mania, quoted in "Protestants See the 'Passion of Christ' Film as a Great Evangelistic Tool," These Last Days Ministries, February 9, 2004, http://www.tldm.org/News6/PassionOfChrist.htm.

7. Roger Ebert, review of *The Passion of the Christ*, rogerebert.com, February 24, 2004, http://rogerebert.suntimes.com/apps/pbcs.dll/article?AID=/20040224/ REVIEWS/402240301/1023.

8. "Some Things You Should Know about Media Violence and Media Literacy," American Academy of Pediatrics, http://www.aap.org/advocacy/childhealthmonth/media.htm.

9. David G. Myers, *The American Paradox: Spiritual Hunger in an Age of Plenty* (New Haven: Yale University Press, 2000), 201.

10. This study is cited in Marc Silver, "Sex and Violence on TV," *U.S. News & World Report*, September 11, 1995, 64.

11. George Gerbner, "The Politics of Media Violence: Some Reflections," in *Mass Communication Research: On Problems and Policies*, ed., C. Hamelink and O. Linne (Norwood, NJ: Ablex, 1994), quoted in Myers, *The American Paradox*, 197–98.

12. John Shelton Lawrence and Robert Jewett, *The Myth of the American Superhero* (Grand Rapids: Eerdmans, 2002), 6.

13. Ibid., 6–7.

14. John Cawelti, *The Six-Gun Mystique* (Bowling Green: BGSU Popular Press, 1970), 39; Richard Slotkin, *Regeneration through Violence: The Mythology of the American Frontier, 1600–1860* (Middletown, CT: Wesleyan University Press, 1973), 5.

15. Carman, "Satan, Bite the Dust," in *Addicted to Jesus*, 1992.

16. Bryan P. Stone, "Religion and Violence in Popular Film," *Journal of Religion and Film* 3, no. 1 (April 1999), par. 1, http://www.unomaha.edu/jrf/Violence.htm.

17. Ibid., par. 16.

18. Ibid., par. 32.

19. Peter T. Chattaway, "The Revenger's Tragedy," *Books & Culture* July–August 2004, 22.

20. David Ansen, "Bloody Good and Bloody Awful," *Newsweek*, August 10, 1992, 52.

21. For a full discussion, see Carl Plantinga, "Spectacles of Death: Clint Eastwood and Violence in *Unforgiven*," *Cinema Journal* 37, no. 2 (1998), 65–83.

22. Jonathan Rosenbaum, "A Depth in the Family: Cronenberg's Latest is a Masterful Blend of Thriller and Art Film," *Chicago Reader*, online version, http://www.chicagoreader.com/movies/archives/2005/0905/050930.html.

23. *Tough Guise: Violence, Media & the Crisis in Masculinity*, video, directed by Sut Jhally, featuring Jackson Katz, 1999. Quotation taken from "Tough Guise: Teacher's Guide: Introduction," http://www.mediaed.org/guides/toughguise/intro.html.

24. William Pollack, *Real Boys: Rescuing Our Sons from The Myths of Boyhood* (New York: Henry Holt and Company, 1998), xxii, xxiv–xxv.

25. Roger Ebert, review of *Fight Club*, rogerebert.com, October 15, 1999, http://rogerebert.suntimes.com/apps/pbcs.dll/article?AID=/19991015/REVIEWS/910150302/1023.

26. Charles Whitehouse, review of *Fight Club*, *Sight and Sound*, December 1999, 46.

27. Ebert, review of *Fight Club*.

28. Pollack, *Real Boys*, 6.

29. Julie Scelfo, "Bad Girls Go Wild," *Newsweek*, June 13, 2005, 66.

30. Ibid., 67.

31. See Brian Godawa, "Appendix: Sex, Violence & Profanity in the Bible," in *Hollywood Worldviews: Watching Films with Wisdom & Discernment* (Downers Grove, IL: InterVarsity Press, 2002), 187–208.

32. Michael Medved, "Values in Popular Culture," Young America's Foundation, C-SPAN, video, 1996.

33. Quoted in Chris Monroe, "*Kingdom of Heaven*: A Spiritual Journey Away from God and Toward Humanism," *Christian Spotlight on the Movies*, April 28, 2005, http://www.christiananswers.net/spotlight/movies/2005/kingdomofheaven2005-interview.html.

34. Alan Riding, "The Crusades as a Lesson in Harmony?" *New York Times*, April 24, 2005, 11.

35. Peter Stanford, "Screen God," *Guardian*, online version, April 24, 2005, http://film.guardian.co.uk/print/0,3858,5178075-3181,00.html.

36. Elliott Ryan, review of *Kingdom of Heaven*, CBN.com, http://www.cbn.com/entertainment/screen/elliott_KingdomofHeaven.asp.

37. Ibid.

38. Stanford, "Screen God."

39. Manohla Dargis, "An Epic Bloodletting Empowered by Faith," *New York Times*, online version, May 6, 2005, http://movies2.nytimes.com/mem/movies/review.html?title1=Kingdom%20of%20Heaven%20(Movie).

40. Michael Karounos, review of *Kingdom of Heaven*, Christian Spotlight on the Movies, http://www.christiananswers.net/spotlight/movies/2005/kingdomofheaven2005.html.

41. Elliott Ryan, review of *Kingdom of Heaven*.

42. Tom Neven, review of *Kingdom of Heaven*, PluggedIn Online, http://www.pluggedinonline.com/movies/movies/a0002146.cfm.

43. Ibid.

44. Annabelle Robertson, "'Kingdom of Heaven' Not the Epic It Could Have Been," crosswalk.com, May 6, 2005, http://www.crosswalk.com/fun/movies/1328564.html?view= print.

45. National Association for the Education of Young Children, "Media Violence in Children's Lives," http://www.naeyc.org/about/positions/PSMEVI98.asp. See also American Psychological Association, "Violence in the Media," http://www.psychologymatters.org/ mediaviolence.html; American Psychiatric Association, "Psychiatric Effects of Media Violence," http://www.psych.org/public_info/medi_violence.cfm.

46. Joel Federman, *National Television Violence Study*, executive summary to vol. 3, Center for Communication and Social Policy, 1998, 5, http://www.ccsp.ucsb.edu/execsum .pdf.

47. Quoted in Myrna Oliver, "George Gerbner, 86; Educator Researched the Influence of TV Viewing on Perceptions," *Los Angeles Times*, online version, December 29, 2005, http://www.latimes.com/news/obituaries/la-me-gerbner29dec29,1,2671282,print .story?coll=la-news -obituaries&ctrack=1&cset=true.

48. Robert N. Bellah, "Righteous Empire," *Christian Century*, March 8, 2003, 20–25.

Conclusion

1. Daniel Fierman and Gillian Flynn, "The Greatest Story Ever Sold," *Entertainment Weekly*, December 3, 1999, 55.

2. Mark Joseph, "Is There Really a Christian Music Boom?" *Christianity Today*, online version, posted February 5, 2002, http://www.christianitytoday.com/ct/2002/104/22.0.html; "Networks Reclaim Water Cooler Title, CBS Claims," Top 5 Network TV Ratings This Week, posted July 20, 2005, http://www.top5s.com/tvnets.htm.

3. Alessandra Stanley, "End Is Expected, but There's Still Time to Debate Morality," *New York Times*, online version, April 13, 2005, http://query.nytimes.com/gst/fullpage .html?res=9C06E6D8123EF930A25757C0A9639C8B63.

4. Bill Mann, "Revelations Not Heavenly," *Press Democrat*, online version, April 10, 2005, http://www.northbay.com/entertainment/mann/10mann_q20q20_qq.html; Mike Duffy, "Wednesday's Best Bets on TV," *Detroit Free Press*, online version, May 11, 2005, http://www .freep.com/entertainment/tvandradio/bet11e_20050511.htm.

5. Craig Detweiler, "'Constantine': Seeing the Supernatural through the Eyes of Hollywood," *Relevant*, January–February, 2005, 51.

6. Jeff Leeds, "Marketing of 'Narnia' Presents Challenge," *New York Times*, October 12, 2005, E1.

7. Peter Travers, review of *The Da Vinci Code*, *Rolling Stone*, online version, 17 May 2006, http://www.rollingstone.com/reviews/movie/_/id/6658038/rid/10345385/; A. O. Scott, "A 'Da Vinci Code' That Takes Longer to Watch Than Read," *New York Times*, online version, May 18, 2006, http://movies2 .nytimes.com/2006/05/18/movies/18code.html?th&emc=th; Charles Honey, "Your Faith Will Be Unshaken," *Grand Rapids Press*, May 18, 2006, A1.

8. Manohla Dargis, "At Cannes, Foreign Art Films Mix with Politics," *New York Times*, online version, May 19, 2006, http://www.nytimes.com/2006/05/19/movies/19cann.html ?th&emc=th; Michael Haag and Veronica Haag with James McConnachie, *The Mini Rough Guide* to The Da Vinci Code: *An Unauthorized Guide to the Book and Movie* (London: Rough Guides/Penguin, 2004, 2006), 76; Scott, "A 'Da Vinci Code' That Takes Longer to Watch Than Read."

9. Julie Bosman, "'Da Vinci' as a Brand: From Soup to Nuts," *New York Times*, online version, May 20, 2006, http://www.nytimes.com/2006/05/20/business/media/20code .html?th&emc=th; Manoh la Dargis and A. O. Scott, "Tales from Cannes Festival: Dystopia, Widows, Da Vinci and Sex," *New York Times*, online version, May 22, 2006, http://www.ny

times.com/2006/05/22/movies/22fest.html?th&emc=th; Scott Bowles, "Critics Can't Break 'Code,'" *USA Today*, May 22, 2006, 1D.

10. Quoted in Sharon Waxman, "The Passion of the Marketers," *New York Times*, July 18, 2005, C3.

11. Joseph Helfgot quoted in Waxman, "The Passion of the Marketers."

12. Waxman, "The Passion of the Marketers."

13. Ibid.

14. Richard Corliss, "The Gospel According to Spider-Man," *Time*, August 9, 2004, 72.

15. David Milch quoted in James Verini, "Divine Purpose," *Los Angeles Times*, December 26, 2004, E40.

16. Dann Halem, "Onward Christian Movies," *Premiere*, March 2004, 45.

17. See Peter J. Boyer, "Hollywood Heresy," *New Yorker*, May 22, 2006, 34–39.

18. Bob Berney quoted in Sean Smith, "Coming to a Theater Near You," *Newsweek*, August 8, 2005, 54.

19. Quoted in "Should Films Be Faith-Explicit? (Part 1)," ChristianityTodayMovies .com, July 11, 2005, http://www.christianitytoday.com/movies/commentaries/filmsfaith explicit1.html.

INDEX